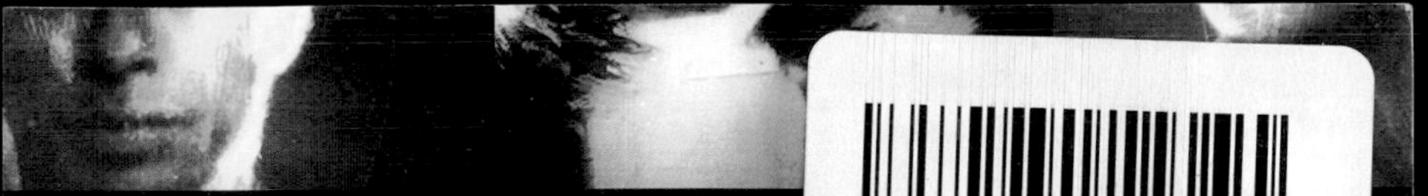

CSI:
CRIME SCENE INVESTIGATION™

serial

WRITTEN BY MAX ALLAN COLLINS
ART BY GABRIEL RODRIGUEZ
AND ASHLEY WOOD

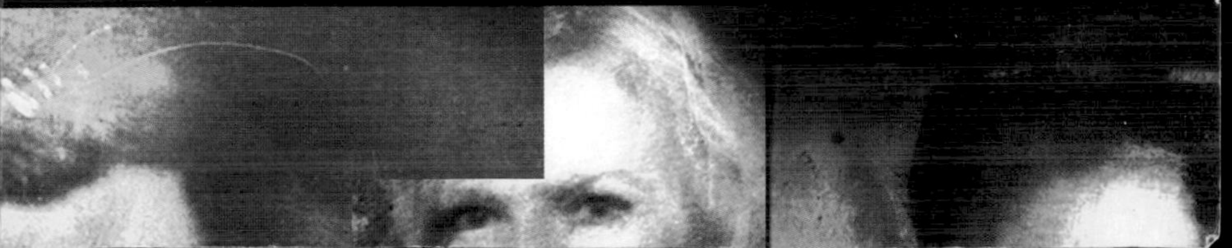

CSI: Crime Scene Investigation

Created by **Anthony E. Zuiker**

Licensed to IDW by CBS Consumer Products

"Serial"

Written by **Max Allan Collins**

Forensics Research/Plot Assist by **Matthew V. Clemens**

Pencils and inks by **Gabriel Rodriguez**

Colors by **Fran Gamboa**

Painted Artwork by **Ashley Wood**

Lettered by **Robbie Robbins**

Edited by **Jeff Mariotte**

Original Series edited by **Kris Oprisko, Jeff Mariotte**

Cover by **Ashley Wood**

Design by **Robbie Robbins and Cindy Chapman**

Special thanks to Maryann Martin CBS Consumer Products
for her invaluable assistance.

www.idwpublishing.com

ISBN: 978-1-60010-203-5
11 10 09 08   1 2 3 4 5

IDW Publishing
Ted Adams, Preside
Robbie Robbins, EVP/Sr. Graphic Art
Chris Ryall, Publisher/Editor-in-Ch
Clifford Meth, EVP of Strategies/Editor
Alan Payne, VP of Sal
Marci Kahn, Executive Assista
Neil Uyetake, Art Direc
Tom Waltz, Edit
Andrew Steven Harris, Edit
Chris Mowry, Graphic Art
Amauri Osorio, Graphic Art
Dene Nee, Graphic Artist/Edit
Matthew Ruzicka, CPA, Controll
Alonzo Simon, Shipping Manag
Kris Oprisko, Editor/Foreign Lic. Re

Originally published as CSI: CRIME SCENE INVESTIGATION: SERIAL Issues # 1 to 5.

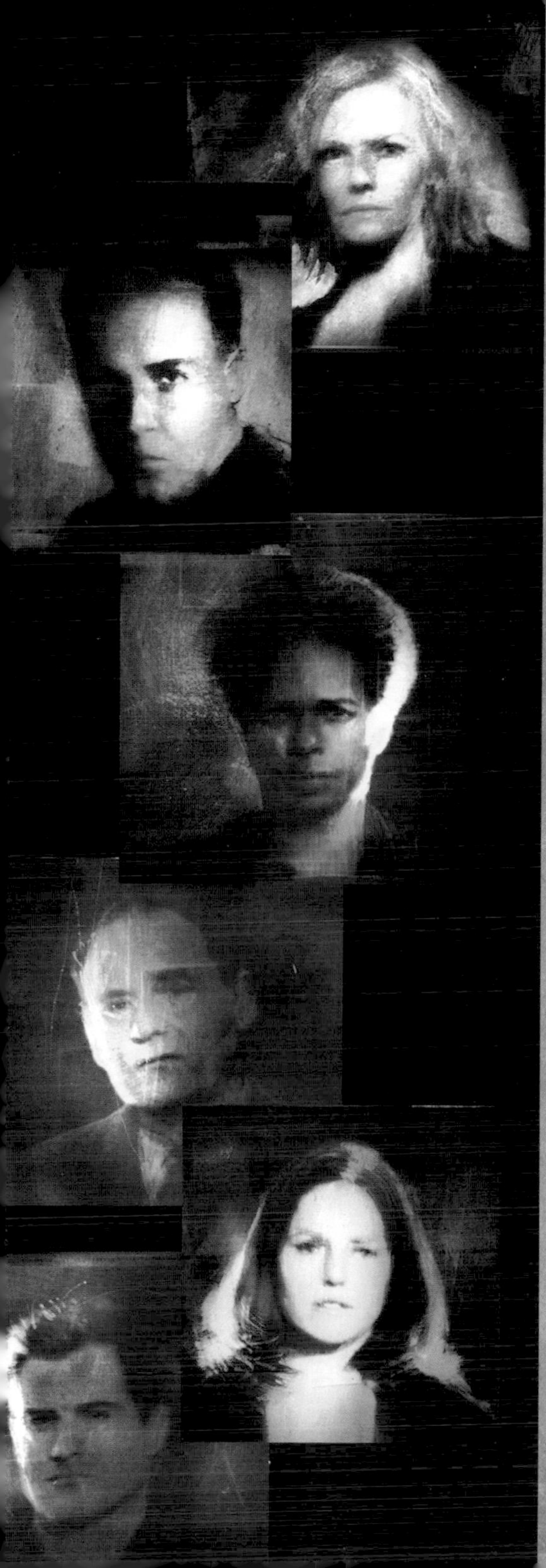

THE Perfect Specimen

CSI was born a year before it ever hit the airwaves. My wife, Jennifer, sat me down to watch *The New Detectives* on Discovery Channel. After the episode featuring the murder of Raiderette Linda Sobek, I knew the arena of "forensics" would be my first idea for television. The more research I did, the more fascinated I was. I found myself enamored with forensic evidence. How a hair follicle "pulled" out of the human head could signify a struggle. This is prevalent if the "tag-cell" is still attached at the end of the strand of hair. I quickly learned that the human body is a perfect specimen. Every facet of the body—from blood, hair, DNA, saliva, bruising, and the like—was designed to tell the well-trained CSI or Forensic Pathologist what occurred without ever being there. The notion that the body "speaks to you" is what drove me to construct a television show about five CSIs who bring peace of mind to the survivors by solving crimes through the use of forensic evidence. Hence, the mantra. "There's always a clue..."

The next day, I phoned the Crime Lab in Las Vegas and asked to ride along. I told the Supervisor, "I want the bloodiest, goriest, and most explicit shift." He told me, "Graveyard." One hour into the first night, we got a "sexual assault" call. A female allegedly picked up another female at a bar and invited her back to her motel to party. When the female walked in, she was surprised by three men. When we arrived, the victim was taken into protective custody and the three men were arrested. However, we couldn't find the primary female. That's where I come in. I was at the scene taking notes for the pilot. The CSI joked, "Hit your knees and look for semen." I replied, "Okay???" I searched around the bed, lifted the bedspread, and saw two sets of eyes. I jumped out of my skin. "She's under the bed!!!" In seconds, CSI and the cops took her down. Afterward, I was told suspects often return to the scene of the crime. I knew right then and there how I would end the pilot script. Shoot a CSI on her first night on the job. That character's name in the pilot was Holly Gribbs. We laid her to rest in episode two.

Enjoy!

--Anthony E. Zuiker

chapter one

Bloody Bonnet

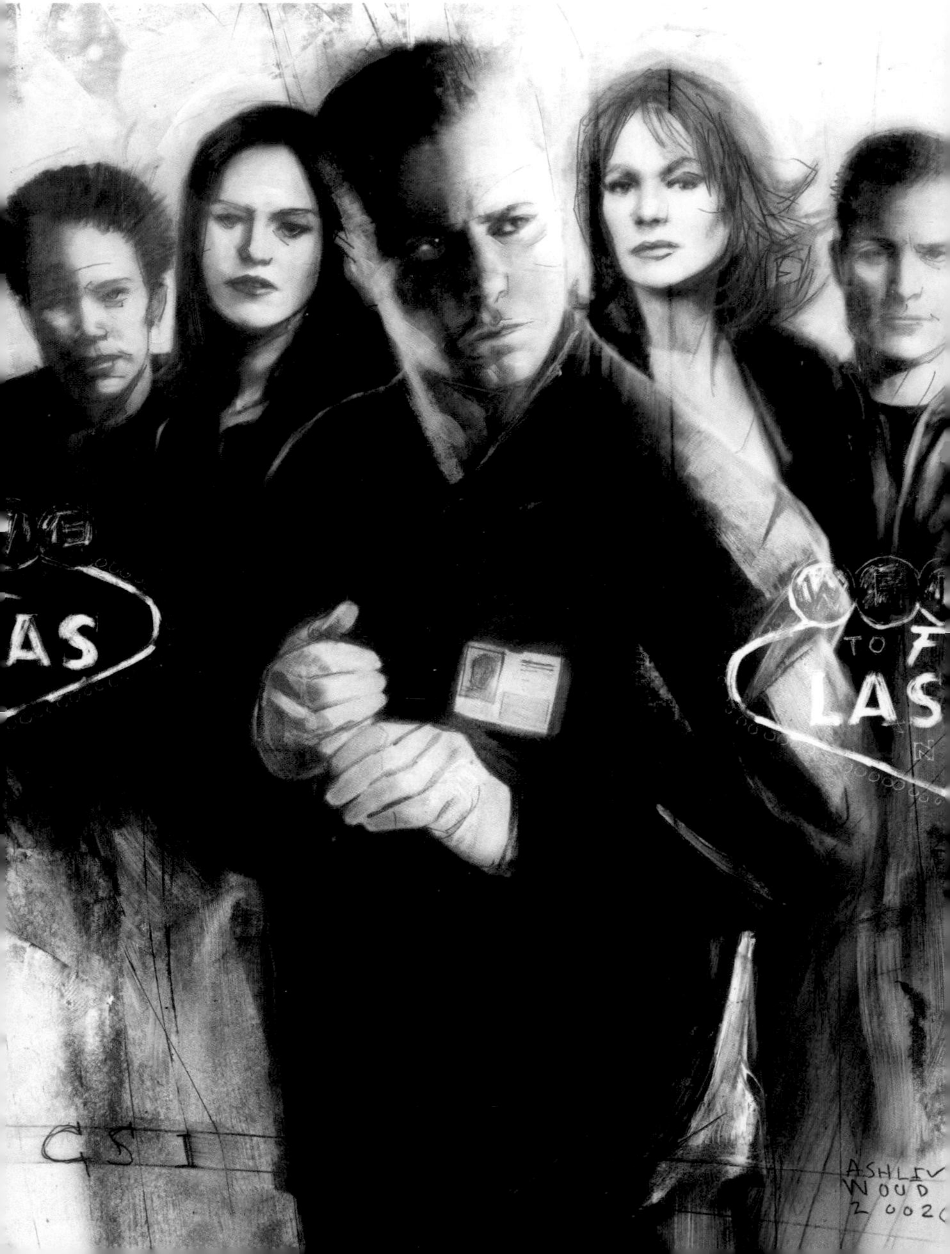
AS
TO
LAS
C S I

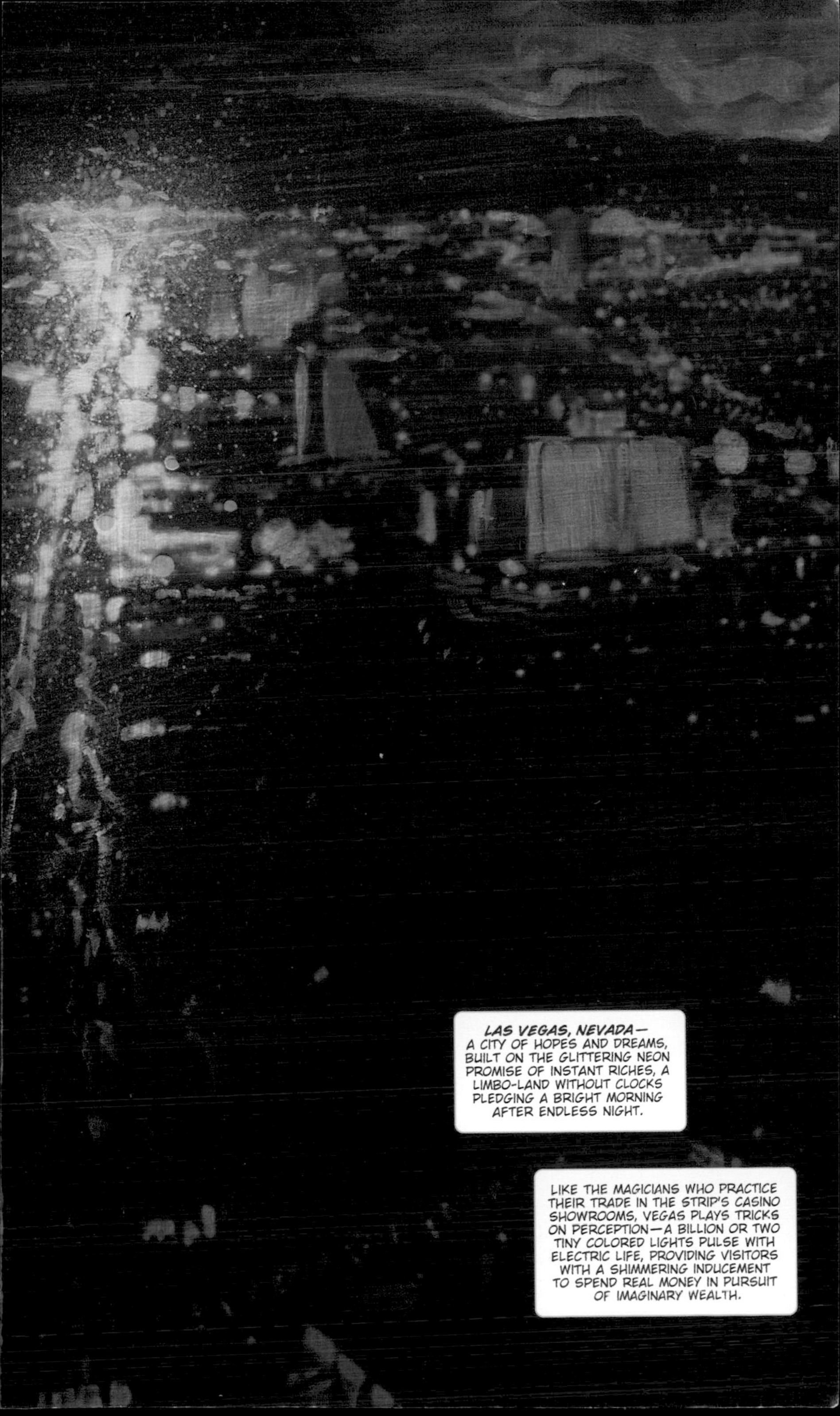
LAS VEGAS, NEVADA— A CITY OF HOPES AND DREAMS, BUILT ON THE GLITTERING NEON PROMISE OF INSTANT RICHES, A LIMBO-LAND WITHOUT CLOCKS PLEDGING A BRIGHT MORNING AFTER ENDLESS NIGHT.
LIKE THE MAGICIANS WHO PRACTICE THEIR TRADE IN THE STRIP'S CASINO SHOWROOMS, VEGAS PLAYS TRICKS ON PERCEPTION—A BILLION OR TWO TINY COLORED LIGHTS PULSE WITH ELECTRIC LIFE, PROVIDING VISITORS WITH A SHIMMERING INDUCEMENT TO SPEND REAL MONEY IN PURSUIT OF IMAGINARY WEALTH.

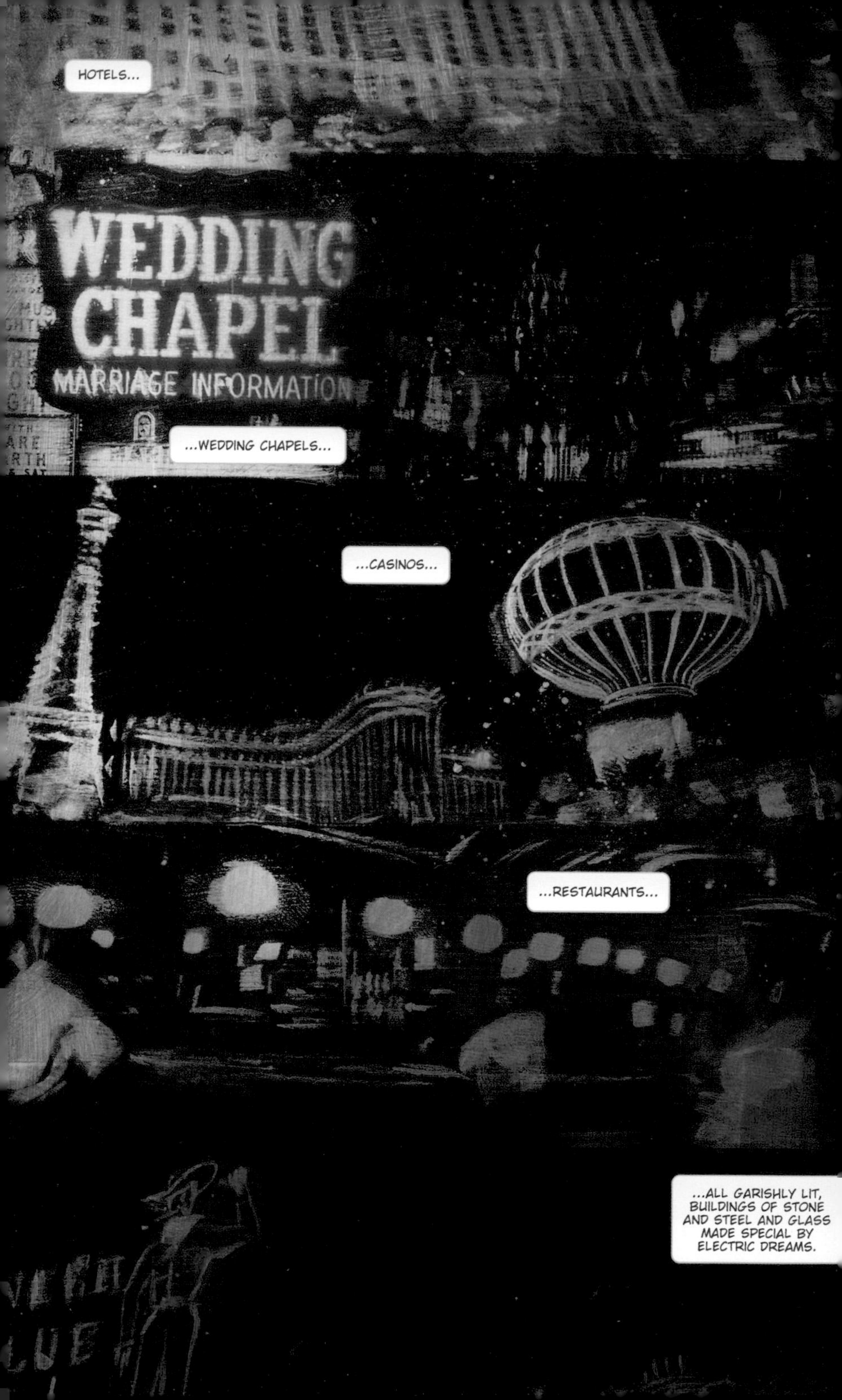
HOTELS...
WEDDING CHAPEL
MARRIAGE INFORMATION
...WEDDING CHAPELS...
...CASINOS...
...RESTAURANTS...
...ALL GARISHLY LIT, BUILDINGS OF STONE AND STEEL AND GLASS MADE SPECIAL BY ELECTRIC DREAMS.

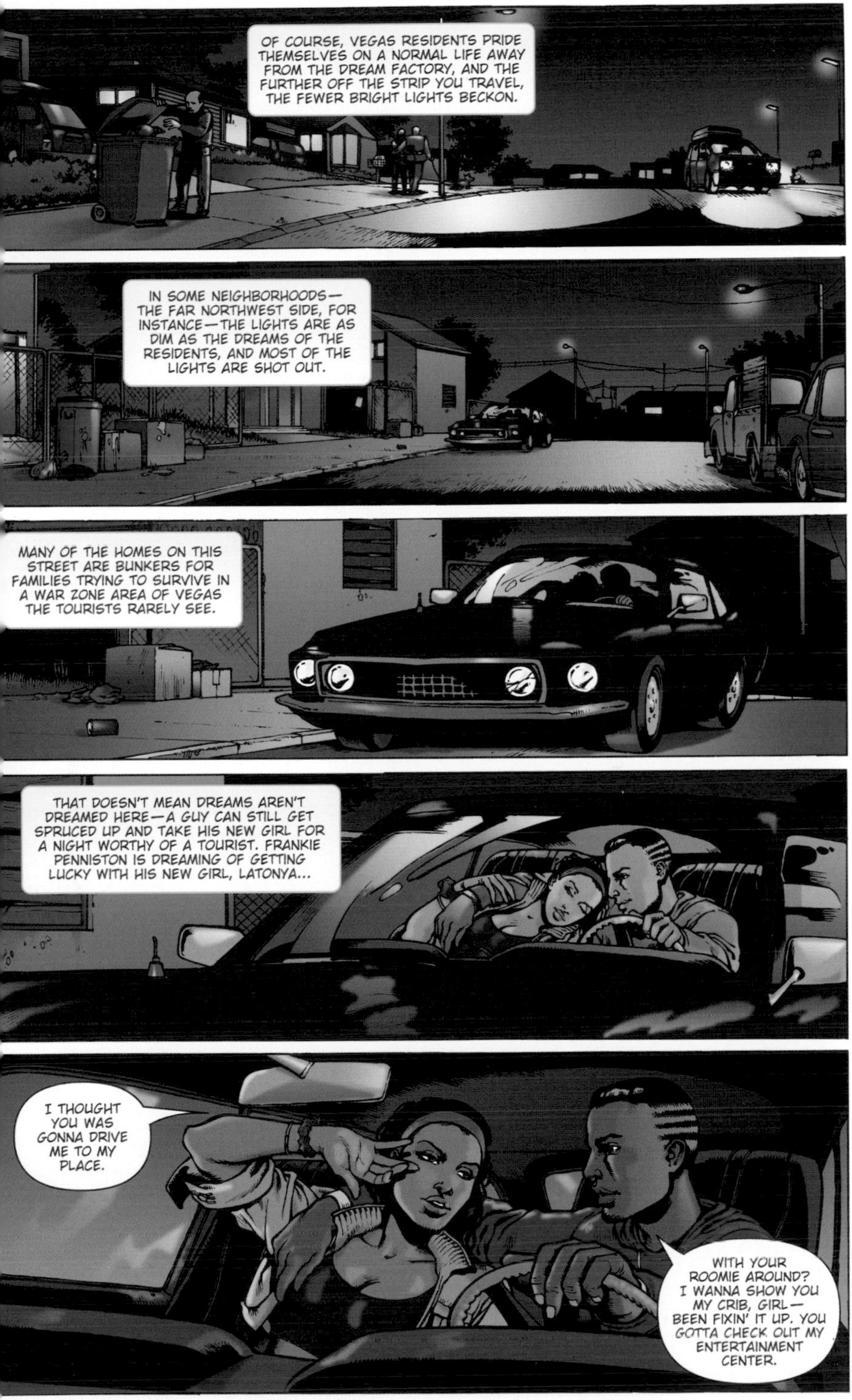

OF COURSE, VEGAS RESIDENTS PRIDE THEMSELVES ON A NORMAL LIFE AWAY FROM THE DREAM FACTORY, AND THE FURTHER OFF THE STRIP YOU TRAVEL, THE FEWER BRIGHT LIGHTS BECKON.
IN SOME NEIGHBORHOODS— THE FAR NORTHWEST SIDE, FOR INSTANCE—THE LIGHTS ARE AS DIM AS THE DREAMS OF THE RESIDENTS, AND MOST OF THE LIGHTS ARE SHOT OUT.
MANY OF THE HOMES ON THIS STREET ARE BUNKERS FOR FAMILIES TRYING TO SURVIVE IN A WAR ZONE AREA OF VEGAS THE TOURISTS RARELY SEE.
THAT DOESN'T MEAN DREAMS AREN'T DREAMED HERE—A GUY CAN STILL GET SPRUCED UP AND TAKE HIS NEW GIRL FOR A NIGHT WORTHY OF A TOURIST. FRANKIE PENNISTON IS DREAMING OF GETTING LUCKY WITH HIS NEW GIRL, LATONYA...
I THOUGHT YOU WAS GONNA DRIVE ME TO MY PLACE.
WITH YOUR ROOMIE AROUND? I WANNA SHOW YOU MY CRIB, GIRL— BEEN FIXIN' IT UP. YOU GOTTA CHECK OUT MY ENTERTAINMENT CENTER.

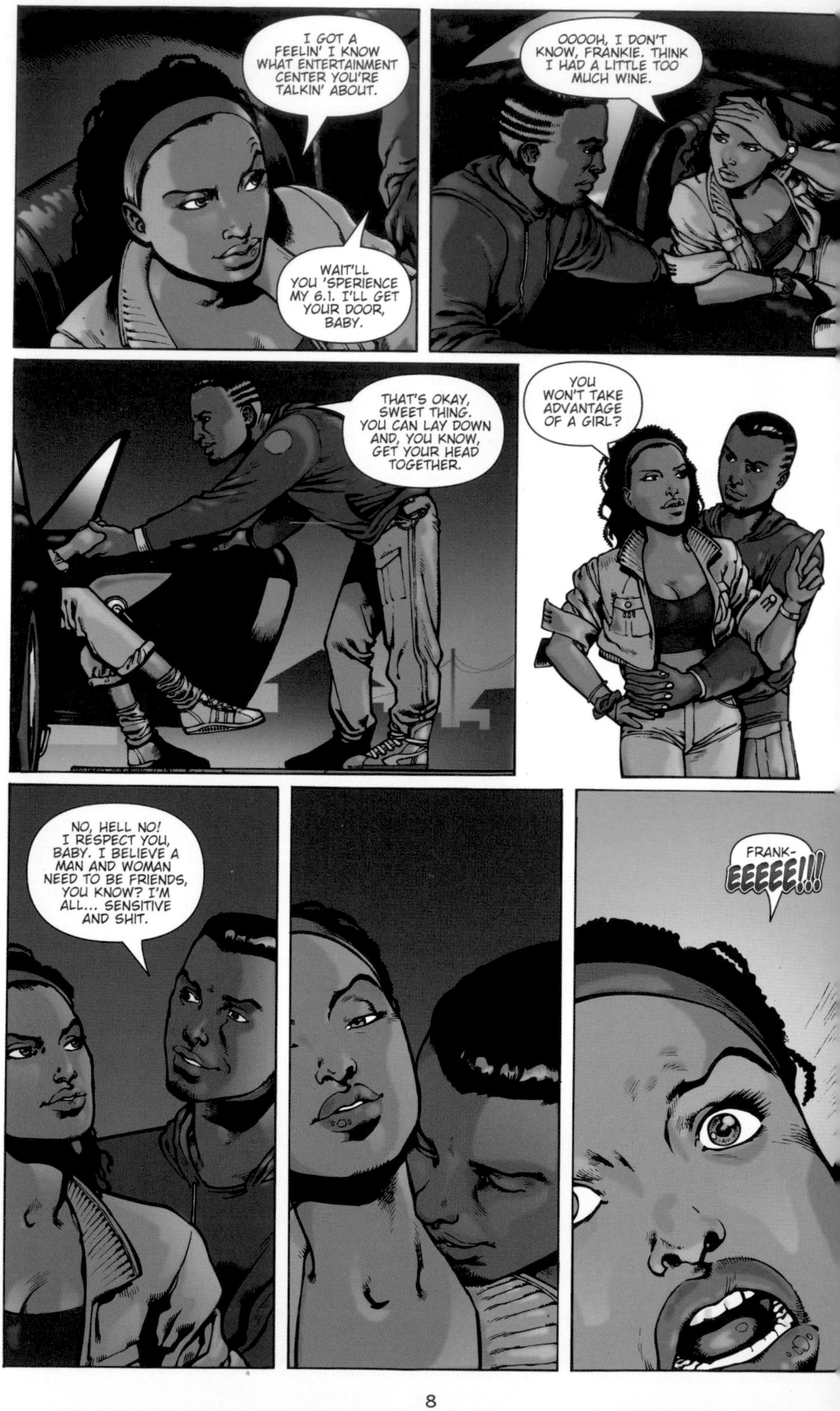
I GOT A FEELIN' I KNOW WHAT ENTERTAINMENT CENTER YOU'RE TALKIN' ABOUT.
WAIT'LL YOU 'SPERIENCE MY 6.1. I'LL GET YOUR DOOR, BABY.
OOOOH, I DON'T KNOW, FRANKIE. THINK I HAD A LITTLE TOO MUCH WINE.
THAT'S OKAY, SWEET THING. YOU CAN LAY DOWN AND, YOU KNOW, GET YOUR HEAD TOGETHER.
YOU WON'T TAKE ADVANTAGE OF A GIRL?
NO, HELL NO! I RESPECT YOU, BABY. I BELIEVE A MAN AND WOMAN NEED TO BE FRIENDS, YOU KNOW? I'M ALL... SENSITIVE AND SHIT.
FRANK-EEEEE!!!

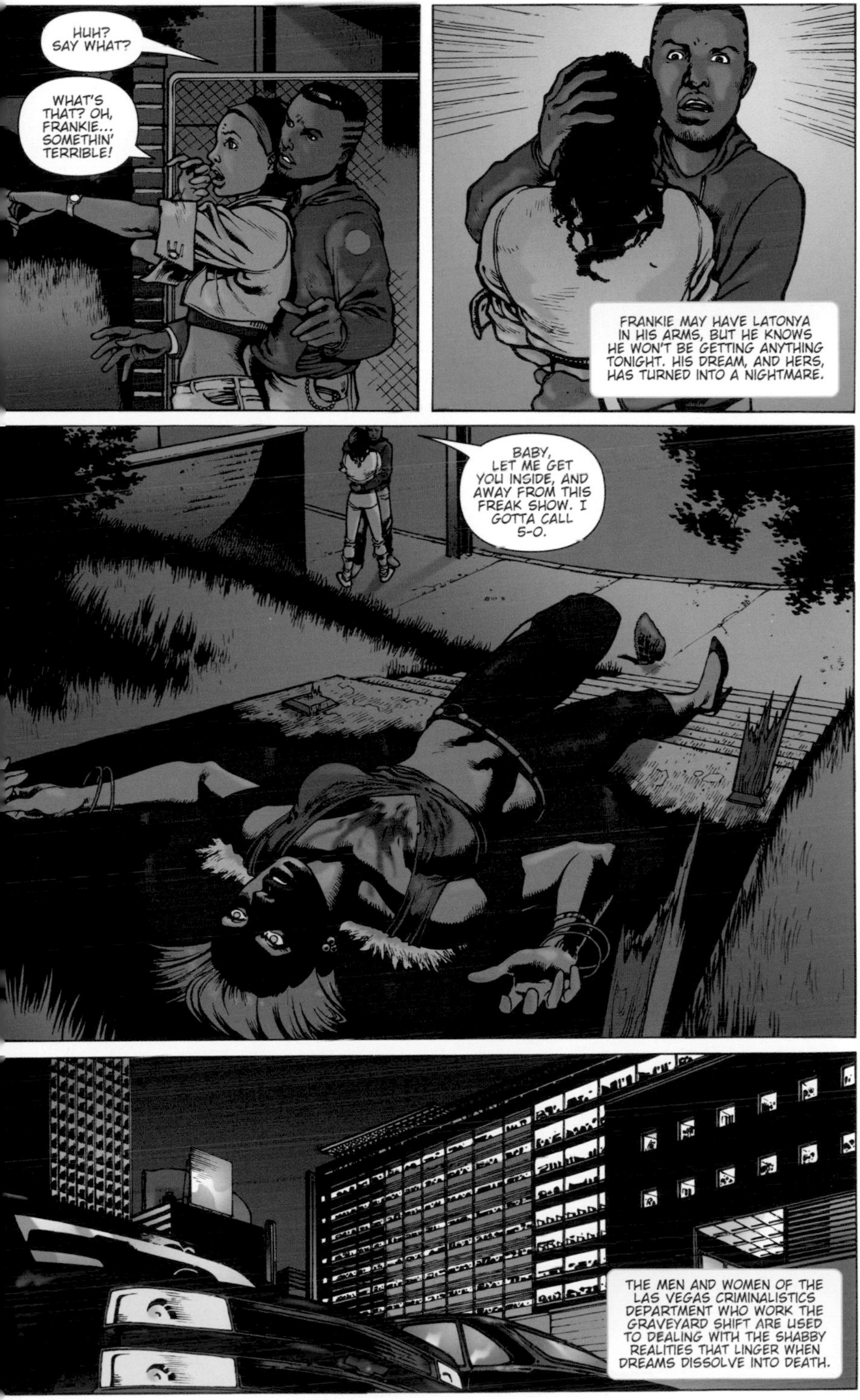
HUH? SAY WHAT?
WHAT'S THAT? OH, FRANKIE... SOMETHIN' TERRIBLE!
FRANKIE MAY HAVE LATONYA IN HIS ARMS, BUT HE KNOWS HE WON'T BE GETTING ANYTHING TONIGHT. HIS DREAM, AND HERS, HAS TURNED INTO A NIGHTMARE.
BABY, LET ME GET YOU INSIDE, AND AWAY FROM THIS FREAK SHOW. I GOTTA CALL 5-O.
THE MEN AND WOMEN OF THE LAS VEGAS CRIMINALISTICS DEPARTMENT WHO WORK THE GRAVEYARD SHIFT ARE USED TO DEALING WITH THE SHABBY REALITIES THAT LINGER WHEN DREAMS DISSOLVE INTO DEATH.

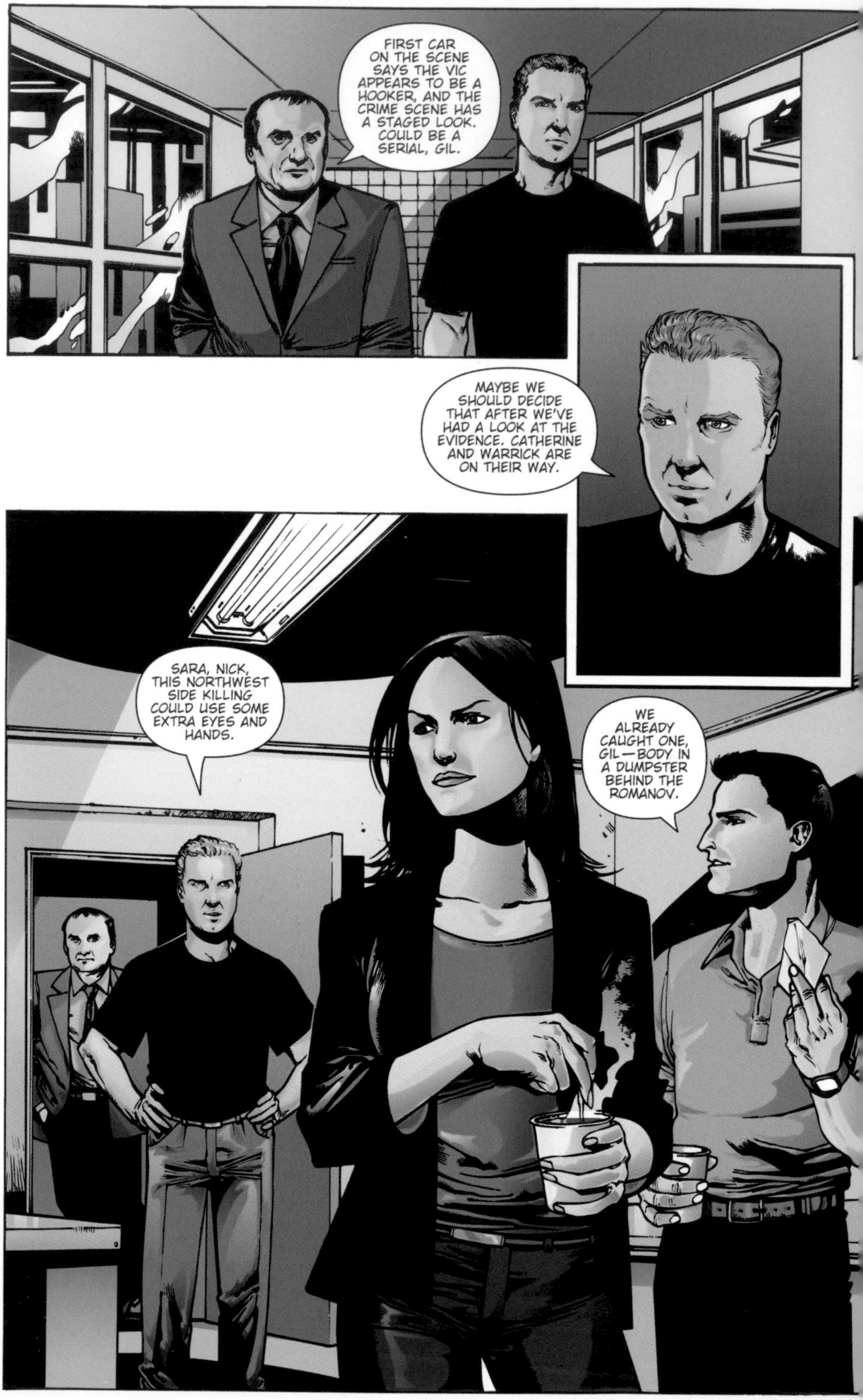
FIRST CAR ON THE SCENE SAYS THE VIC APPEARS TO BE A HOOKER, AND THE CRIME SCENE HAS A STAGED LOOK. COULD BE A SERIAL, GIL.
MAYBE WE SHOULD DECIDE THAT AFTER WE'VE HAD A LOOK AT THE EVIDENCE. CATHERINE AND WARRICK ARE ON THEIR WAY.
SARA, NICK, THIS NORTHWEST SIDE KILLING COULD USE SOME EXTRA EYES AND HANDS.
WE ALREADY CAUGHT ONE, GIL—BODY IN A DUMPSTER BEHIND THE ROMANOV.

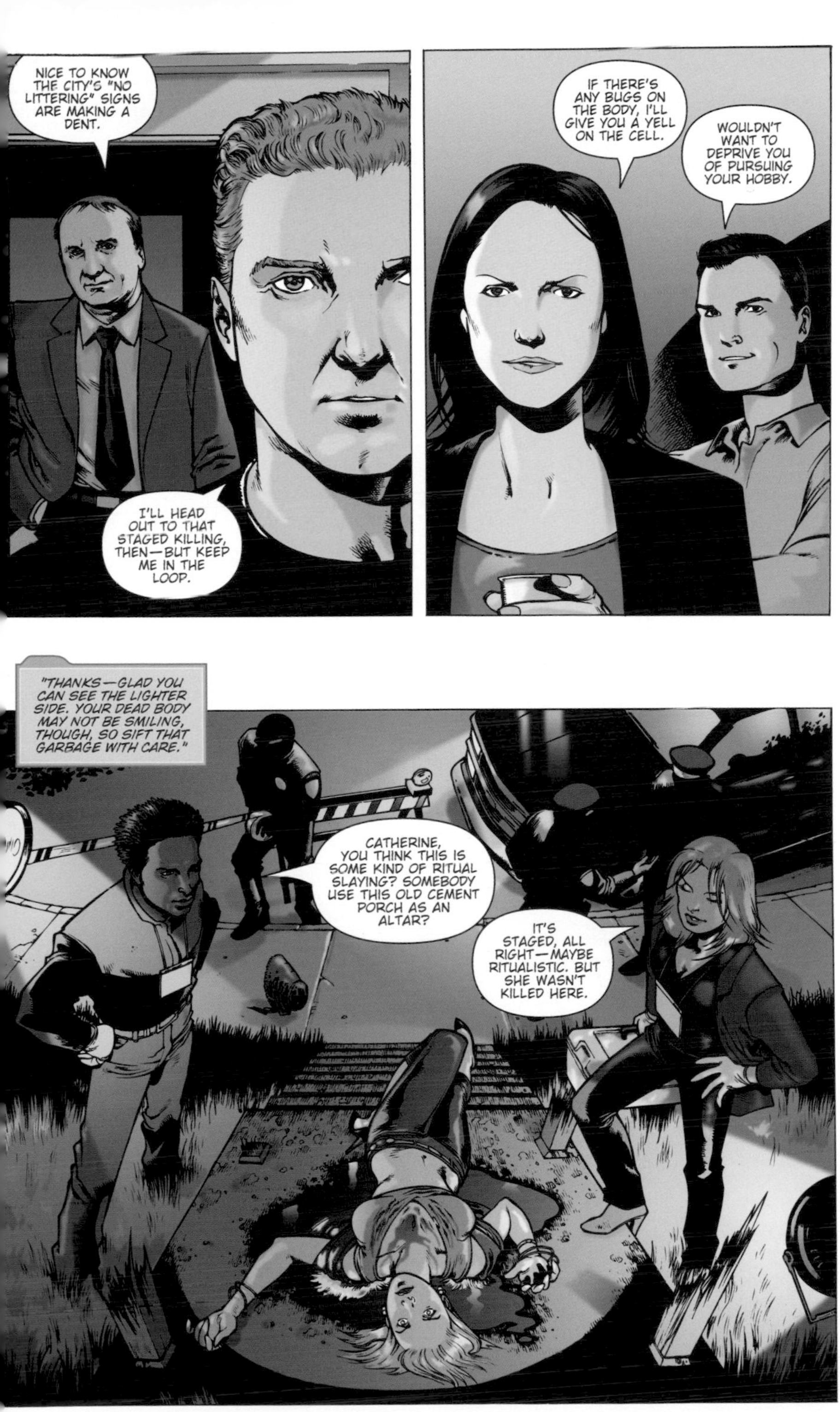
NICE TO KNOW THE CITY'S "NO LITTERING" SIGNS ARE MAKING A DENT.
I'LL HEAD OUT TO THAT STAGED KILLING, THEN—BUT KEEP ME IN THE LOOP.
IF THERE'S ANY BUGS ON THE BODY, I'LL GIVE YOU A YELL ON THE CELL.
WOULDN'T WANT TO DEPRIVE YOU OF PURSUING YOUR HOBBY.
"THANKS—GLAD YOU CAN SEE THE LIGHTER SIDE. YOUR DEAD BODY MAY NOT BE SMILING, THOUGH, SO SIFT THAT GARBAGE WITH CARE."
CATHERINE, YOU THINK THIS IS SOME KIND OF RITUAL SLAYING? SOMEBODY USE THIS OLD CEMENT PORCH AS AN ALTAR?
IT'S STAGED, ALL RIGHT—MAYBE RITUALISTIC. BUT SHE WASN'T KILLED HERE.

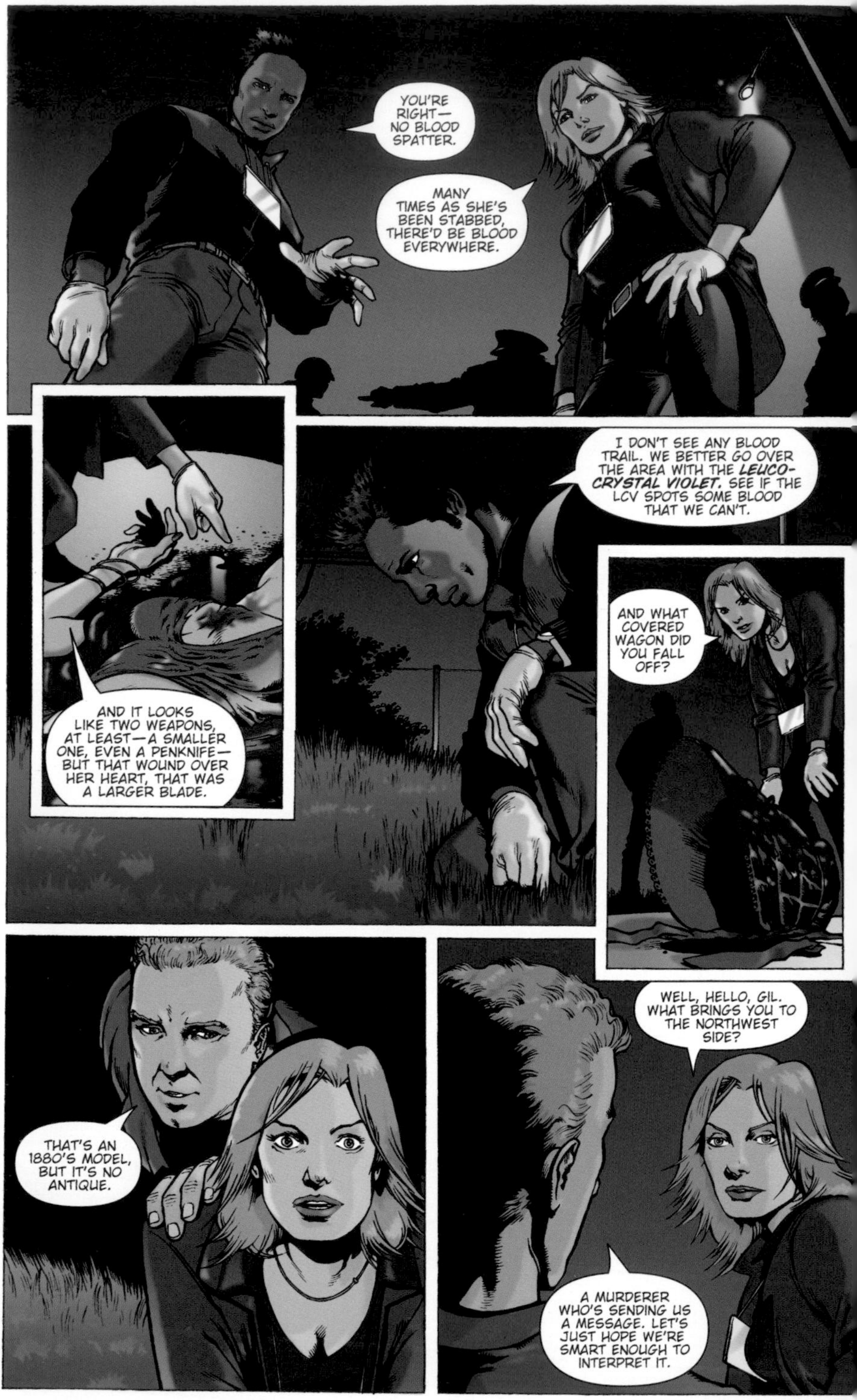
YOU'RE RIGHT— NO BLOOD SPATTER.
MANY TIMES AS SHE'S BEEN STABBED, THERE'D BE BLOOD EVERYWHERE.
AND IT LOOKS LIKE TWO WEAPONS, AT LEAST—A SMALLER ONE, EVEN A PENKNIFE—BUT THAT WOUND OVER HER HEART, THAT WAS A LARGER BLADE.
I DON'T SEE ANY BLOOD TRAIL. WE BETTER GO OVER THE AREA WITH THE LEUCO-CRYSTAL VIOLET. SEE IF THE LCV SPOTS SOME BLOOD THAT WE CAN'T.
AND WHAT COVERED WAGON DID YOU FALL OFF?
THAT'S AN 1880'S MODEL, BUT IT'S NO ANTIQUE.
WELL, HELLO, GIL. WHAT BRINGS YOU TO THE NORTHWEST SIDE?
A MURDERER WHO'S SENDING US A MESSAGE. LET'S JUST HOPE WE'RE SMART ENOUGH TO INTERPRET IT.

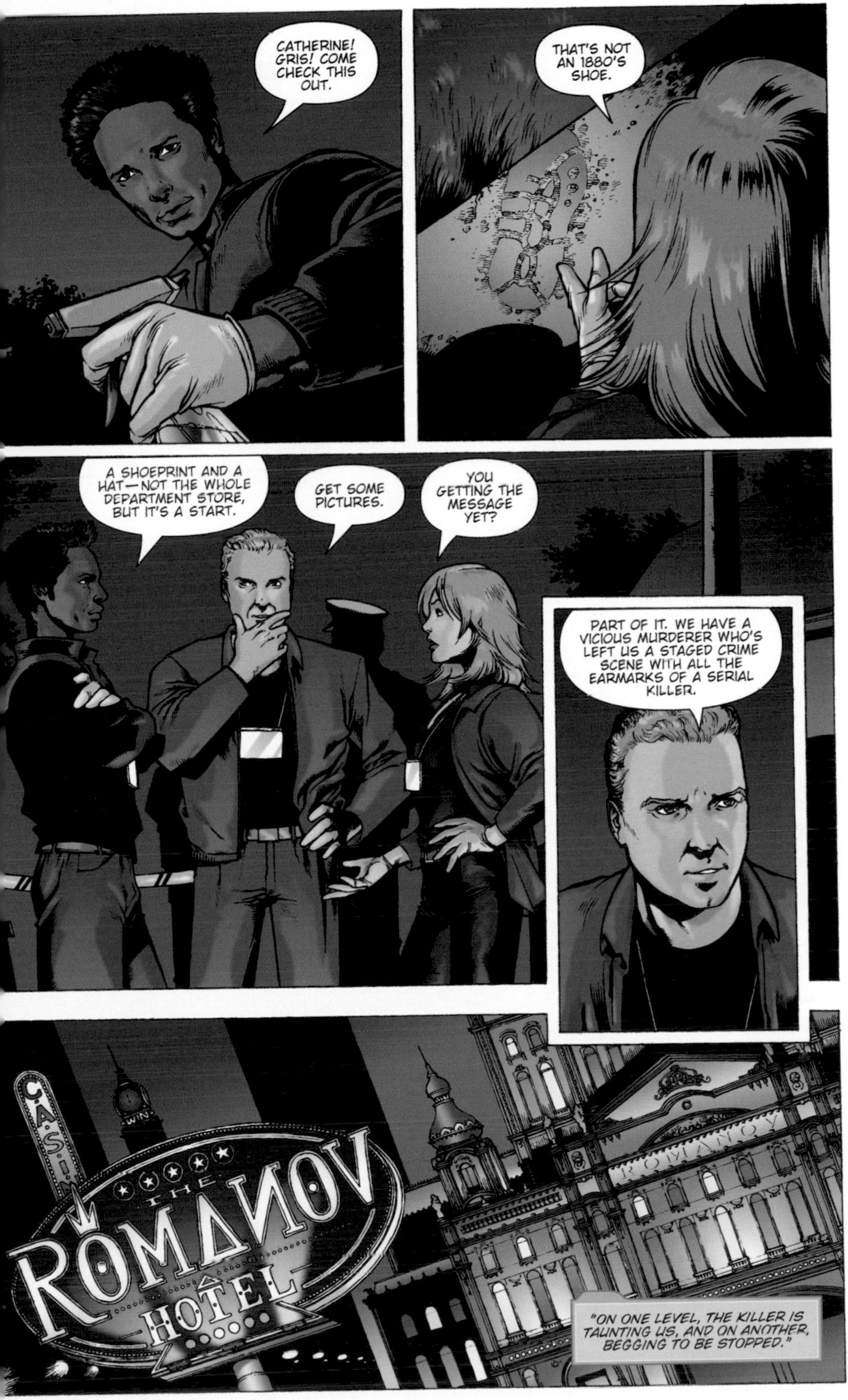

CATHERINE! GRIS! COME CHECK THIS OUT.
THAT'S NOT AN 1880'S SHOE.
A SHOEPRINT AND A HAT—NOT THE WHOLE DEPARTMENT STORE, BUT IT'S A START.
GET SOME PICTURES.
YOU GETTING THE MESSAGE YET?
PART OF IT. WE HAVE A VICIOUS MURDERER WHO'S LEFT US A STAGED CRIME SCENE WITH ALL THE EARMARKS OF A SERIAL KILLER.
CASINO
THE ROMANOV HOTEL
ROMANOV
"ON ONE LEVEL, THE KILLER IS TAUNTING US, AND ON ANOTHER, BEGGING TO BE STOPPED."

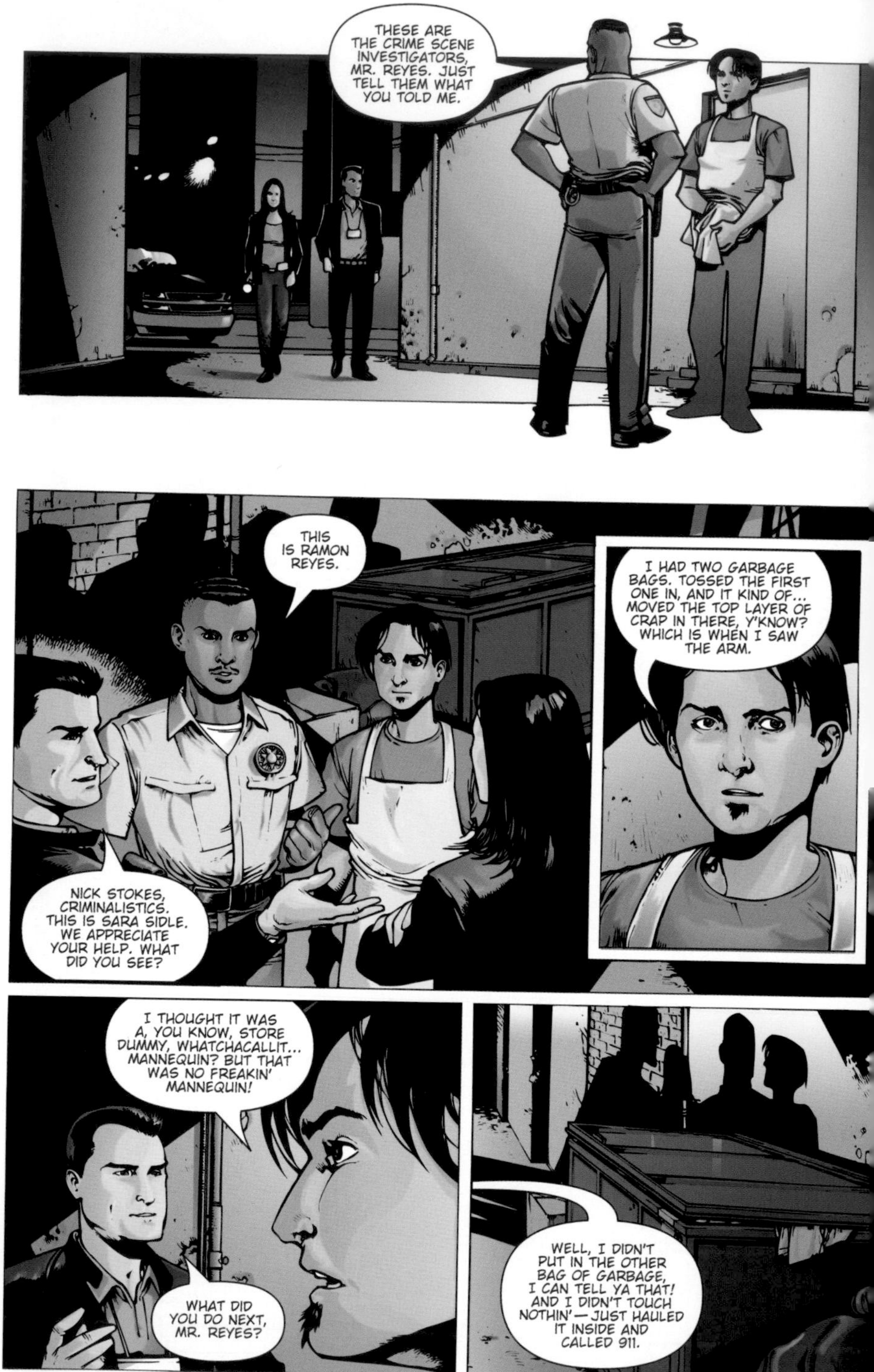

THESE ARE THE CRIME SCENE INVESTIGATORS, MR. REYES. JUST TELL THEM WHAT YOU TOLD ME.
THIS IS RAMON REYES.
NICK STOKES, CRIMINALISTICS. THIS IS SARA SIDLE. WE APPRECIATE YOUR HELP. WHAT DID YOU SEE?
I HAD TWO GARBAGE BAGS. TOSSED THE FIRST ONE IN, AND IT KIND OF... MOVED THE TOP LAYER OF CRAP IN THERE, Y'KNOW? WHICH IS WHEN I SAW THE ARM.
I THOUGHT IT WAS A, YOU KNOW, STORE DUMMY, WHATCHACALLIT... MANNEQUIN? BUT THAT WAS NO FREAKIN' MANNEQUIN!
WHAT DID YOU DO NEXT, MR. REYES?
WELL, I DIDN'T PUT IN THE OTHER BAG OF GARBAGE, I CAN TELL YA THAT! AND I DIDN'T TOUCH NOTHIN'— JUST HAULED IT INSIDE AND CALLED 911.

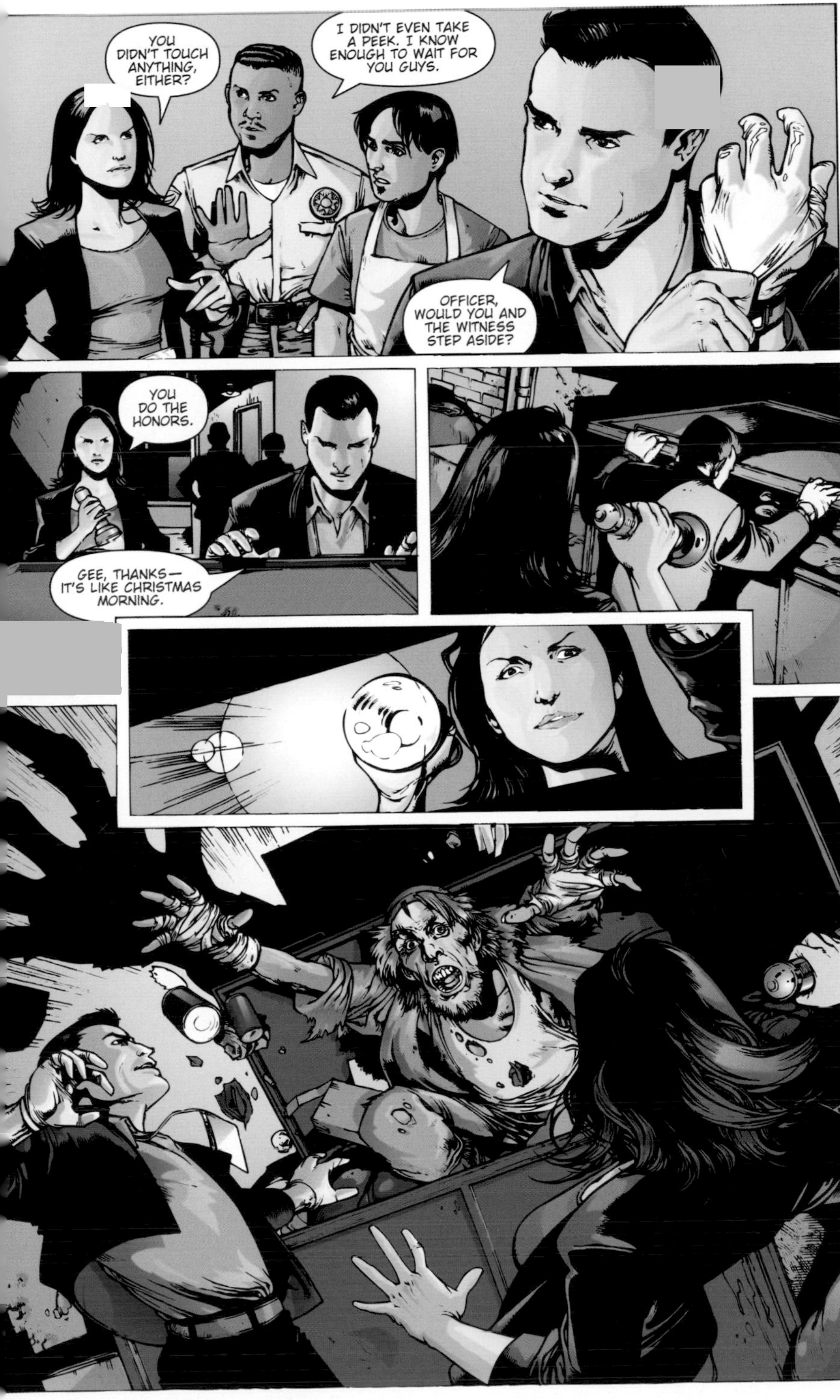
YOU DIDN'T TOUCH ANYTHING, EITHER?
I DIDN'T EVEN TAKE A PEEK. I KNOW ENOUGH TO WAIT FOR YOU GUYS.
OFFICER, WOULD YOU AND THE WITNESS STEP ASIDE?
YOU DO THE HONORS.
GEE, THANKS— IT'S LIKE CHRISTMAS MORNING.

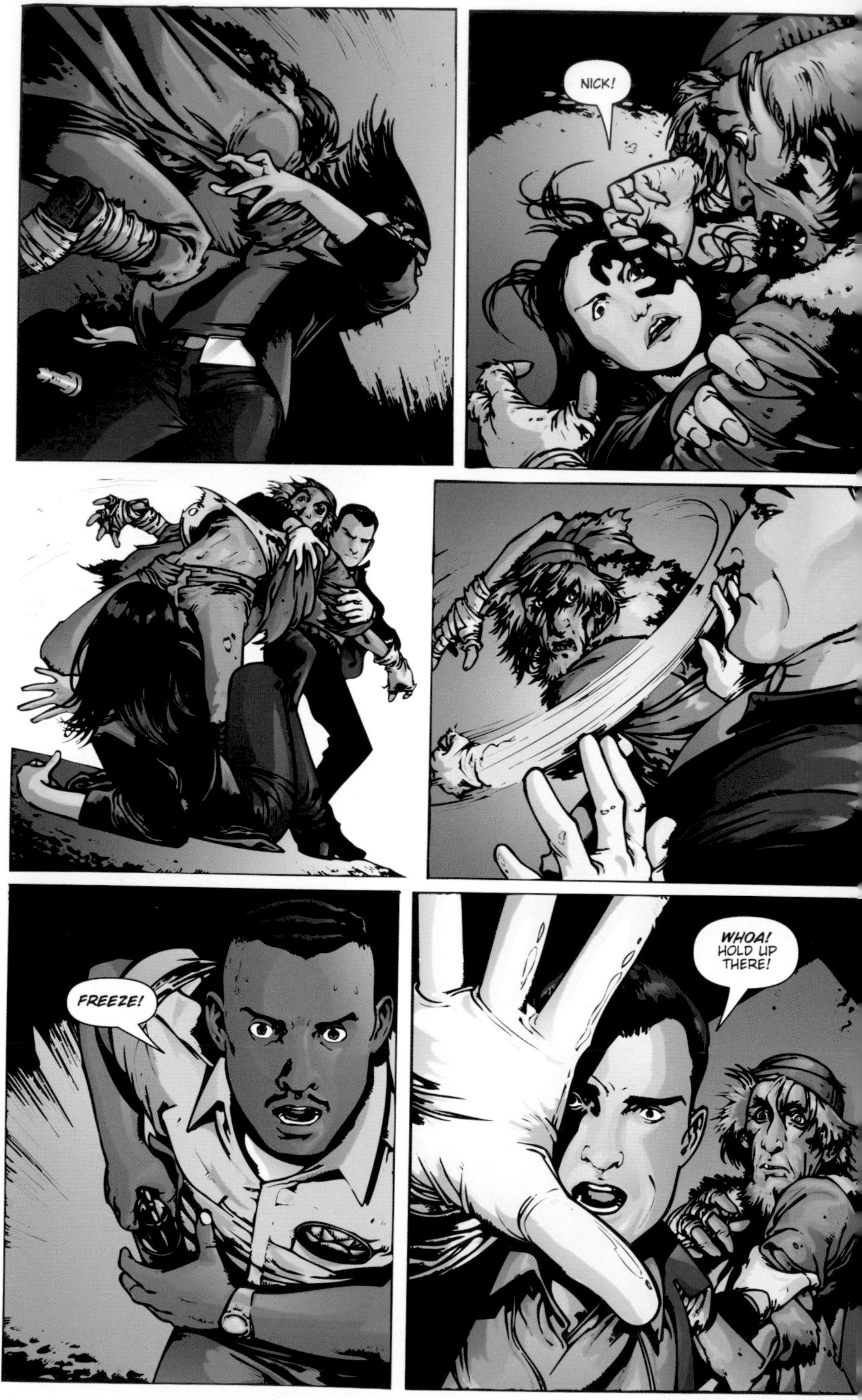
NICK!
FREEZE!
WHOA! HOLD UP THERE!

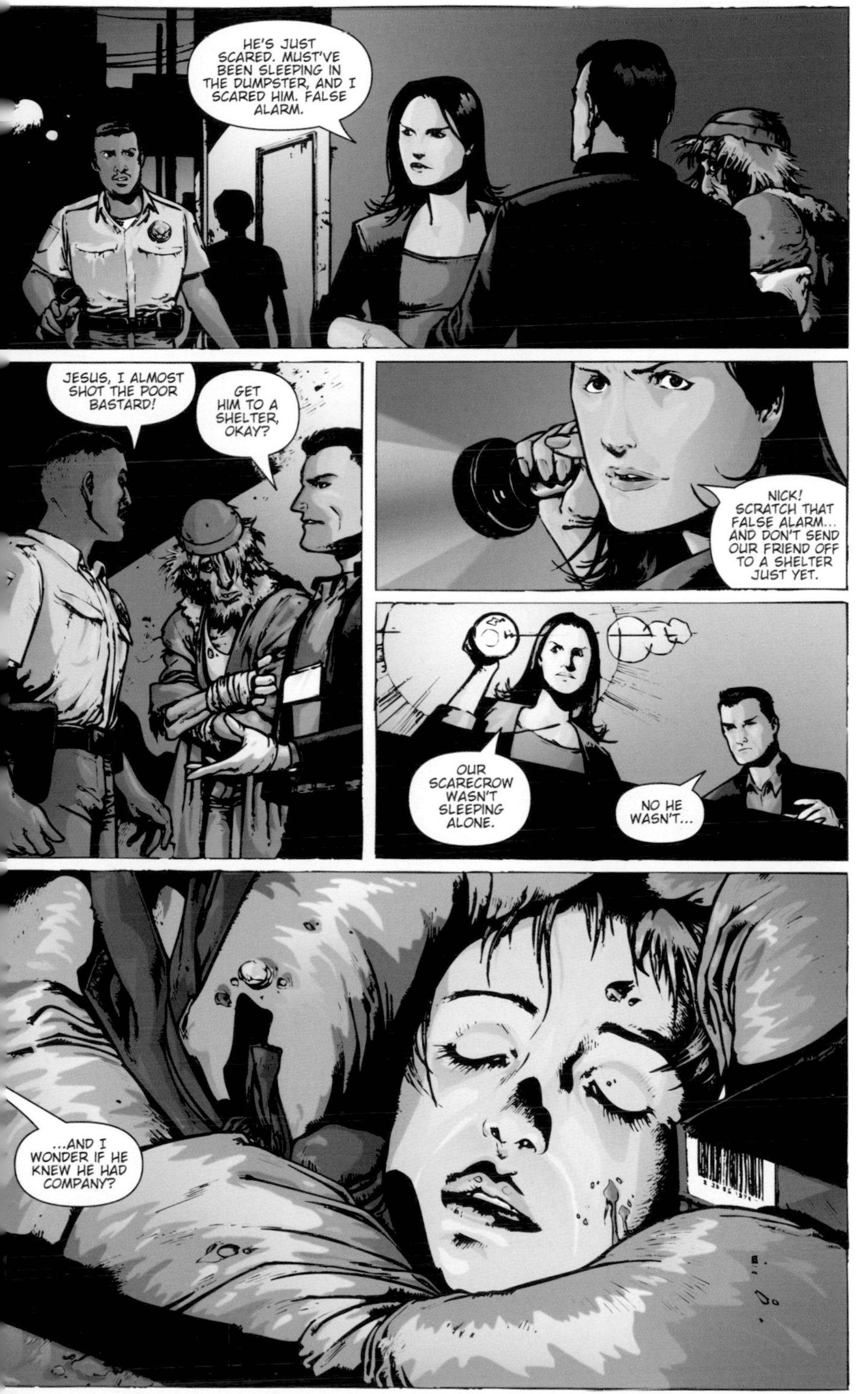

HE'S JUST SCARED. MUST'VE BEEN SLEEPING IN THE DUMPSTER, AND I SCARED HIM. FALSE ALARM.
JESUS, I ALMOST SHOT THE POOR BASTARD!
GET HIM TO A SHELTER, OKAY?
NICK! SCRATCH THAT FALSE ALARM... AND DON'T SEND OUR FRIEND OFF TO A SHELTER JUST YET.
OUR SCARECROW WASN'T SLEEPING ALONE.
NO HE WASN'T...
...AND I WONDER IF HE KNEW HE HAD COMPANY?

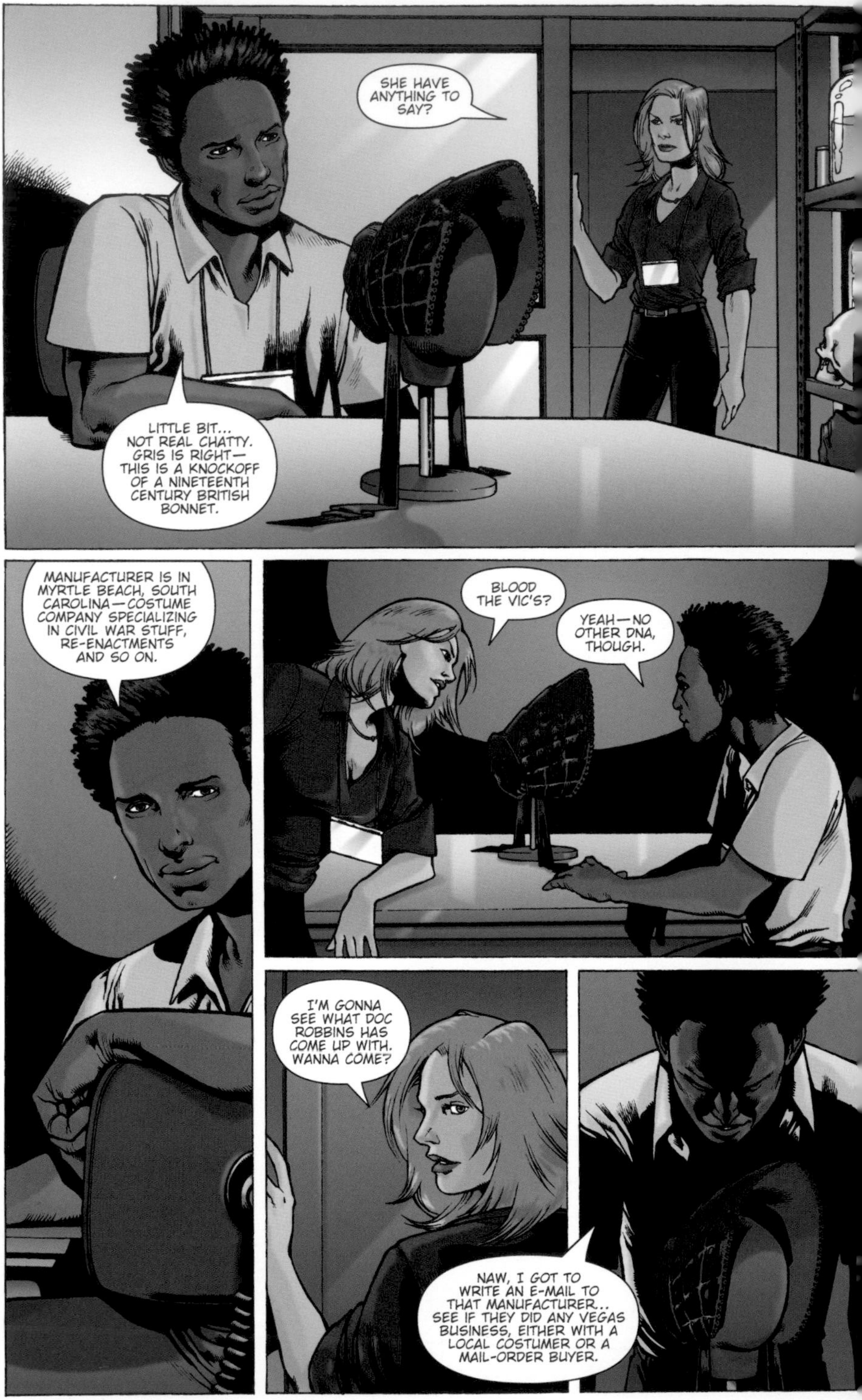
SHE HAVE ANYTHING TO SAY?
LITTLE BIT... NOT REAL CHATTY. GRIS IS RIGHT— THIS IS A KNOCKOFF OF A NINETEENTH CENTURY BRITISH BONNET.
MANUFACTURER IS IN MYRTLE BEACH, SOUTH CAROLINA—COSTUME COMPANY SPECIALIZING IN CIVIL WAR STUFF, RE-ENACTMENTS AND SO ON.
BLOOD THE VIC'S?
YEAH—NO OTHER DNA, THOUGH.
I'M GONNA SEE WHAT DOC ROBBINS HAS COME UP WITH. WANNA COME?
NAW, I GOT TO WRITE AN E-MAIL TO THAT MANUFACTURER... SEE IF THEY DID ANY VEGAS BUSINESS, EITHER WITH A LOCAL COSTUMER OR A MAIL-ORDER BUYER.

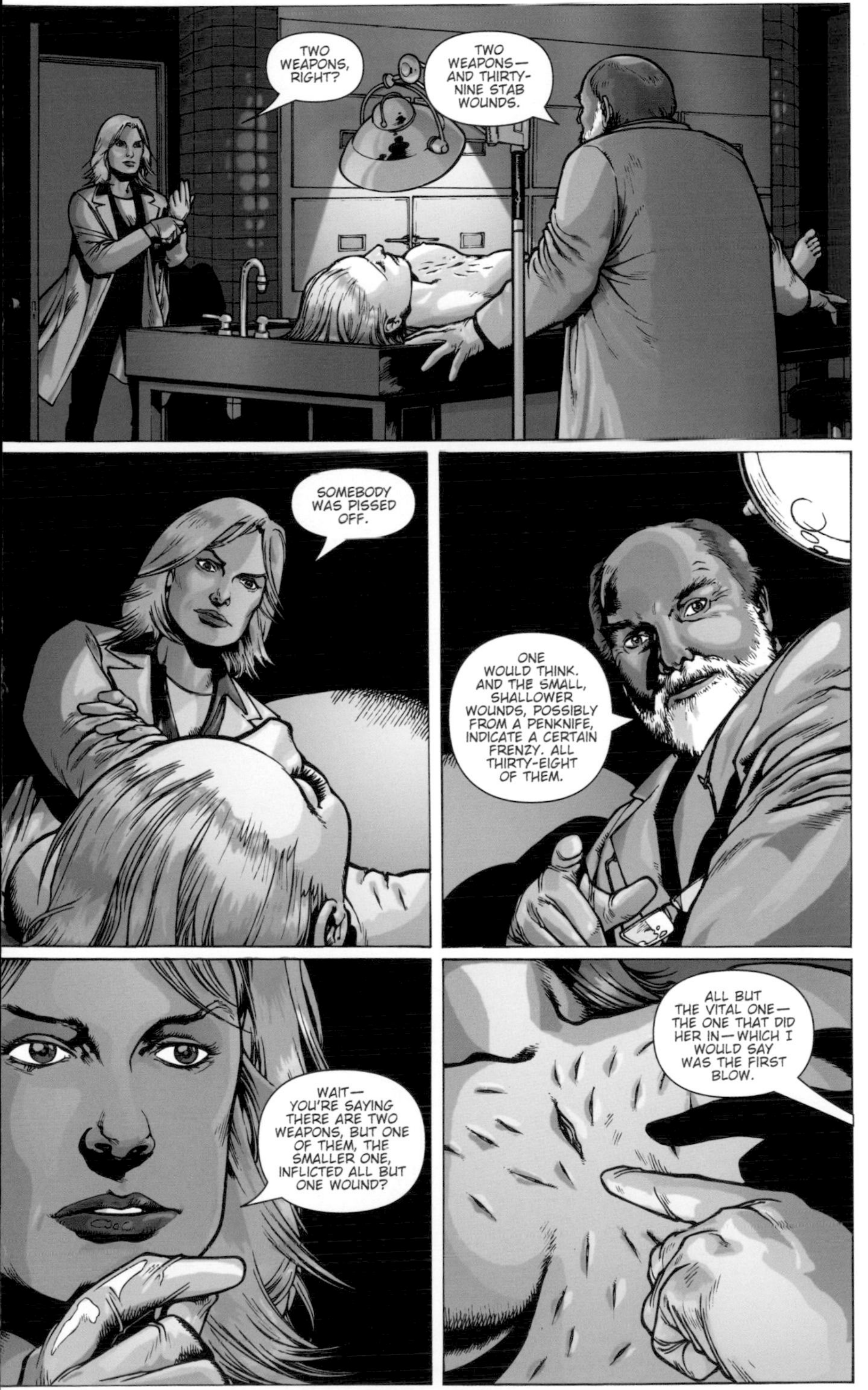
TWO WEAPONS, RIGHT?
TWO WEAPONS— AND THIRTY-NINE STAB WOUNDS.
SOMEBODY WAS PISSED OFF.
ONE WOULD THINK. AND THE SMALL, SHALLOWER WOUNDS, POSSIBLY FROM A PENKNIFE, INDICATE A CERTAIN FRENZY. ALL THIRTY-EIGHT OF THEM.
WAIT— YOU'RE SAYING THERE ARE TWO WEAPONS, BUT ONE OF THEM, THE SMALLER ONE, INFLICTED ALL BUT ONE WOUND?
ALL BUT THE VITAL ONE— THE ONE THAT DID HER IN— WHICH I WOULD SAY WAS THE FIRST BLOW.

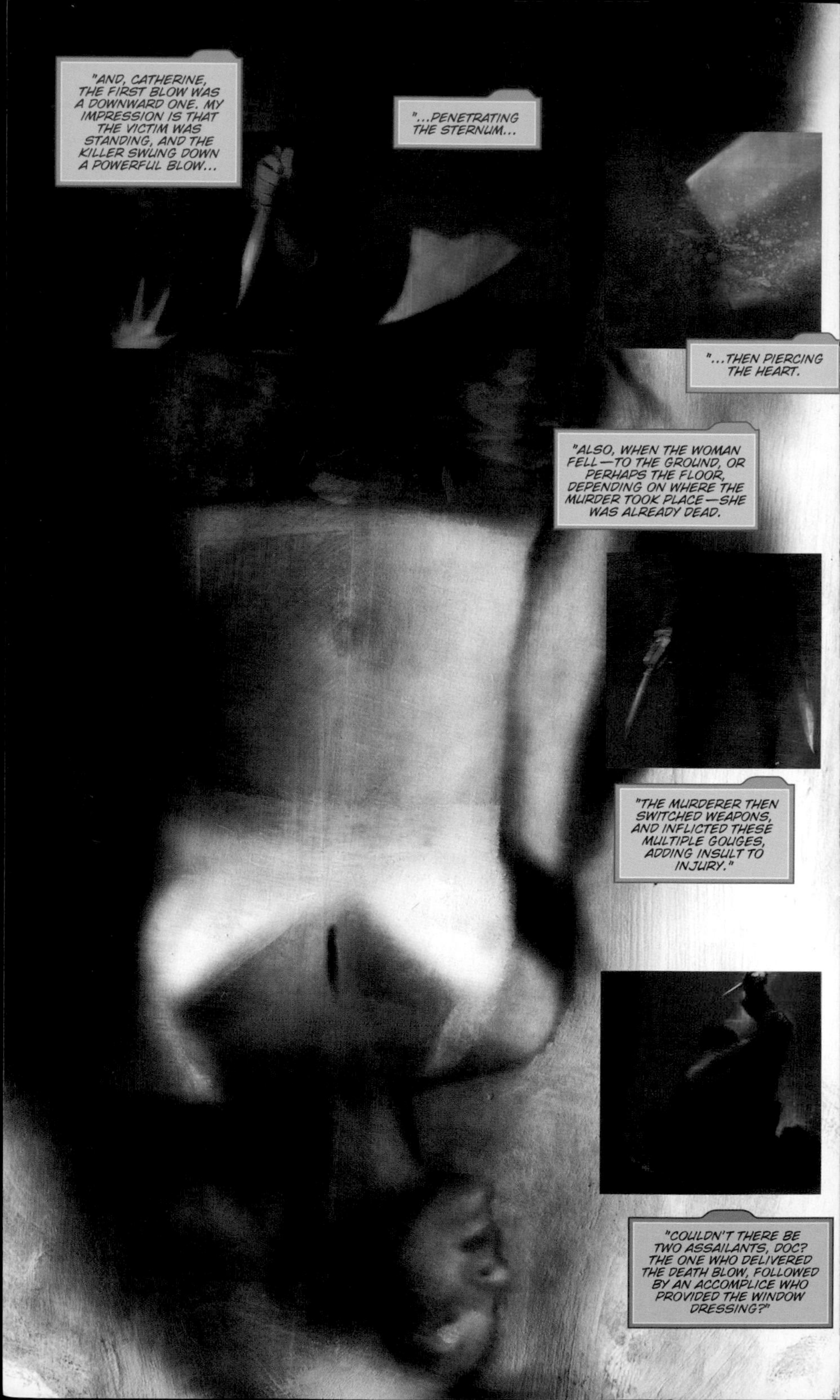
"AND, CATHERINE, THE FIRST BLOW WAS A DOWNWARD ONE. MY IMPRESSION IS THAT THE VICTIM WAS STANDING, AND THE KILLER SWUNG DOWN A POWERFUL BLOW...
"...PENETRATING THE STERNUM...
"...THEN PIERCING THE HEART.
"ALSO, WHEN THE WOMAN FELL—TO THE GROUND, OR PERHAPS THE FLOOR, DEPENDING ON WHERE THE MURDER TOOK PLACE—SHE WAS ALREADY DEAD.
"THE MURDERER THEN SWITCHED WEAPONS, AND INFLICTED THESE MULTIPLE GOUGES, ADDING INSULT TO INJURY."
"COULDN'T THERE BE TWO ASSAILANTS, DOC? THE ONE WHO DELIVERED THE DEATH BLOW, FOLLOWED BY AN ACCOMPLICE WHO PROVIDED THE WINDOW DRESSING?"

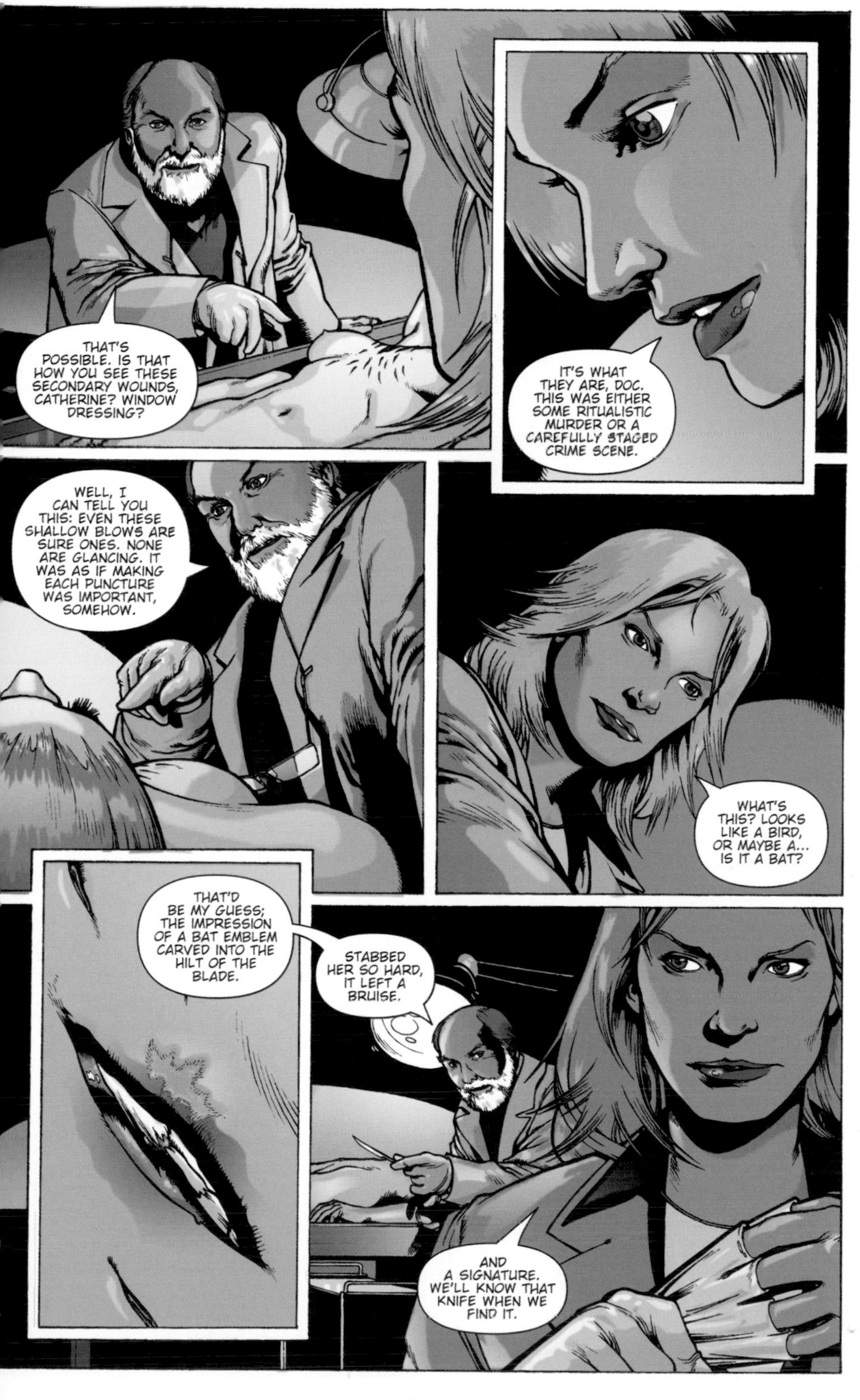
THAT'S POSSIBLE. IS THAT HOW YOU SEE THESE SECONDARY WOUNDS, CATHERINE? WINDOW DRESSING?
IT'S WHAT THEY ARE, DOC. THIS WAS EITHER SOME RITUALISTIC MURDER OR A CAREFULLY STAGED CRIME SCENE.
WELL, I CAN TELL YOU THIS: EVEN THESE SHALLOW BLOWS ARE SURE ONES. NONE ARE GLANCING. IT WAS AS IF MAKING EACH PUNCTURE WAS IMPORTANT, SOMEHOW.
WHAT'S THIS? LOOKS LIKE A BIRD, OR MAYBE A... IS IT A BAT?
THAT'D BE MY GUESS; THE IMPRESSION OF A BAT EMBLEM CARVED INTO THE HILT OF THE BLADE.
STABBED HER SO HARD, IT LEFT A BRUISE.
AND A SIGNATURE. WE'LL KNOW THAT KNIFE WHEN WE FIND IT.

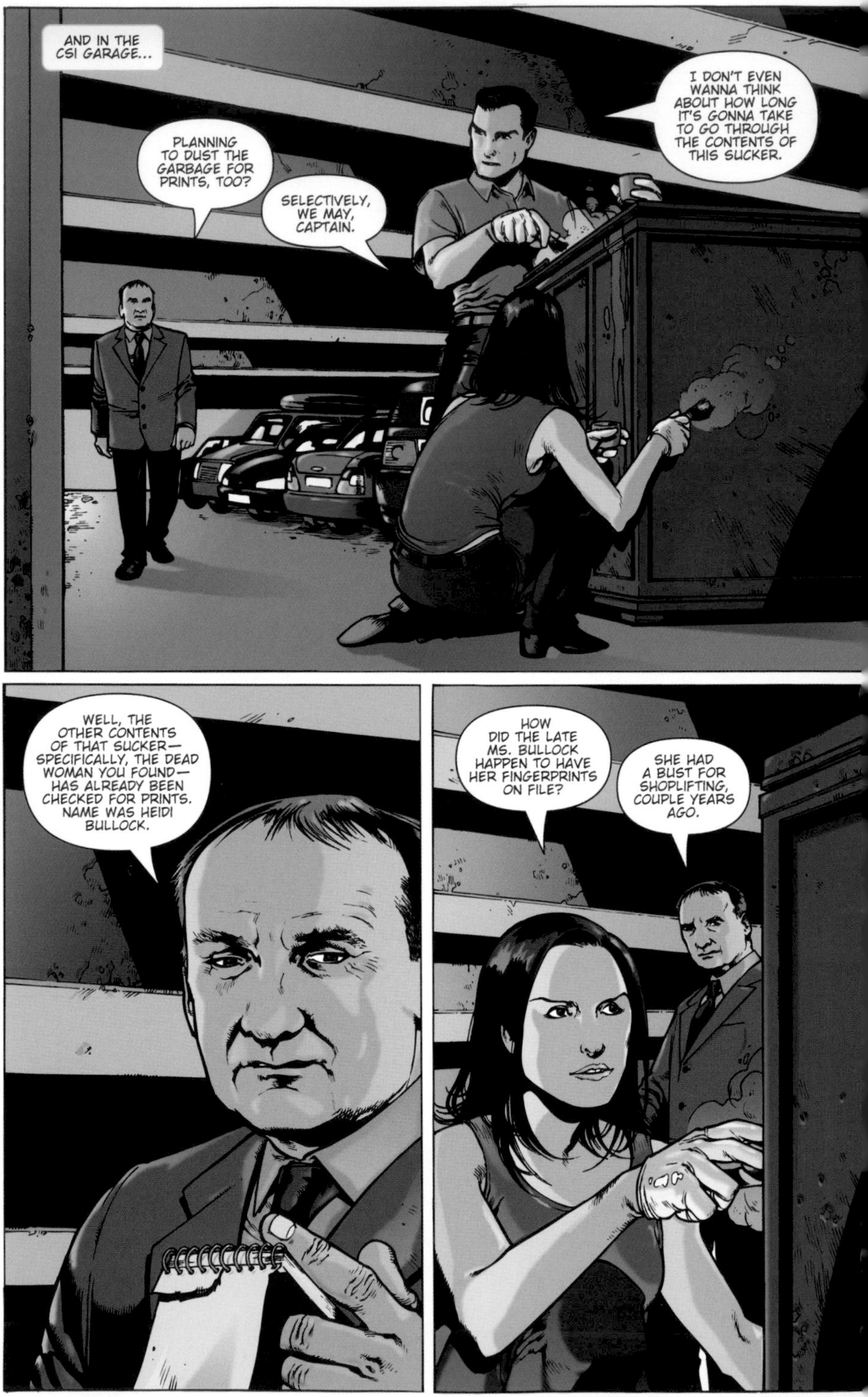
AND IN THE CSI GARAGE...
PLANNING TO DUST THE GARBAGE FOR PRINTS, TOO?
SELECTIVELY, WE MAY, CAPTAIN.
I DON'T EVEN WANNA THINK ABOUT HOW LONG IT'S GONNA TAKE TO GO THROUGH THE CONTENTS OF THIS SUCKER.
WELL, THE OTHER CONTENTS OF THAT SUCKER—SPECIFICALLY, THE DEAD WOMAN YOU FOUND—HAS ALREADY BEEN CHECKED FOR PRINTS. NAME WAS HEIDI BULLOCK.
HOW DID THE LATE MS. BULLOCK HAPPEN TO HAVE HER FINGERPRINTS ON FILE?
SHE HAD A BUST FOR SHOPLIFTING, COUPLE YEARS AGO.

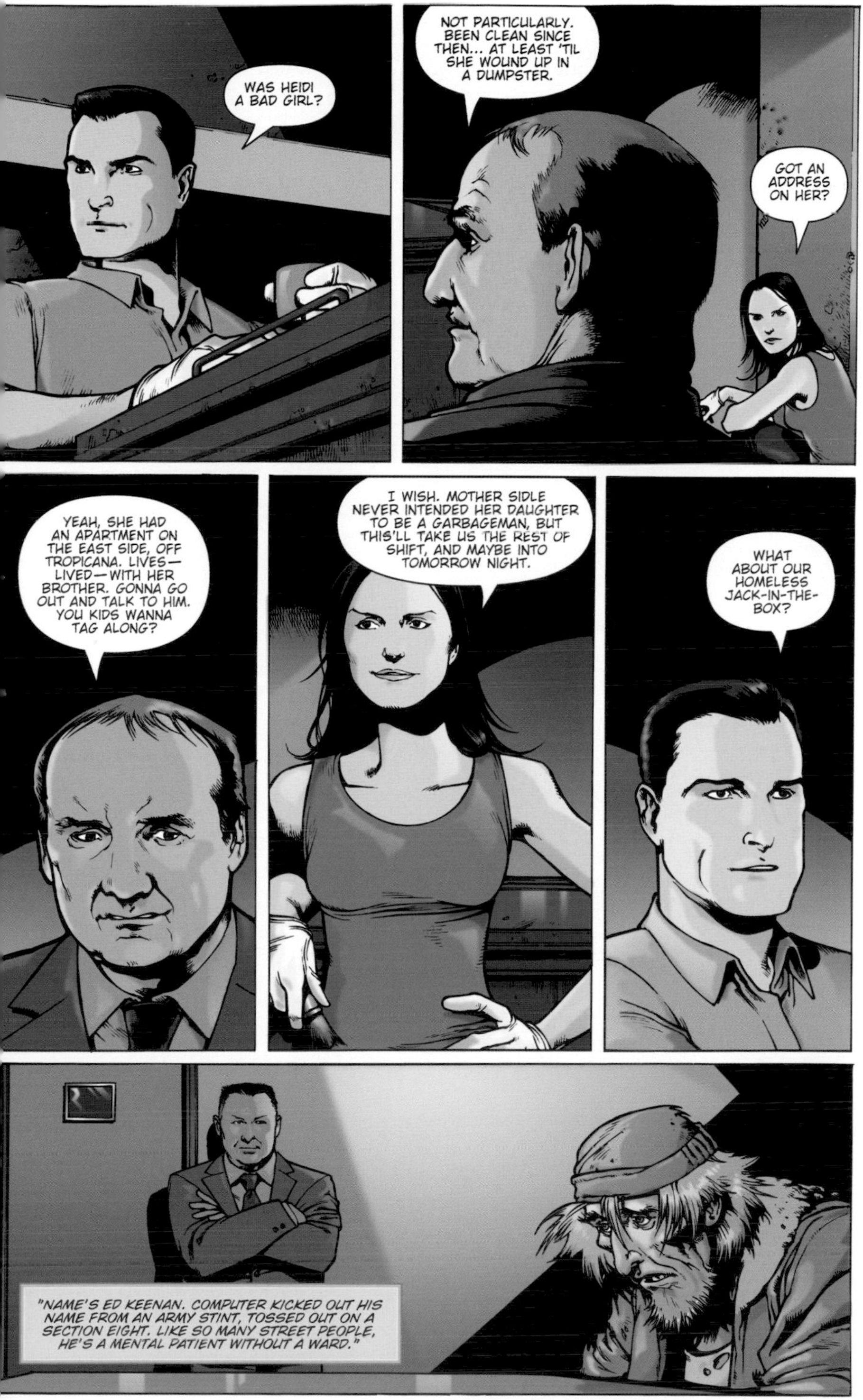
WAS HEIDI A BAD GIRL?
NOT PARTICULARLY. BEEN CLEAN SINCE THEN... AT LEAST 'TIL SHE WOUND UP IN A DUMPSTER.
GOT AN ADDRESS ON HER?
YEAH, SHE HAD AN APARTMENT ON THE EAST SIDE, OFF TROPICANA. LIVES—LIVED—WITH HER BROTHER. GONNA GO OUT AND TALK TO HIM. YOU KIDS WANNA TAG ALONG?
I WISH. MOTHER SIDLE NEVER INTENDED HER DAUGHTER TO BE A GARBAGEMAN, BUT THIS'LL TAKE US THE REST OF SHIFT, AND MAYBE INTO TOMORROW NIGHT.
WHAT ABOUT OUR HOMELESS JACK-IN-THE-BOX?
"NAME'S ED KEENAN. COMPUTER KICKED OUT HIS NAME FROM AN ARMY STINT, TOSSED OUT ON A SECTION EIGHT. LIKE SO MANY STREET PEOPLE, HE'S A MENTAL PATIENT WITHOUT A WARD."

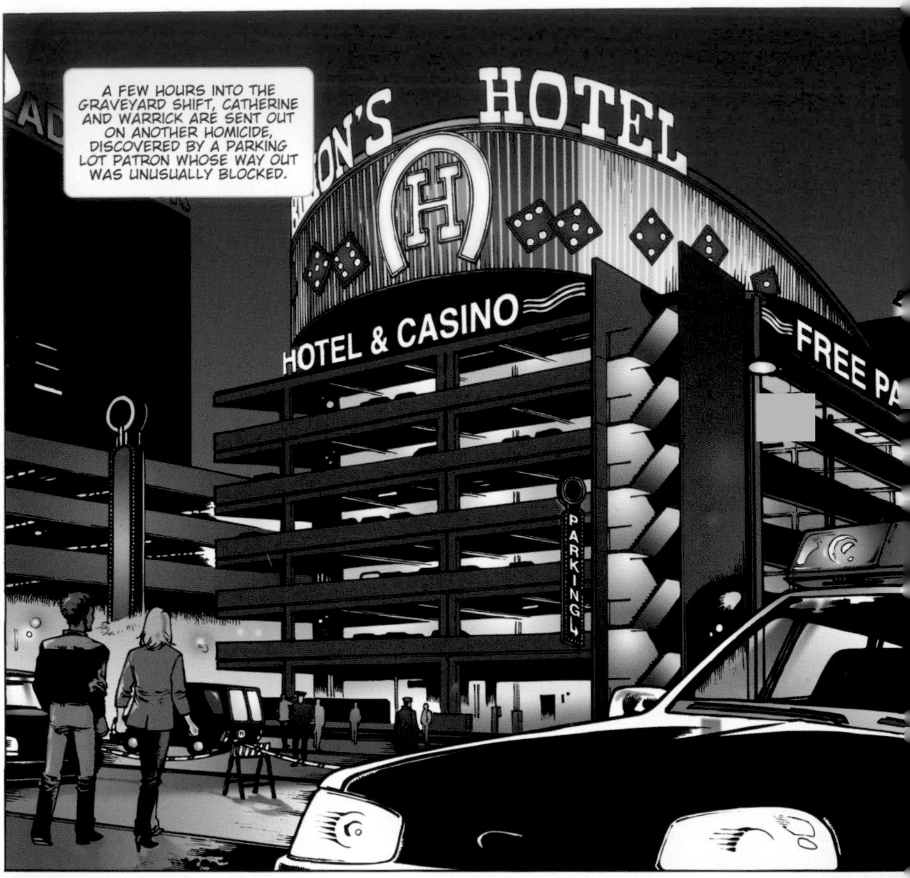
A FEW HOURS INTO THE GRAVEYARD SHIFT, CATHERINE AND WARRICK ARE SENT OUT ON ANOTHER HOMICIDE, DISCOVERED BY A PARKING LOT PATRON WHOSE WAY OUT WAS UNUSUALLY BLOCKED.
HOTEL
HOTEL & CASINO
FREE PA
PARKING

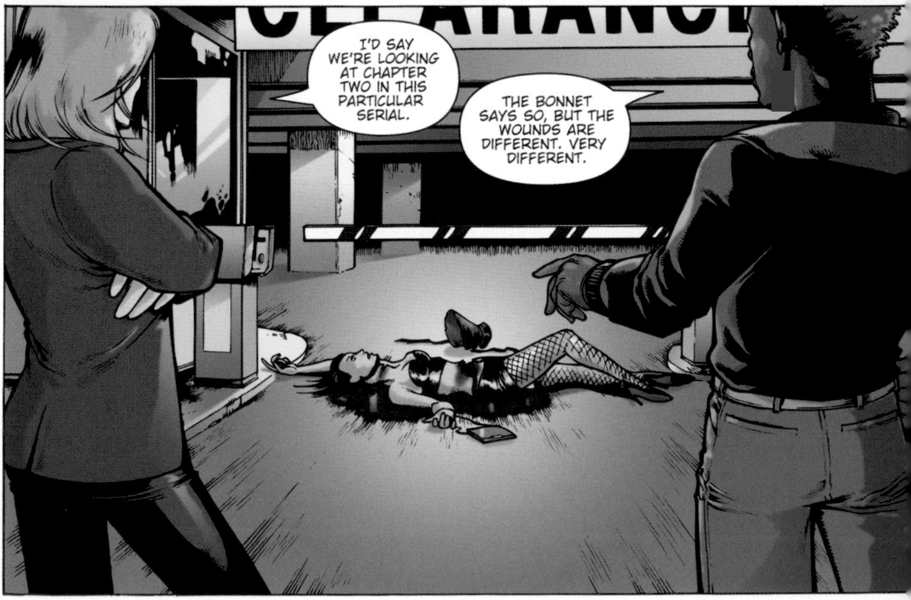
I'D SAY WE'RE LOOKING AT CHAPTER TWO IN THIS PARTICULAR SERIAL.
THE BONNET SAYS SO, BUT THE WOUNDS ARE DIFFERENT. VERY DIFFERENT.

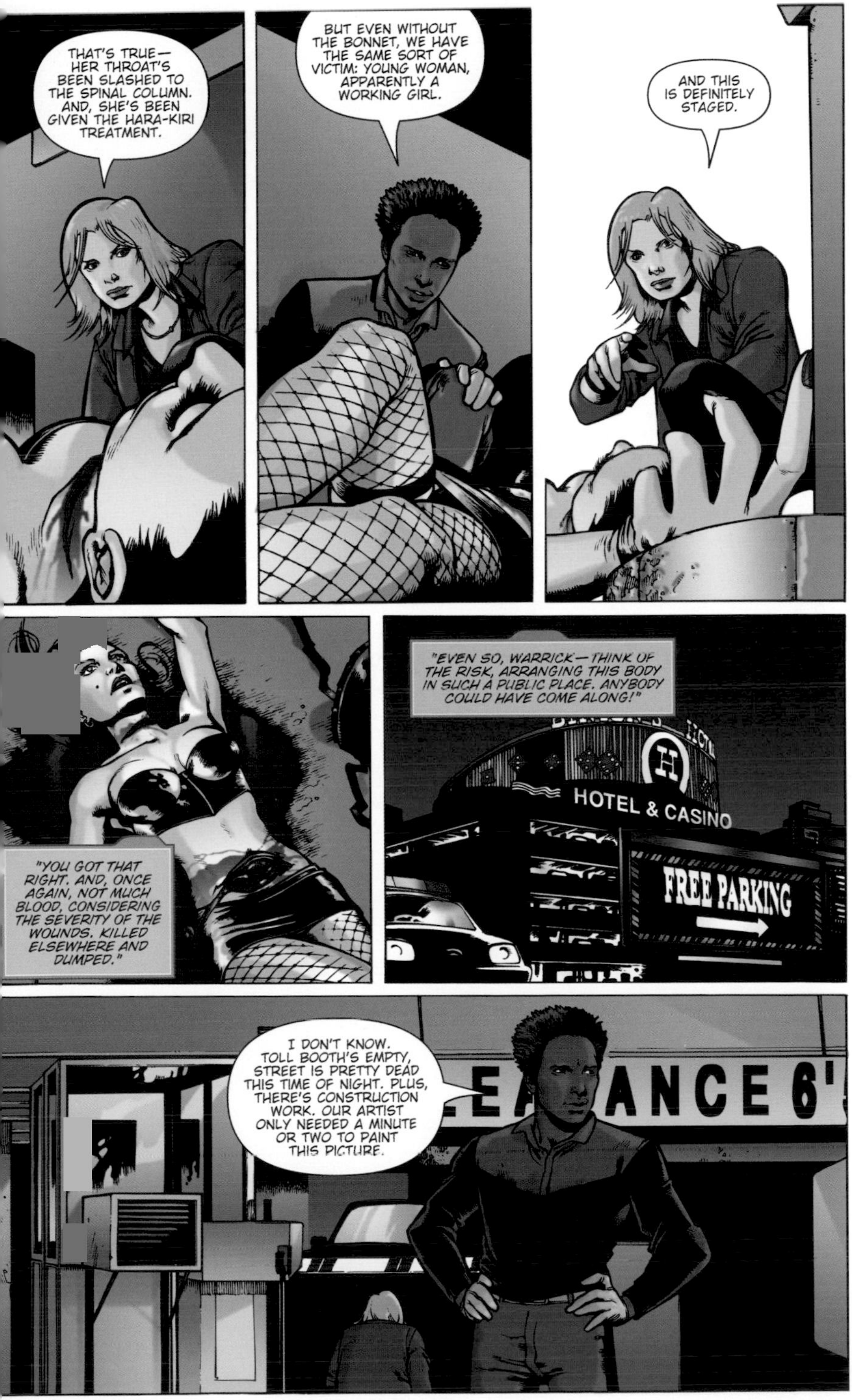
THAT'S TRUE— HER THROAT'S BEEN SLASHED TO THE SPINAL COLUMN. AND, SHE'S BEEN GIVEN THE HARA-KIRI TREATMENT.
BUT EVEN WITHOUT THE BONNET, WE HAVE THE SAME SORT OF VICTIM: YOUNG WOMAN, APPARENTLY A WORKING GIRL.
AND THIS IS DEFINITELY STAGED.
"YOU GOT THAT RIGHT. AND, ONCE AGAIN, NOT MUCH BLOOD, CONSIDERING THE SEVERITY OF THE WOUNDS. KILLED ELSEWHERE AND DUMPED."
"EVEN SO, WARRICK—THINK OF THE RISK, ARRANGING THIS BODY IN SUCH A PUBLIC PLACE. ANYBODY COULD HAVE COME ALONG!"
HOTEL & CASINO
FREE PARKING
I DON'T KNOW. TOLL BOOTH'S EMPTY, STREET IS PRETTY DEAD THIS TIME OF NIGHT. PLUS, THERE'S CONSTRUCTION WORK. OUR ARTIST ONLY NEEDED A MINUTE OR TWO TO PAINT THIS PICTURE.
ANCE 6'

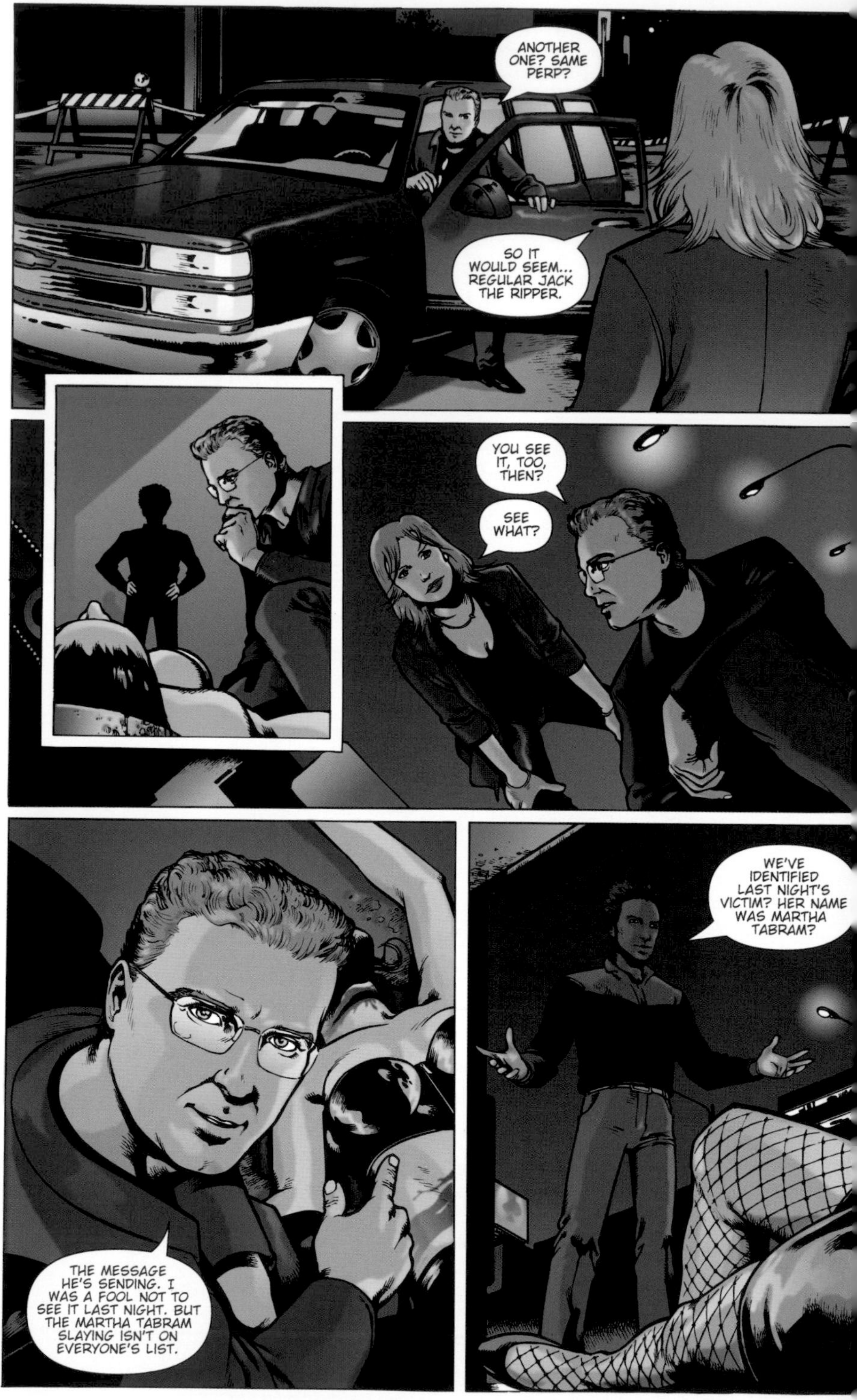
ANOTHER ONE? SAME PERP?
SO IT WOULD SEEM... REGULAR JACK THE RIPPER.
YOU SEE IT, TOO, THEN?
SEE WHAT?
THE MESSAGE HE'S SENDING. I WAS A FOOL NOT TO SEE IT LAST NIGHT. BUT THE MARTHA TABRAM SLAYING ISN'T ON EVERYONE'S LIST.
WE'VE IDENTIFIED LAST NIGHT'S VICTIM? HER NAME WAS MARTHA TABRAM?

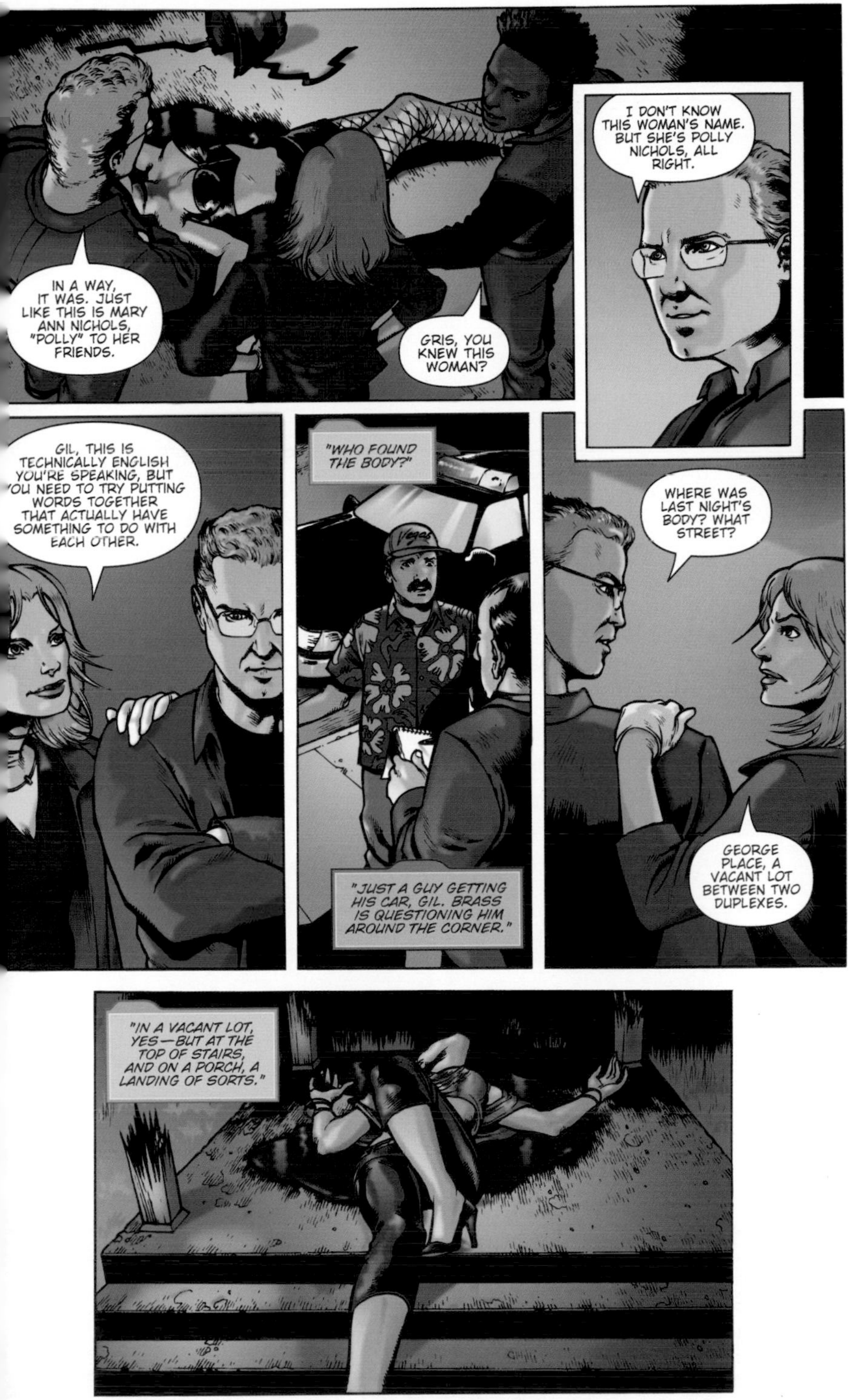
IN A WAY, IT WAS. JUST LIKE THIS IS MARY ANN NICHOLS, "POLLY" TO HER FRIENDS.
GRIS, YOU KNEW THIS WOMAN?
I DON'T KNOW THIS WOMAN'S NAME. BUT SHE'S POLLY NICHOLS, ALL RIGHT.
GIL, THIS IS TECHNICALLY ENGLISH YOU'RE SPEAKING, BUT YOU NEED TO TRY PUTTING WORDS TOGETHER THAT ACTUALLY HAVE SOMETHING TO DO WITH EACH OTHER.
"WHO FOUND THE BODY?"
"JUST A GUY GETTING HIS CAR, GIL. BRASS IS QUESTIONING HIM AROUND THE CORNER."
WHERE WAS LAST NIGHT'S BODY? WHAT STREET?
GEORGE PLACE, A VACANT LOT BETWEEN TWO DUPLEXES.
"IN A VACANT LOT, YES—BUT AT THE TOP OF STAIRS, AND ON A PORCH, A LANDING OF SORTS."

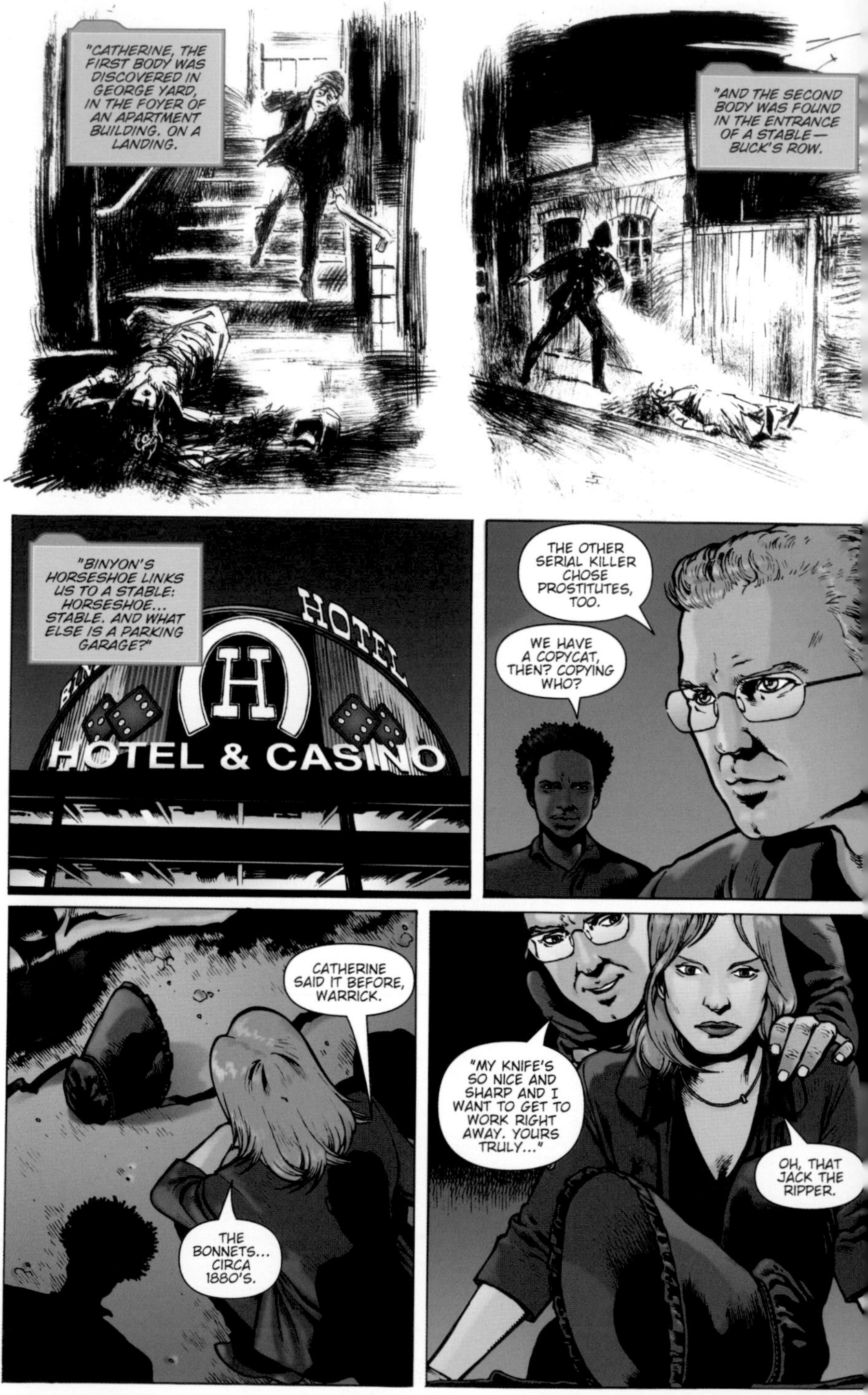

"CATHERINE, THE FIRST BODY WAS DISCOVERED IN GEORGE YARD, IN THE FOYER OF AN APARTMENT BUILDING. ON A LANDING.
"AND THE SECOND BODY WAS FOUND IN THE ENTRANCE OF A STABLE— BUCK'S ROW.
"BINYON'S HORSESHOE LINKS US TO A STABLE: HORSESHOE... STABLE. AND WHAT ELSE IS A PARKING GARAGE?"
HOTEL
H
HOTEL & CASINO
THE OTHER SERIAL KILLER CHOSE PROSTITUTES, TOO.
WE HAVE A COPYCAT, THEN? COPYING WHO?
CATHERINE SAID IT BEFORE, WARRICK.
THE BONNETS... CIRCA 1880'S.
"MY KNIFE'S SO NICE AND SHARP AND I WANT TO GET TO WORK RIGHT AWAY. YOURS TRULY..."
OH, THAT JACK THE RIPPER.

chapter two

Ripper Mania

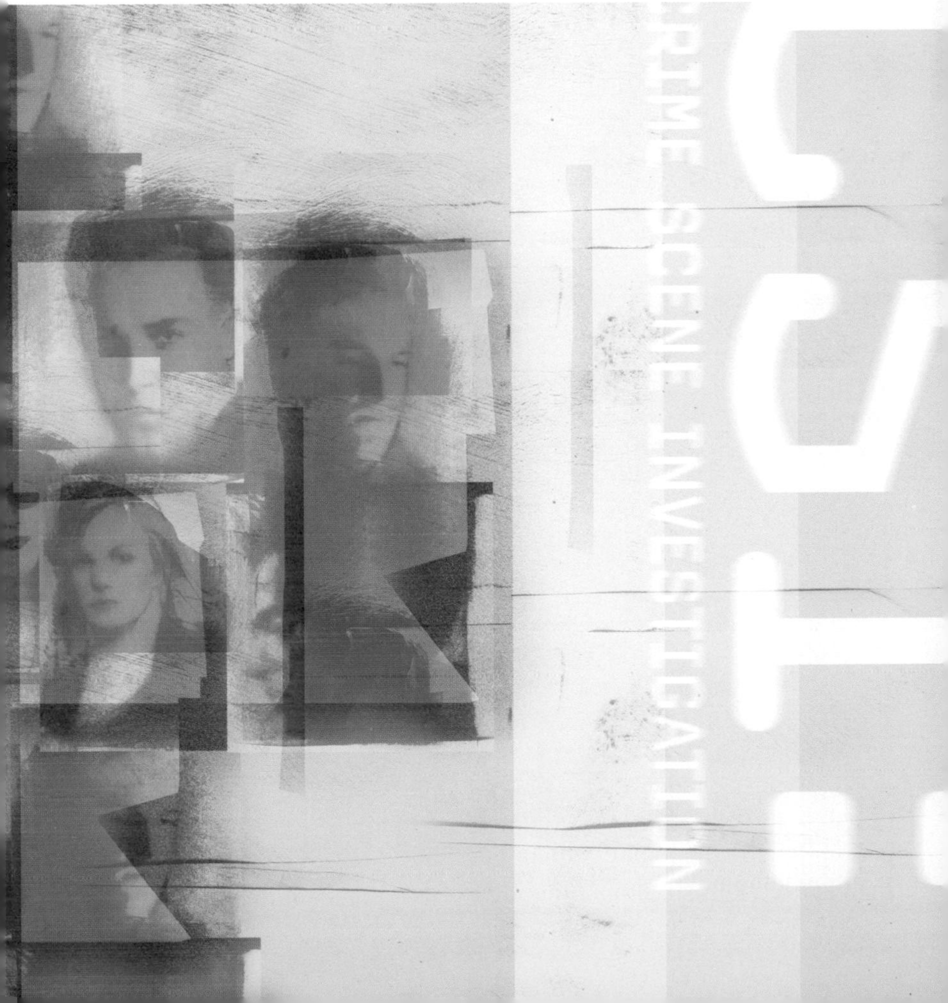
CRIME SCENE INVESTIGATION

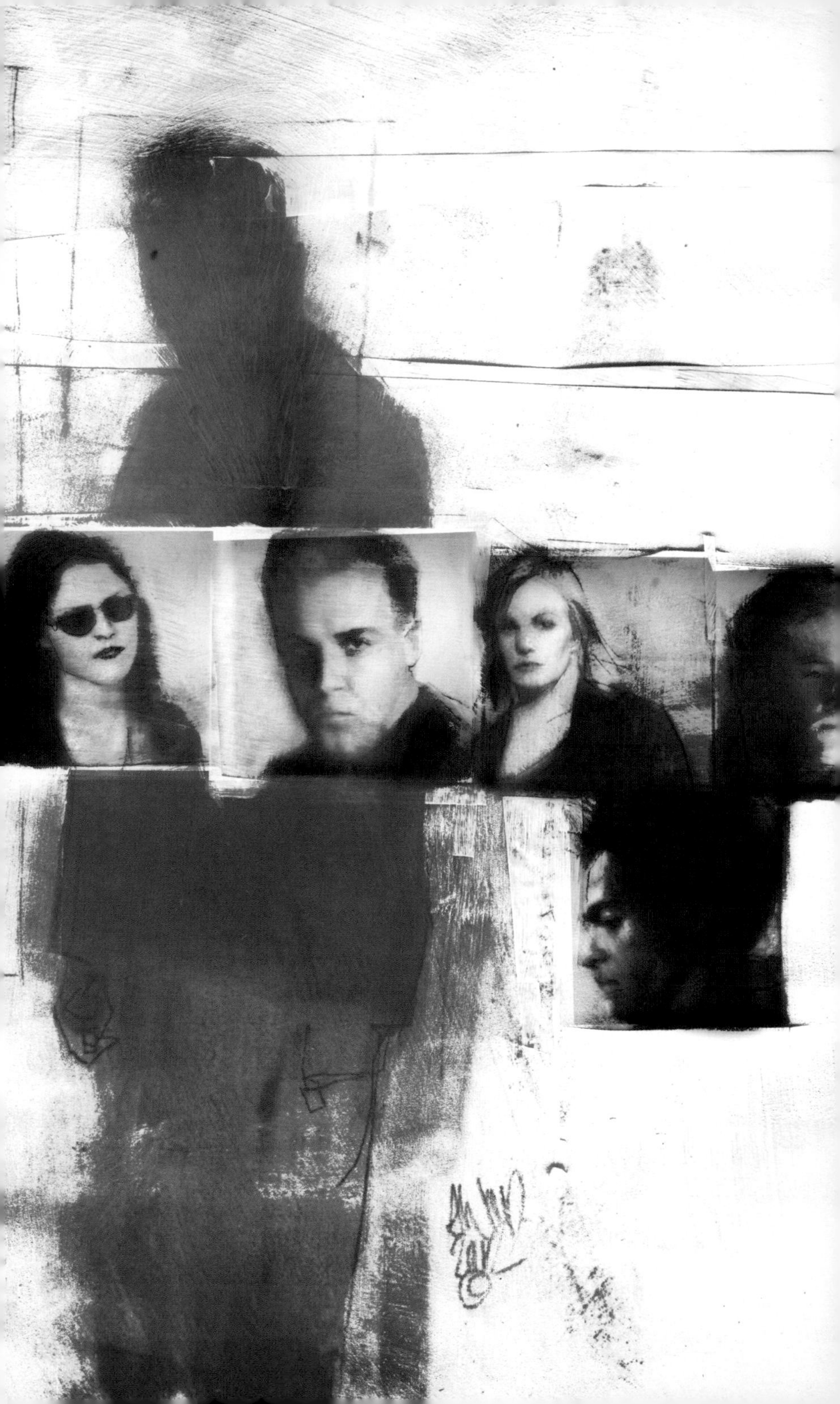

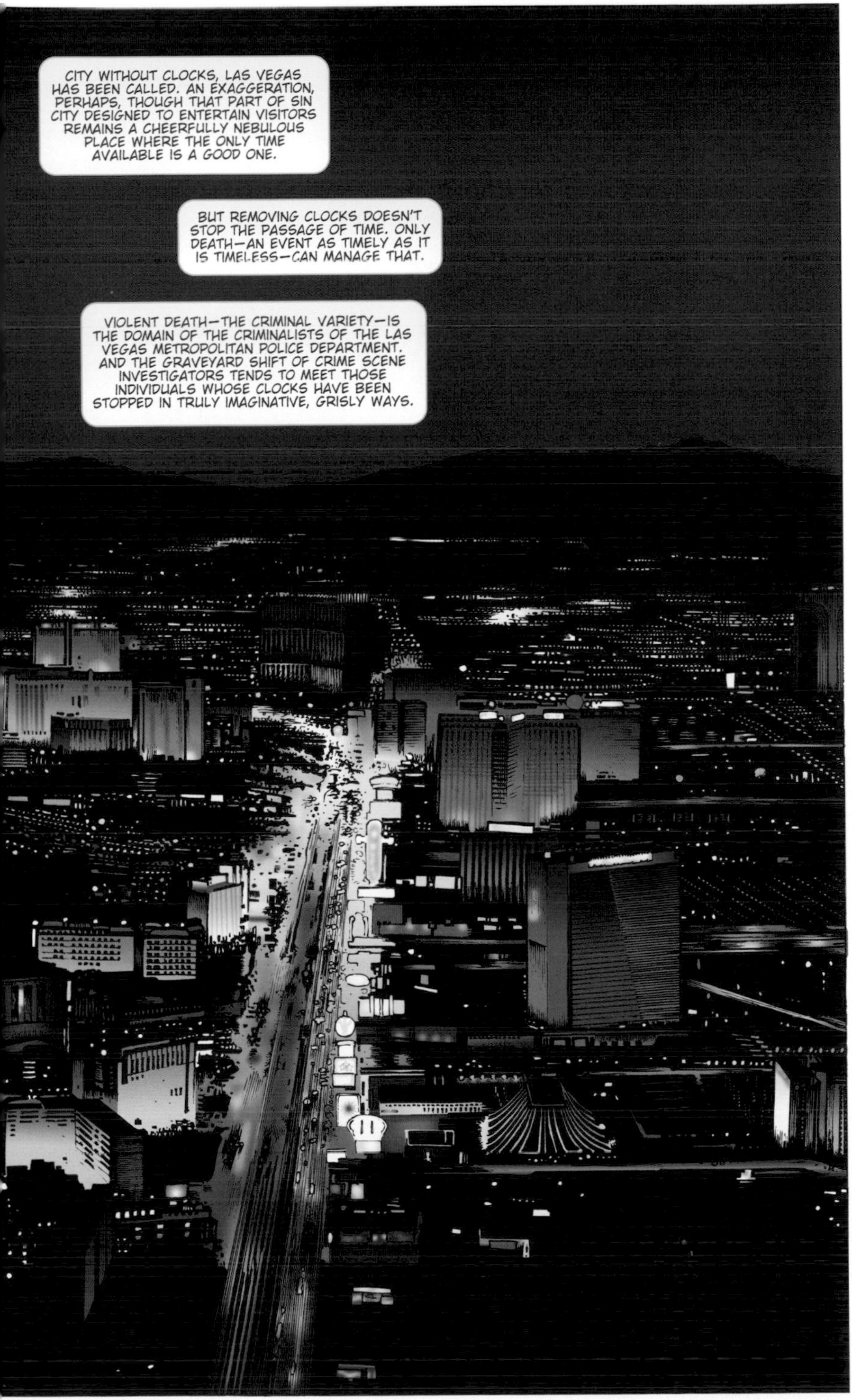
CITY WITHOUT CLOCKS, LAS VEGAS HAS BEEN CALLED. AN EXAGGERATION, PERHAPS, THOUGH THAT PART OF SIN CITY DESIGNED TO ENTERTAIN VISITORS REMAINS A CHEERFULLY NEBULOUS PLACE WHERE THE ONLY TIME AVAILABLE IS A GOOD ONE.
BUT REMOVING CLOCKS DOESN'T STOP THE PASSAGE OF TIME. ONLY DEATH—AN EVENT AS TIMELY AS IT IS TIMELESS—CAN MANAGE THAT.
VIOLENT DEATH—THE CRIMINAL VARIETY—IS THE DOMAIN OF THE CRIMINALISTS OF THE LAS VEGAS METROPOLITAN POLICE DEPARTMENT. AND THE GRAVEYARD SHIFT OF CRIME SCENE INVESTIGATORS TENDS TO MEET THOSE INDIVIDUALS WHOSE CLOCKS HAVE BEEN STOPPED IN TRULY IMAGINATIVE, GRISLY WAYS.

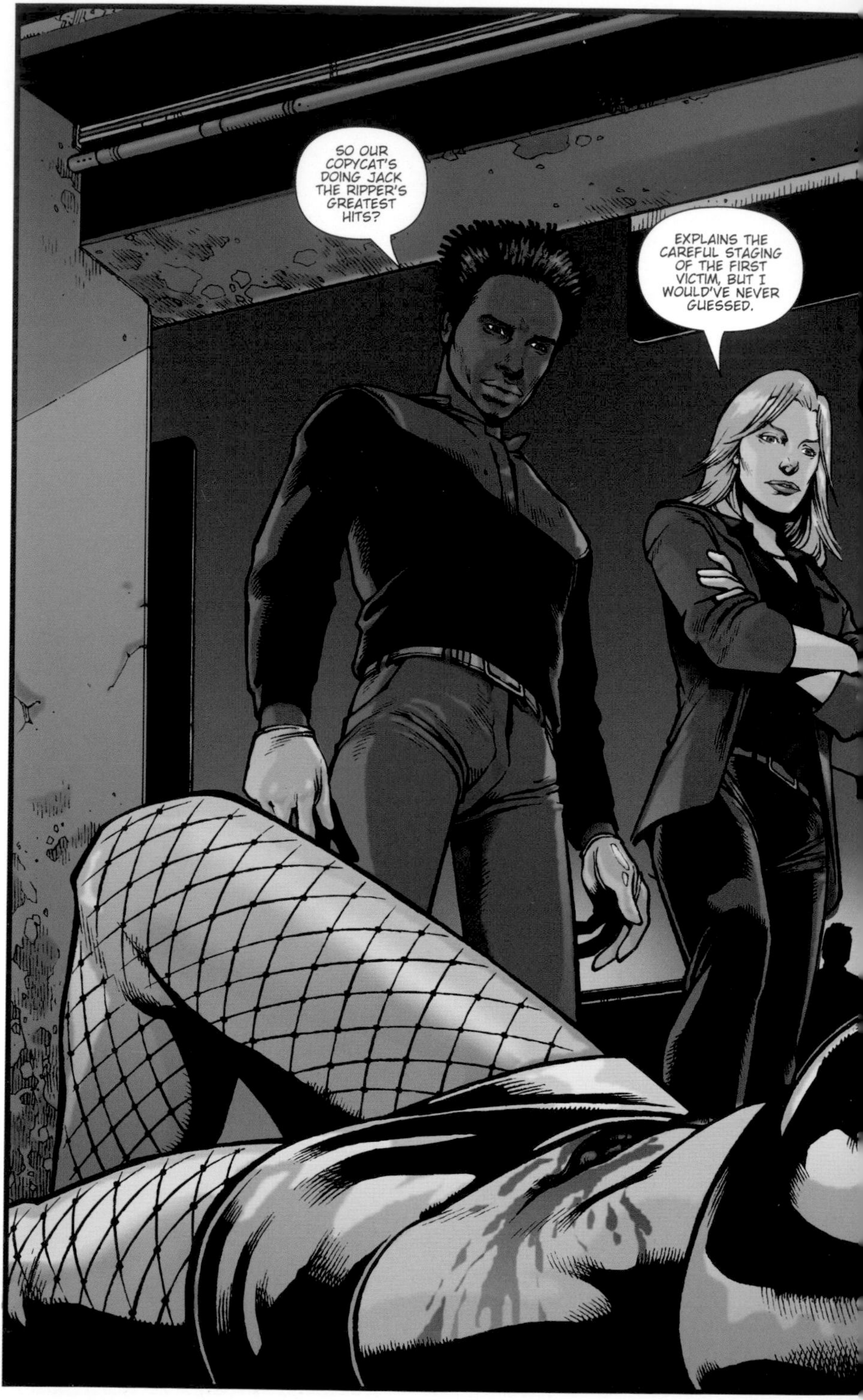
SO OUR COPYCAT'S DOING JACK THE RIPPER'S GREATEST HITS?
EXPLAINS THE CAREFUL STAGING OF THE FIRST VICTIM, BUT I WOULD'VE NEVER GUESSED.

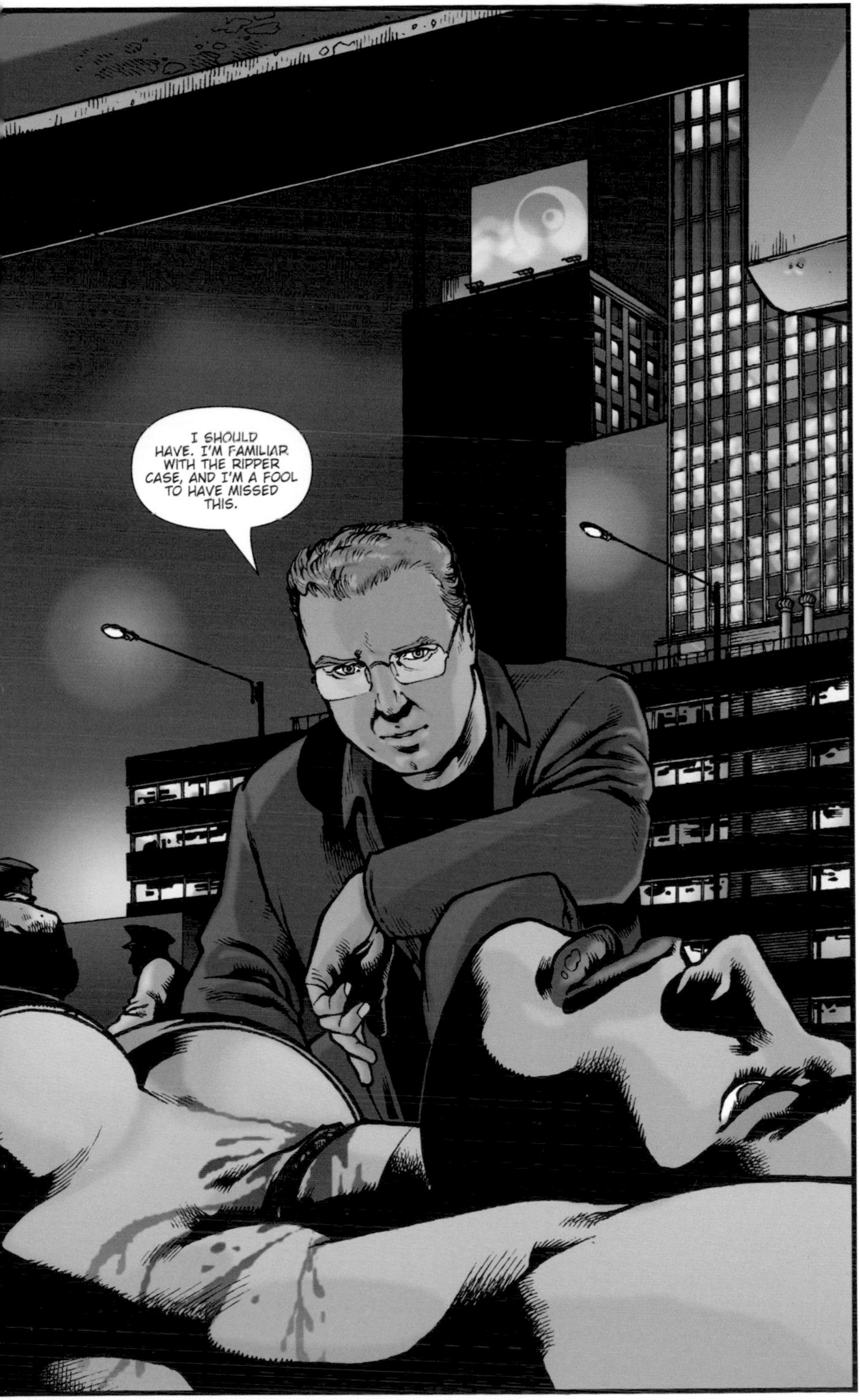
I SHOULD HAVE. I'M FAMILIAR WITH THE RIPPER CASE, AND I'M A FOOL TO HAVE MISSED THIS.

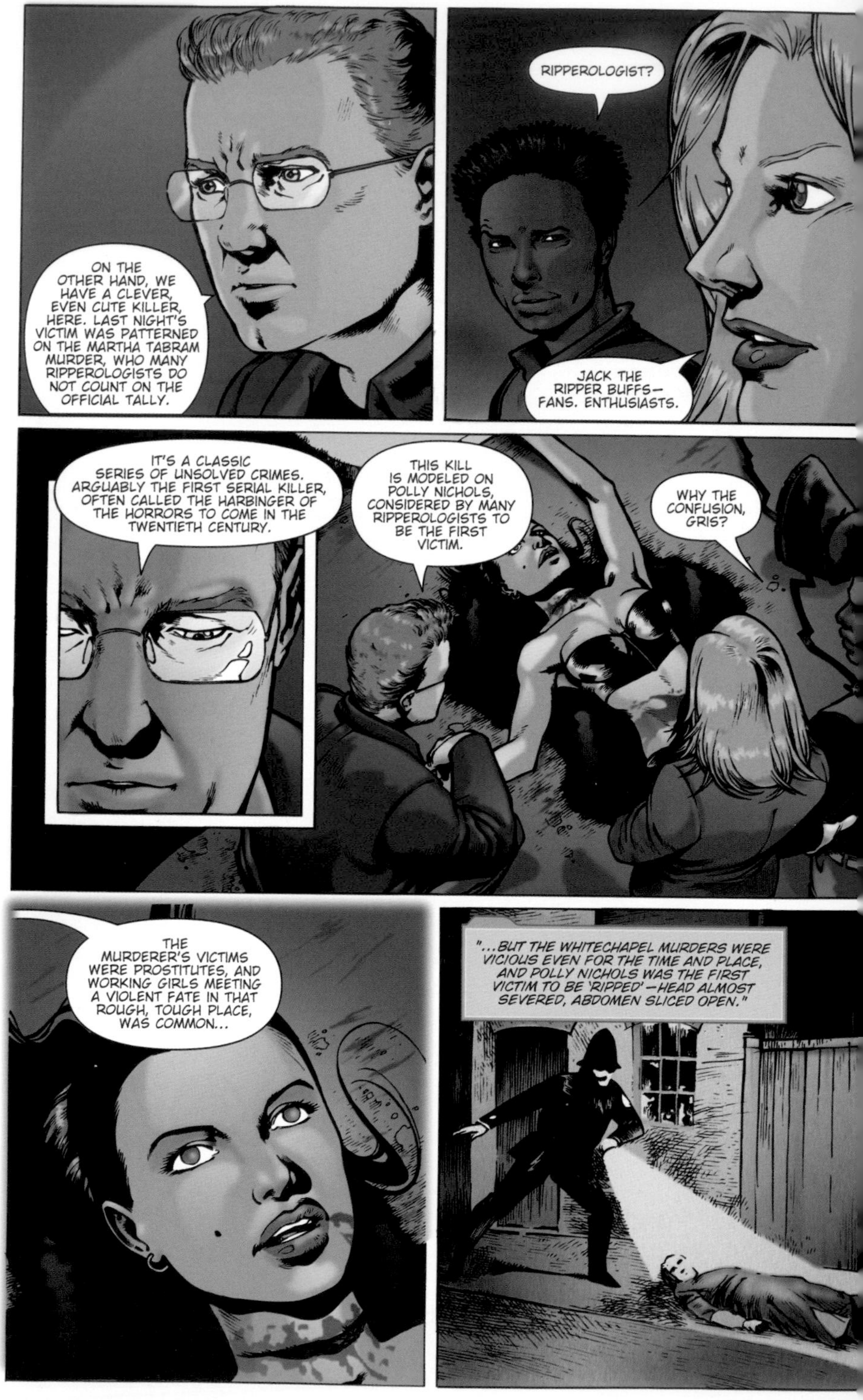
ON THE OTHER HAND, WE HAVE A CLEVER, EVEN CUTE KILLER, HERE. LAST NIGHT'S VICTIM WAS PATTERNED ON THE MARTHA TABRAM MURDER, WHO MANY RIPPEROLOGISTS DO NOT COUNT ON THE OFFICIAL TALLY.
RIPPEROLOGIST?
JACK THE RIPPER BUFFS—FANS. ENTHUSIASTS.
IT'S A CLASSIC SERIES OF UNSOLVED CRIMES. ARGUABLY THE FIRST SERIAL KILLER, OFTEN CALLED THE HARBINGER OF THE HORRORS TO COME IN THE TWENTIETH CENTURY.
THIS KILL IS MODELED ON POLLY NICHOLS, CONSIDERED BY MANY RIPPEROLOGISTS TO BE THE FIRST VICTIM.
WHY THE CONFUSION, GRIS?
THE MURDERER'S VICTIMS WERE PROSTITUTES, AND WORKING GIRLS MEETING A VIOLENT FATE IN THAT ROUGH, TOUGH PLACE, WAS COMMON...
"...BUT THE WHITECHAPEL MURDERS WERE VICIOUS EVEN FOR THE TIME AND PLACE, AND POLLY NICHOLS WAS THE FIRST VICTIM TO BE 'RIPPED'—HEAD ALMOST SEVERED, ABDOMEN SLICED OPEN."

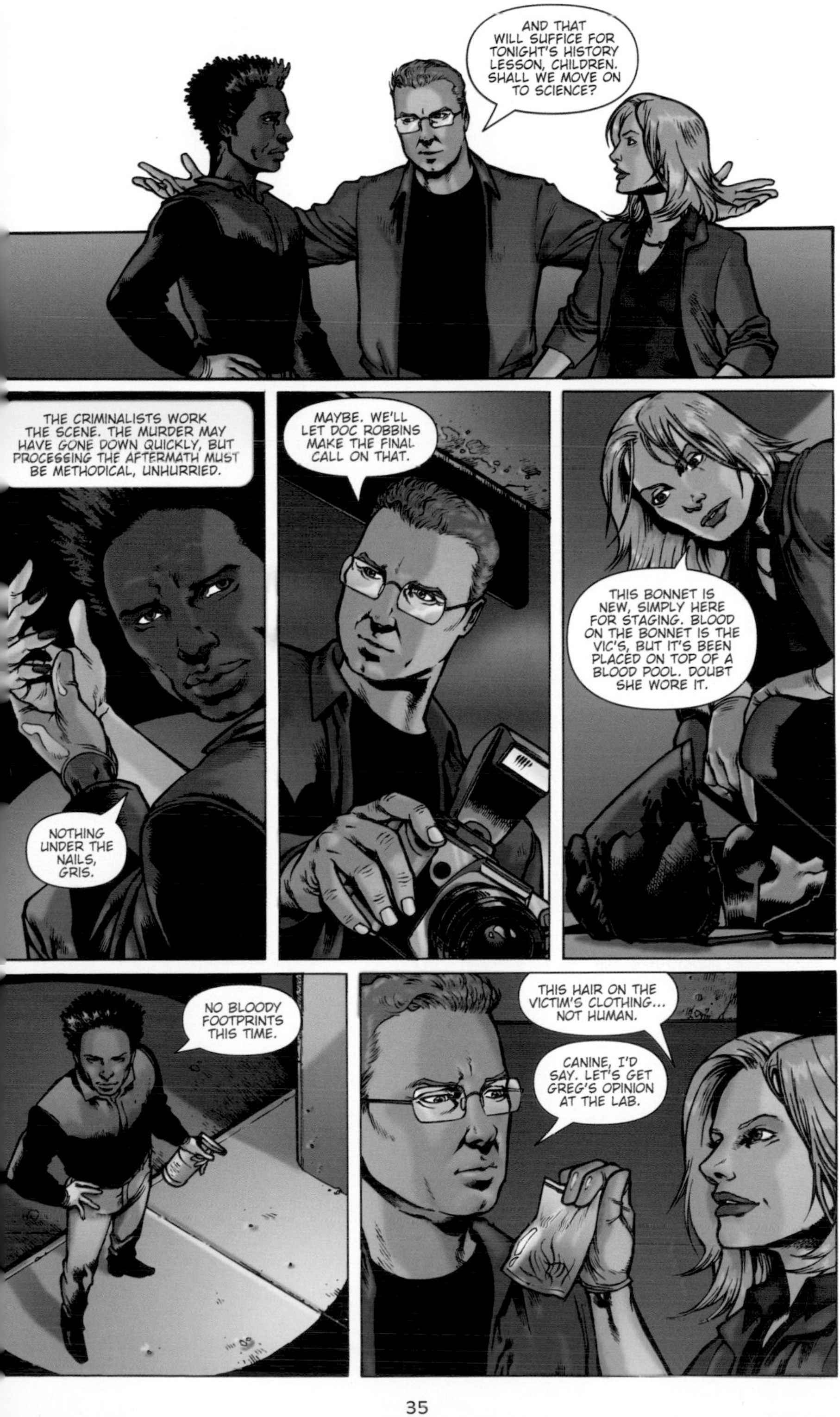
AND THAT WILL SUFFICE FOR TONIGHT'S HISTORY LESSON, CHILDREN. SHALL WE MOVE ON TO SCIENCE?
THE CRIMINALISTS WORK THE SCENE. THE MURDER MAY HAVE GONE DOWN QUICKLY, BUT PROCESSING THE AFTERMATH MUST BE METHODICAL, UNHURRIED.
NOTHING UNDER THE NAILS, GRIS.
MAYBE. WE'LL LET DOC ROBBINS MAKE THE FINAL CALL ON THAT.
THIS BONNET IS NEW, SIMPLY HERE FOR STAGING. BLOOD ON THE BONNET IS THE VIC'S, BUT IT'S BEEN PLACED ON TOP OF A BLOOD POOL. DOUBT SHE WORE IT.
NO BLOODY FOOTPRINTS THIS TIME.
THIS HAIR ON THE VICTIM'S CLOTHING... NOT HUMAN.
CANINE, I'D SAY. LET'S GET GREG'S OPINION AT THE LAB.

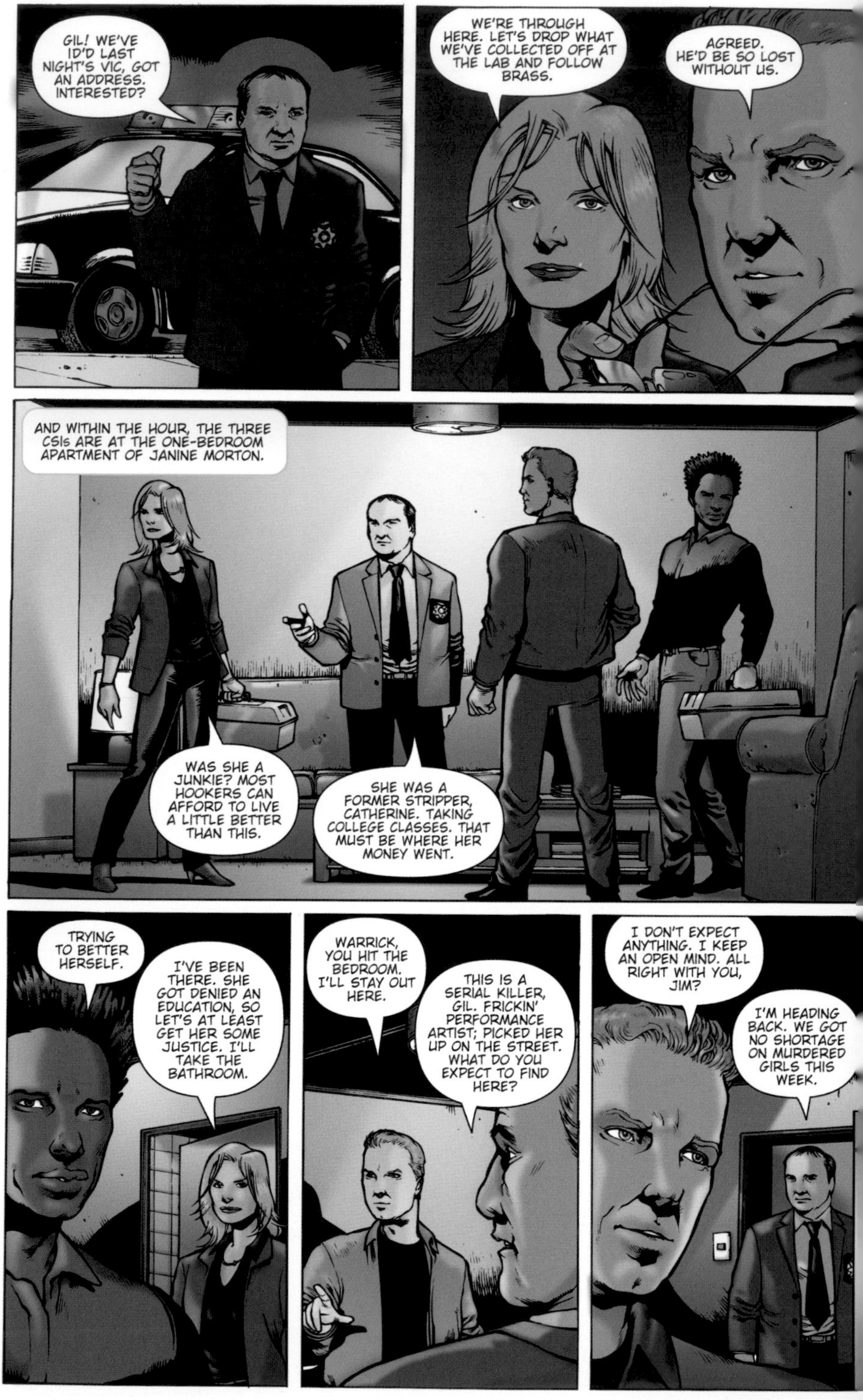

GIL! WE'VE ID'D LAST NIGHT'S VIC, GOT AN ADDRESS. INTERESTED?
WE'RE THROUGH HERE. LET'S DROP WHAT WE'VE COLLECTED OFF AT THE LAB AND FOLLOW BRASS.
AGREED. HE'D BE SO LOST WITHOUT US.
AND WITHIN THE HOUR, THE THREE CSIs ARE AT THE ONE-BEDROOM APARTMENT OF JANINE MORTON.
WAS SHE A JUNKIE? MOST HOOKERS CAN AFFORD TO LIVE A LITTLE BETTER THAN THIS.
SHE WAS A FORMER STRIPPER, CATHERINE. TAKING COLLEGE CLASSES. THAT MUST BE WHERE HER MONEY WENT.
TRYING TO BETTER HERSELF.
I'VE BEEN THERE. SHE GOT DENIED AN EDUCATION, SO LET'S AT LEAST GET HER SOME JUSTICE. I'LL TAKE THE BATHROOM.
WARRICK, YOU HIT THE BEDROOM. I'LL STAY OUT HERE.
THIS IS A SERIAL KILLER, GIL. FRICKIN' PERFORMANCE ARTIST; PICKED HER UP ON THE STREET. WHAT DO YOU EXPECT TO FIND HERE?
I DON'T EXPECT ANYTHING. I KEEP AN OPEN MIND. ALL RIGHT WITH YOU, JIM?
I'M HEADING BACK. WE GOT NO SHORTAGE ON MURDERED GIRLS THIS WEEK.

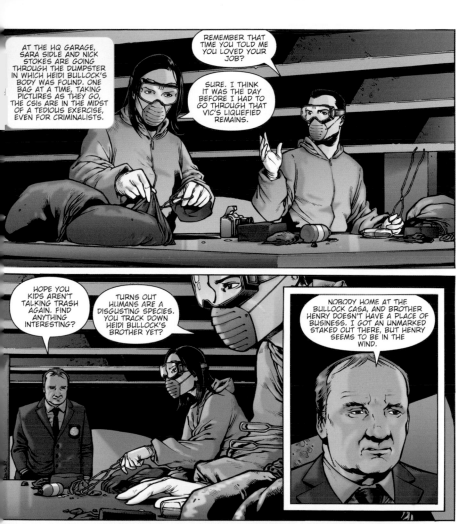

AT THE HQ GARAGE, SARA SIDLE AND NICK STOKES ARE GOING THROUGH THE DUMPSTER IN WHICH HEIDI BULLOCK'S BODY WAS FOUND. ONE BAG AT A TIME, TAKING PICTURES AS THEY GO, THE CSIs ARE IN THE MIDST OF A TEDIOUS EXERCISE, EVEN FOR CRIMINALISTS.

REMEMBER THAT TIME YOU TOLD ME YOU LOVED YOUR JOB?

SURE. I THINK IT WAS THE DAY BEFORE I HAD TO GO THROUGH THAT VIC'S LIQUEFIED REMAINS.

HOPE YOU KIDS AREN'T TALKING TRASH AGAIN. FIND ANYTHING INTERESTING?

TURNS OUT HUMANS ARE A DISGUSTING SPECIES. YOU TRACK DOWN HEIDI BULLOCK'S BROTHER YET?

NOBODY HOME AT THE BULLOCK CASA, AND BROTHER HENRY DOESN'T HAVE A PLACE OF BUSINESS. I GOT AN UNMARKED STAKED OUT THERE, BUT HENRY SEEMS TO BE IN THE WIND.

WE LIFTED A PALM PRINT FROM THE SIDE OF THE DUMPSTER. RUNNING IT THROUGH AFIS NOW.

YOU TALK TO DOC ROBBINS?

YEAH. SHE WAS STRANGLED. WHOEVER DID IT LEFT THE CORD AROUND HER NECK. THIN CORD, PROBABLY OFF A VENETIAN BLIND.

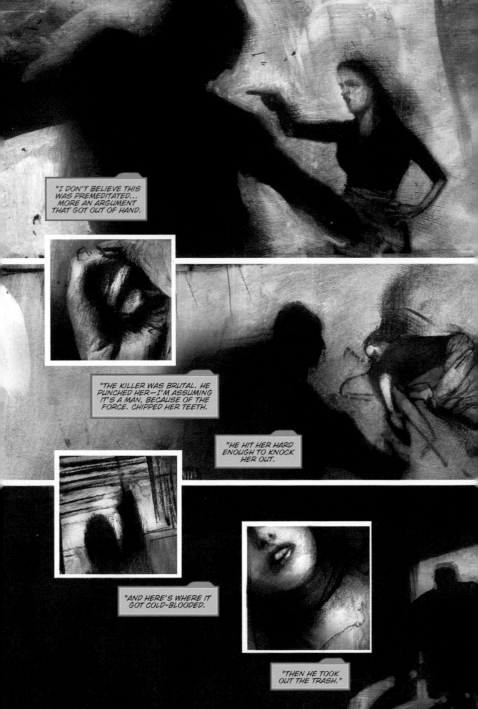

"I DON'T BELIEVE THIS WAS PREMEDITATED... MORE AN ARGUMENT THAT GOT OUT OF HAND.

"THE KILLER WAS BRUTAL. HE PUNCHED HER—I'M ASSUMING IT'S A MAN, BECAUSE OF THE FORCE. CHIPPED HER TEETH.

"HE HIT HER HARD ENOUGH TO KNOCK HER OUT.

"AND HERE'S WHERE IT GOT COLD-BLOODED.

"THEN HE TOOK OUT THE TRASH."

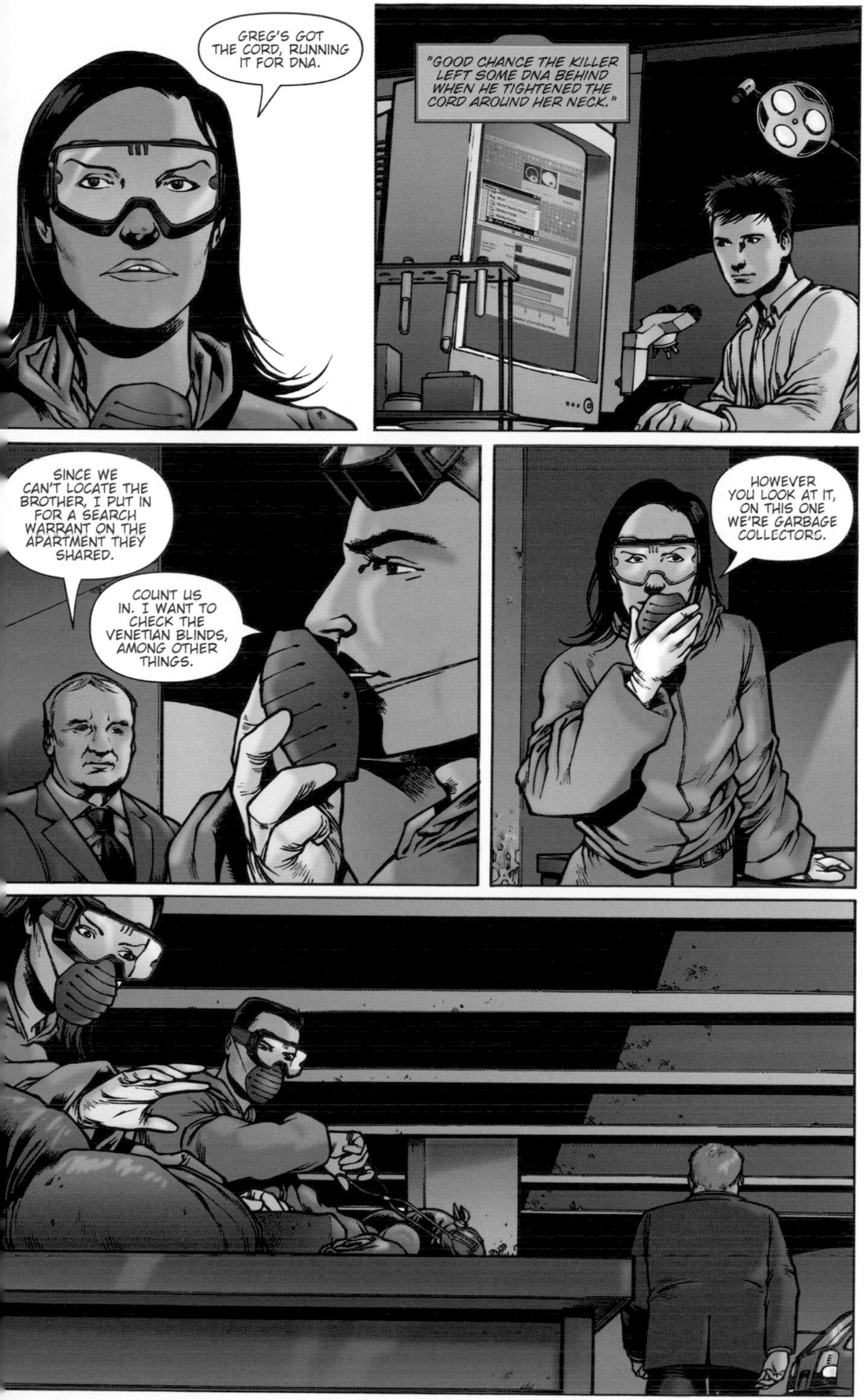
GREG'S GOT THE CORD, RUNNING IT FOR DNA.
"GOOD CHANCE THE KILLER LEFT SOME DNA BEHIND WHEN HE TIGHTENED THE CORD AROUND HER NECK."
SINCE WE CAN'T LOCATE THE BROTHER, I PUT IN FOR A SEARCH WARRANT ON THE APARTMENT THEY SHARED.
COUNT US IN. I WANT TO CHECK THE VENETIAN BLINDS, AMONG OTHER THINGS.
HOWEVER YOU LOOK AT IT, ON THIS ONE WE'RE GARBAGE COLLECTORS.

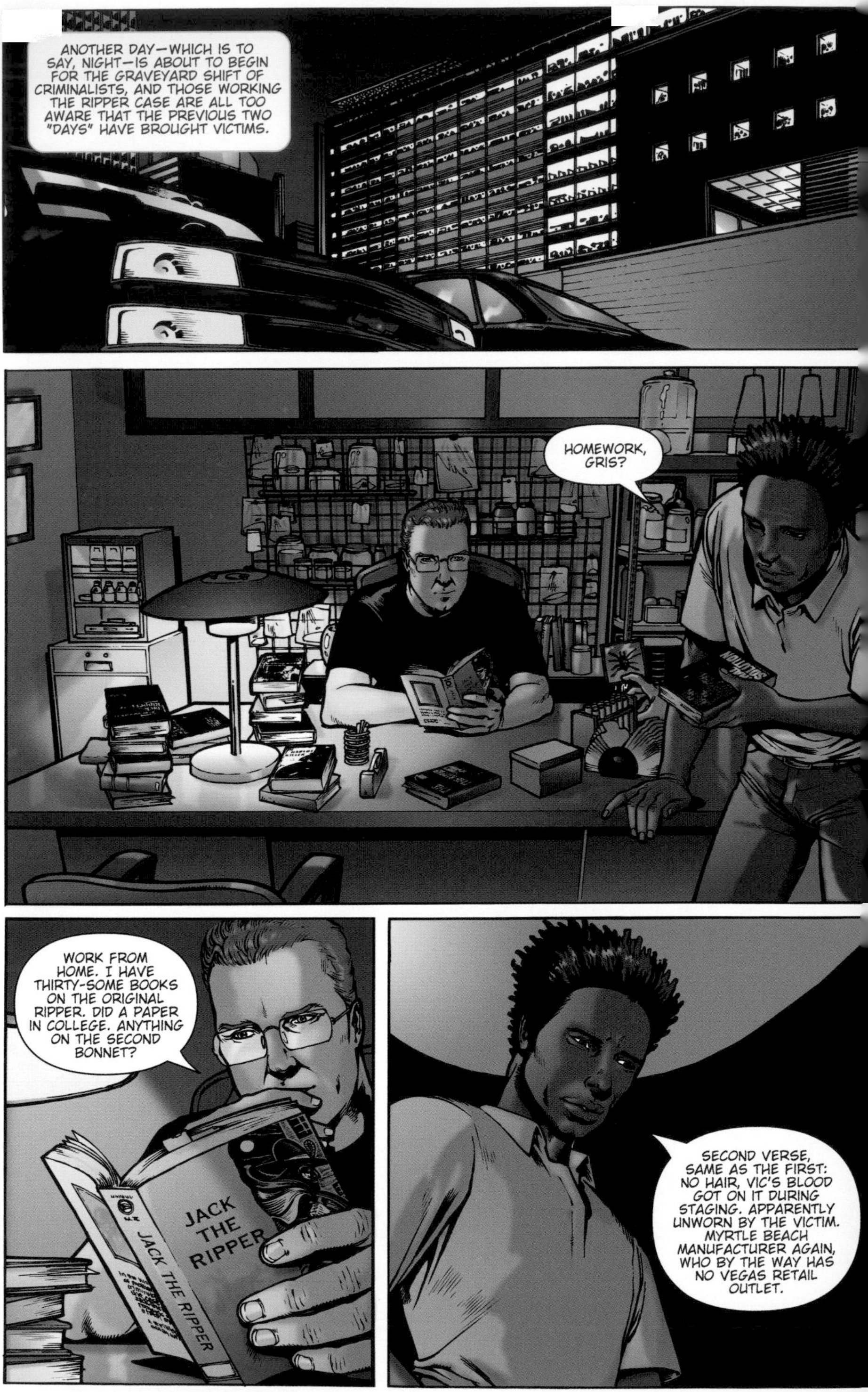
ANOTHER DAY—WHICH IS TO SAY, NIGHT—IS ABOUT TO BEGIN FOR THE GRAVEYARD SHIFT OF CRIMINALISTS, AND THOSE WORKING THE RIPPER CASE ARE ALL TOO AWARE THAT THE PREVIOUS TWO "DAYS" HAVE BROUGHT VICTIMS.
HOMEWORK, GRIS?
WORK FROM HOME. I HAVE THIRTY-SOME BOOKS ON THE ORIGINAL RIPPER. DID A PAPER IN COLLEGE. ANYTHING ON THE SECOND BONNET?
JACK THE RIPPER
JACK THE RIPPER
SECOND VERSE, SAME AS THE FIRST: NO HAIR, VIC'S BLOOD GOT ON IT DURING STAGING. APPARENTLY UNWORN BY THE VICTIM. MYRTLE BEACH MANUFACTURER AGAIN, WHO BY THE WAY HAS NO VEGAS RETAIL OUTLET.

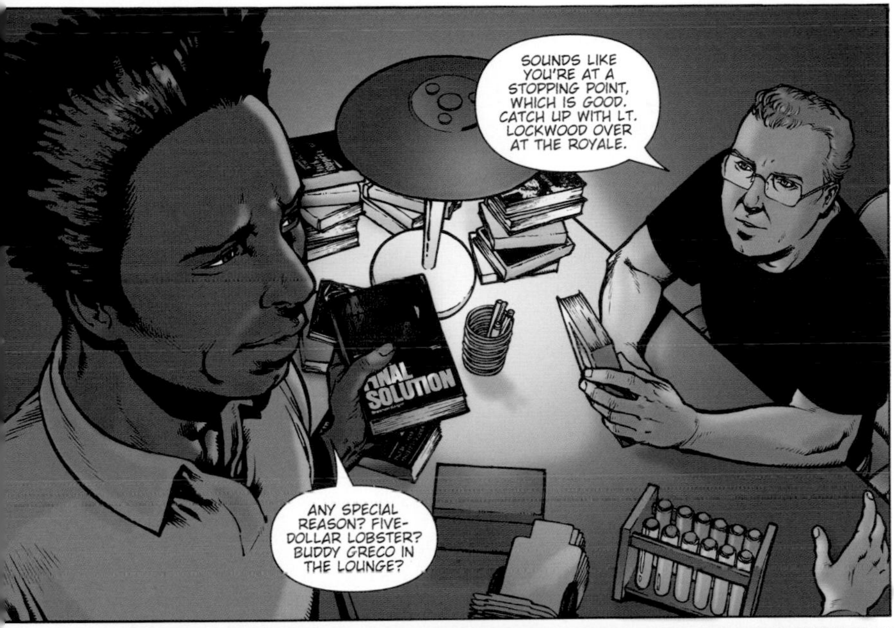
SOUNDS LIKE YOU'RE AT A STOPPING POINT, WHICH IS GOOD. CATCH UP WITH LT. LOCKWOOD OVER AT THE ROYALE.
ANY SPECIAL REASON? FIVE-DOLLAR LOBSTER? BUDDY GRECO IN THE LOUNGE?
SOLUTION

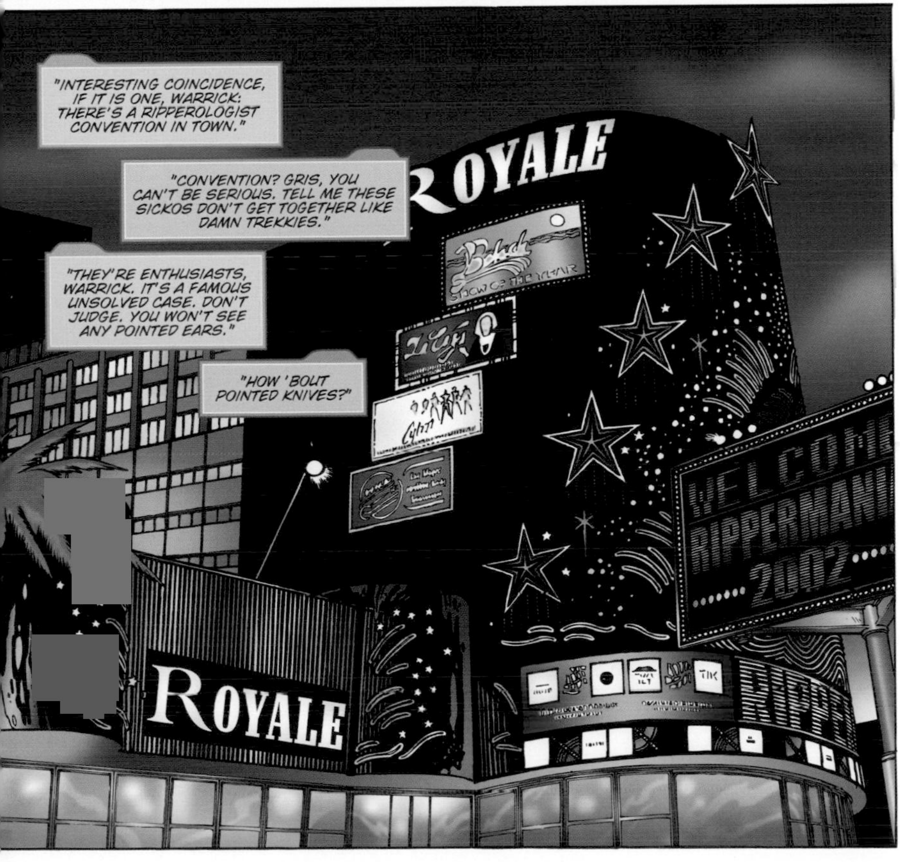
"INTERESTING COINCIDENCE, IF IT IS ONE, WARRICK: THERE'S A RIPPEROLOGIST CONVENTION IN TOWN."
"CONVENTION? GRIS, YOU CAN'T BE SERIOUS. TELL ME THESE SICKOS DON'T GET TOGETHER LIKE DAMN TREKKIES."
"THEY'RE ENTHUSIASTS, WARRICK. IT'S A FAMOUS UNSOLVED CASE. DON'T JUDGE. YOU WON'T SEE ANY POINTED EARS."
"HOW 'BOUT POINTED KNIVES?"
ROYALE
ROYALE

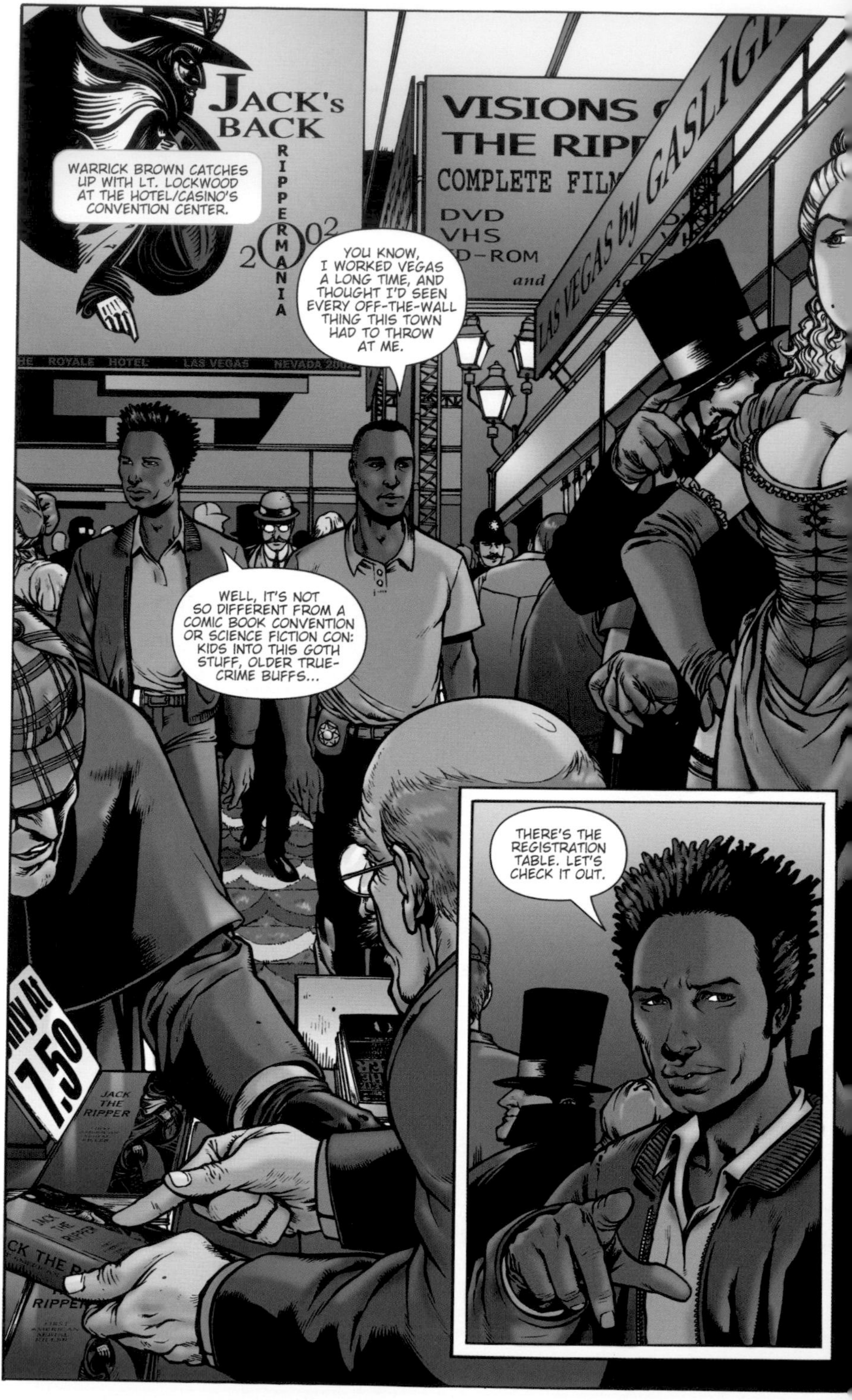
JACK's BACK
RIPPERMANIA
2002
WARRICK BROWN CATCHES UP WITH LT. LOCKWOOD AT THE HOTEL/CASINO'S CONVENTION CENTER.
VISIONS
THE RIPP
COMPLETE FILM
DVD
VHS
and
LAS VEGAS by GASLIG
YOU KNOW, I WORKED VEGAS A LONG TIME, AND THOUGHT I'D SEEN EVERY OFF-THE-WALL THING THIS TOWN HAD TO THROW AT ME.
THE ROYALE HOTEL LAS VEGAS NEVADA 2002
WELL, IT'S NOT SO DIFFERENT FROM A COMIC BOOK CONVENTION OR SCIENCE FICTION CON: KIDS INTO THIS GOTH STUFF, OLDER TRUE-CRIME BUFFS...
THERE'S THE REGISTRATION TABLE. LET'S CHECK IT OUT.
7.50
JACK THE RIPPER
JACK THE RIPPER
RIPPER

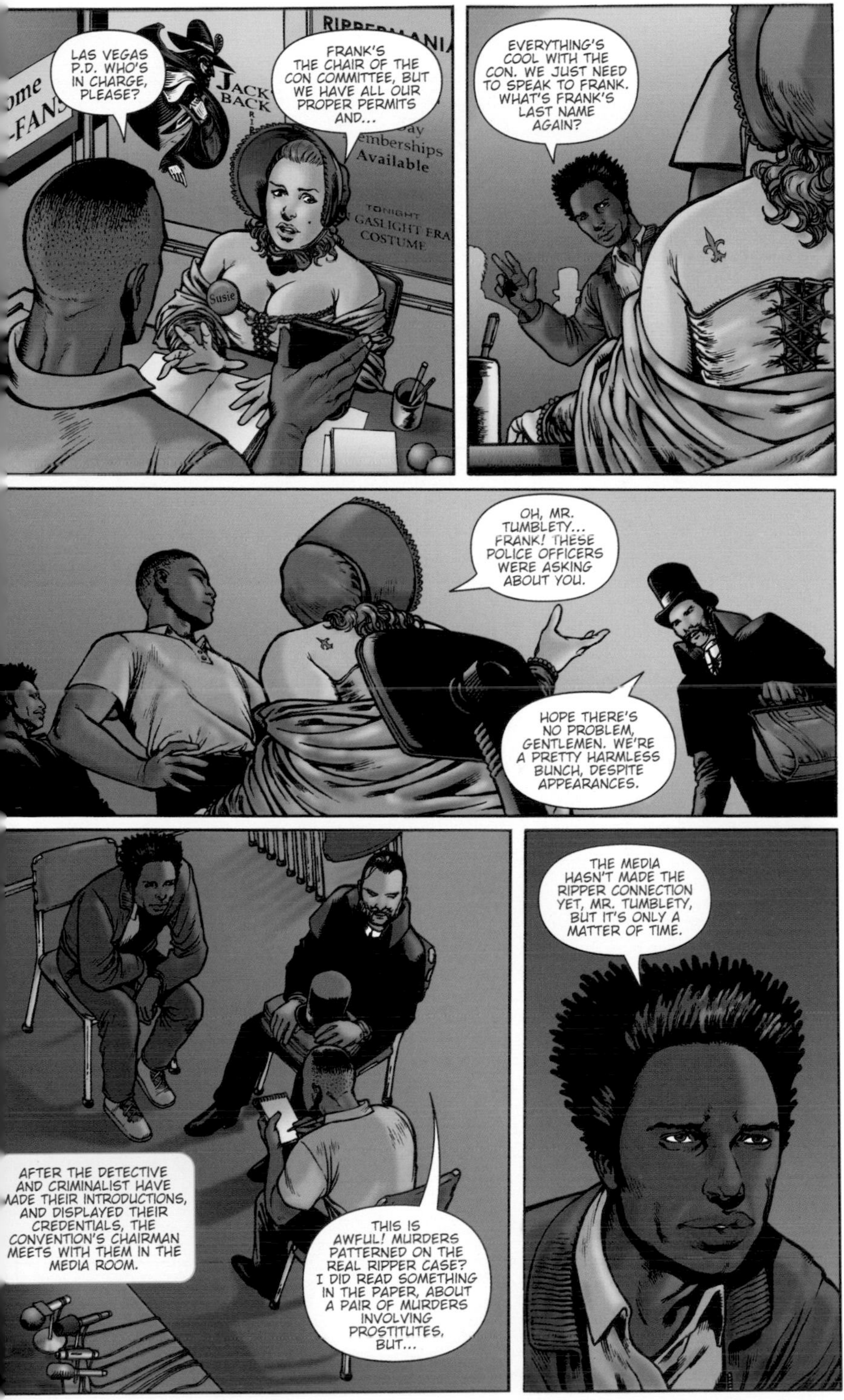
RIPPERMANIA
LAS VEGAS P.D. WHO'S IN CHARGE, PLEASE?
FRANK'S THE CHAIR OF THE CON COMMITTEE, BUT WE HAVE ALL OUR PROPER PERMITS AND...
Available
TONIGHT
COSTUME
Susie
EVERYTHING'S COOL WITH THE CON. WE JUST NEED TO SPEAK TO FRANK. WHAT'S FRANK'S LAST NAME AGAIN?
OH, MR. TUMBLETY... FRANK! THESE POLICE OFFICERS WERE ASKING ABOUT YOU.
HOPE THERE'S NO PROBLEM, GENTLEMEN. WE'RE A PRETTY HARMLESS BUNCH, DESPITE APPEARANCES.
AFTER THE DETECTIVE AND CRIMINALIST HAVE MADE THEIR INTRODUCTIONS, AND DISPLAYED THEIR CREDENTIALS, THE CONVENTION'S CHAIRMAN MEETS WITH THEM IN THE MEDIA ROOM.
THIS IS AWFUL! MURDERS PATTERNED ON THE REAL RIPPER CASE? I DID READ SOMETHING IN THE PAPER, ABOUT A PAIR OF MURDERS INVOLVING PROSTITUTES, BUT...
THE MEDIA HASN'T MADE THE RIPPER CONNECTION YET, MR. TUMBLETY, BUT IT'S ONLY A MATTER OF TIME.

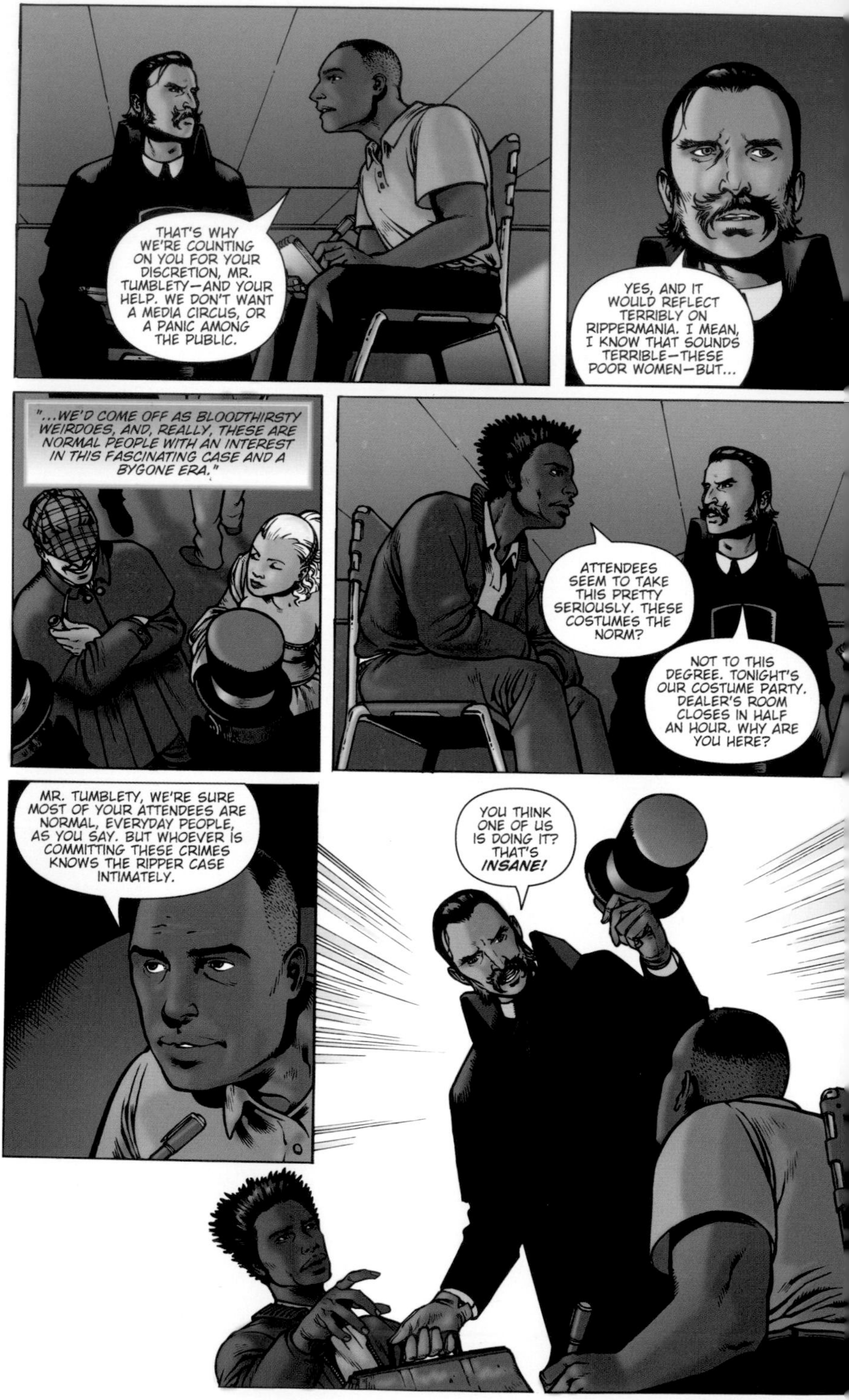
THAT'S WHY WE'RE COUNTING ON YOU FOR YOUR DISCRETION, MR. TUMBLETY—AND YOUR HELP. WE DON'T WANT A MEDIA CIRCUS, OR A PANIC AMONG THE PUBLIC.
YES, AND IT WOULD REFLECT TERRIBLY ON RIPPERMANIA. I MEAN, I KNOW THAT SOUNDS TERRIBLE—THESE POOR WOMEN—BUT...
"...WE'D COME OFF AS BLOODTHIRSTY WEIRDOES, AND, REALLY, THESE ARE NORMAL PEOPLE WITH AN INTEREST IN THIS FASCINATING CASE AND A BYGONE ERA."
ATTENDEES SEEM TO TAKE THIS PRETTY SERIOUSLY. THESE COSTUMES THE NORM?
NOT TO THIS DEGREE. TONIGHT'S OUR COSTUME PARTY. DEALER'S ROOM CLOSES IN HALF AN HOUR. WHY ARE YOU HERE?
MR. TUMBLETY, WE'RE SURE MOST OF YOUR ATTENDEES ARE NORMAL, EVERYDAY PEOPLE, AS YOU SAY. BUT WHOEVER IS COMMITTING THESE CRIMES KNOWS THE RIPPER CASE INTIMATELY.
YOU THINK ONE OF US IS DOING IT? THAT'S *INSANE!*

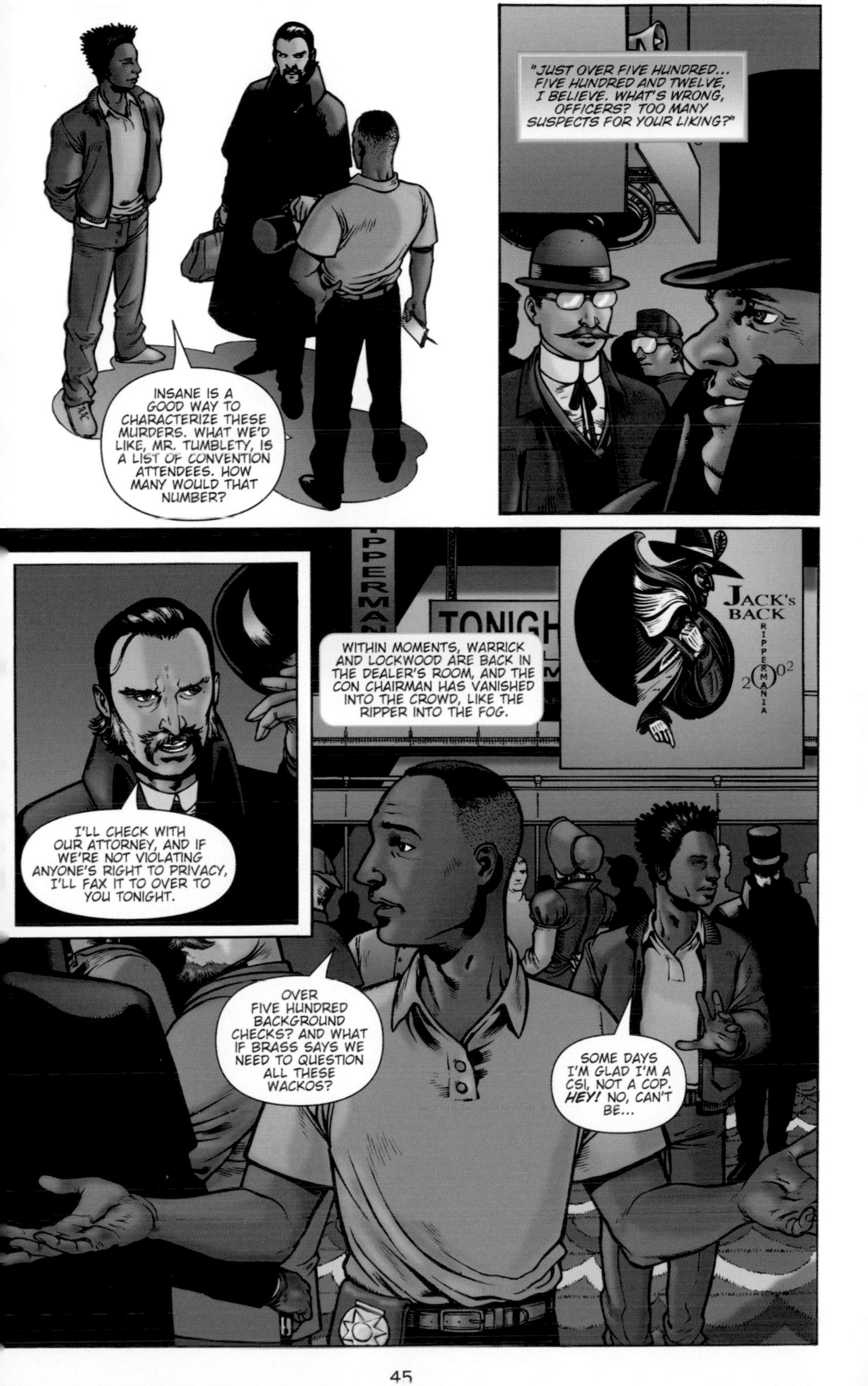
INSANE IS A GOOD WAY TO CHARACTERIZE THESE MURDERS. WHAT WE'D LIKE, MR. TUMBLETY, IS A LIST OF CONVENTION ATTENDEES. HOW MANY WOULD THAT NUMBER?
"JUST OVER FIVE HUNDRED... FIVE HUNDRED AND TWELVE, I BELIEVE. WHAT'S WRONG, OFFICERS? TOO MANY SUSPECTS FOR YOUR LIKING?"
I'LL CHECK WITH OUR ATTORNEY, AND IF WE'RE NOT VIOLATING ANYONE'S RIGHT TO PRIVACY, I'LL FAX IT TO OVER TO YOU TONIGHT.
RIPPERMAN
TONIGH
JACK'S BACK
RIPPERMANIA
2002
WITHIN MOMENTS, WARRICK AND LOCKWOOD ARE BACK IN THE DEALER'S ROOM, AND THE CON CHAIRMAN HAS VANISHED INTO THE CROWD, LIKE THE RIPPER INTO THE FOG.
OVER FIVE HUNDRED BACKGROUND CHECKS? AND WHAT IF BRASS SAYS WE NEED TO QUESTION ALL THESE WACKOS?
SOME DAYS I'M GLAD I'M A CSI, NOT A COP. HEY! NO, CAN'T BE...

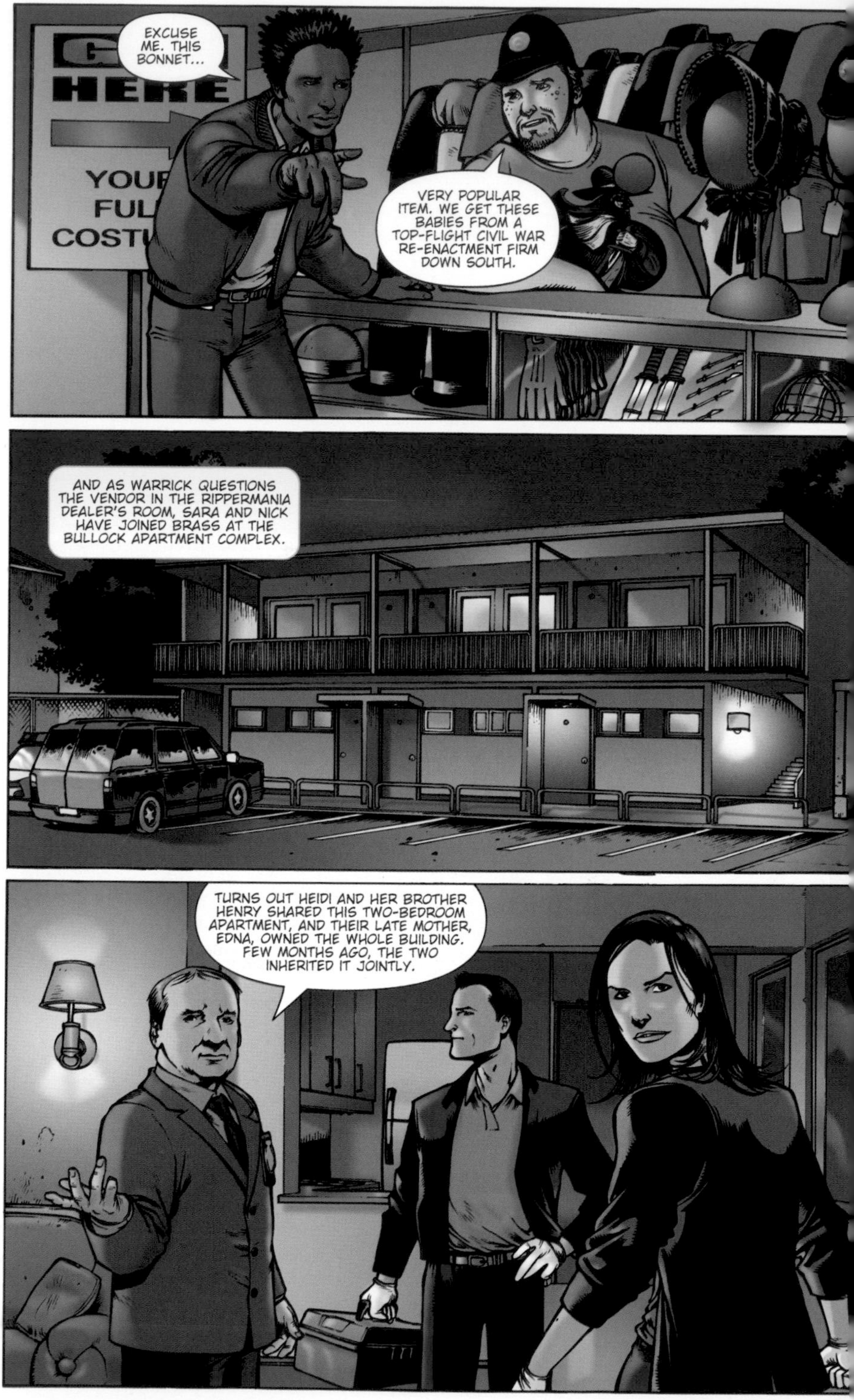
EXCUSE ME. THIS BONNET...
HERE
VERY POPULAR ITEM. WE GET THESE BABIES FROM A TOP-FLIGHT CIVIL WAR RE-ENACTMENT FIRM DOWN SOUTH.
AND AS WARRICK QUESTIONS THE VENDOR IN THE RIPPERMANIA DEALER'S ROOM, SARA AND NICK HAVE JOINED BRASS AT THE BULLOCK APARTMENT COMPLEX.
TURNS OUT HEIDI AND HER BROTHER HENRY SHARED THIS TWO-BEDROOM APARTMENT, AND THEIR LATE MOTHER, EDNA, OWNED THE WHOLE BUILDING. FEW MONTHS AGO, THE TWO INHERITED IT JOINTLY.

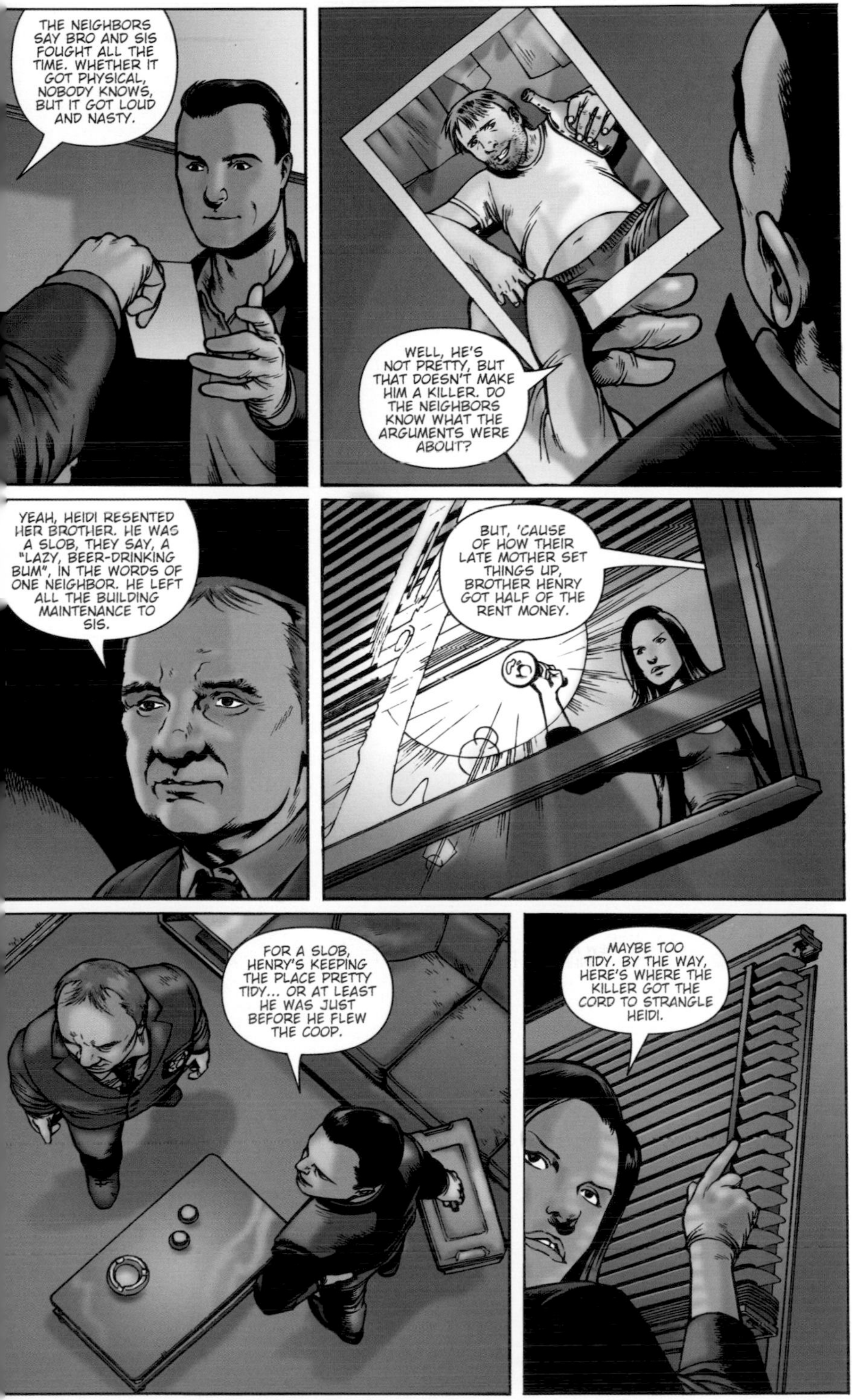
THE NEIGHBORS SAY BRO AND SIS FOUGHT ALL THE TIME. WHETHER IT GOT PHYSICAL, NOBODY KNOWS, BUT IT GOT LOUD AND NASTY.
WELL, HE'S NOT PRETTY, BUT THAT DOESN'T MAKE HIM A KILLER. DO THE NEIGHBORS KNOW WHAT THE ARGUMENTS WERE ABOUT?
YEAH, HEIDI RESENTED HER BROTHER. HE WAS A SLOB, THEY SAY, A "LAZY, BEER-DRINKING BUM", IN THE WORDS OF ONE NEIGHBOR. HE LEFT ALL THE BUILDING MAINTENANCE TO SIS.
BUT, 'CAUSE OF HOW THEIR LATE MOTHER SET THINGS UP, BROTHER HENRY GOT HALF OF THE RENT MONEY.
FOR A SLOB, HENRY'S KEEPING THE PLACE PRETTY TIDY... OR AT LEAST HE WAS JUST BEFORE HE FLEW THE COOP.
MAYBE TOO TIDY. BY THE WAY, HERE'S WHERE THE KILLER GOT THE CORD TO STRANGLE HEIDI.

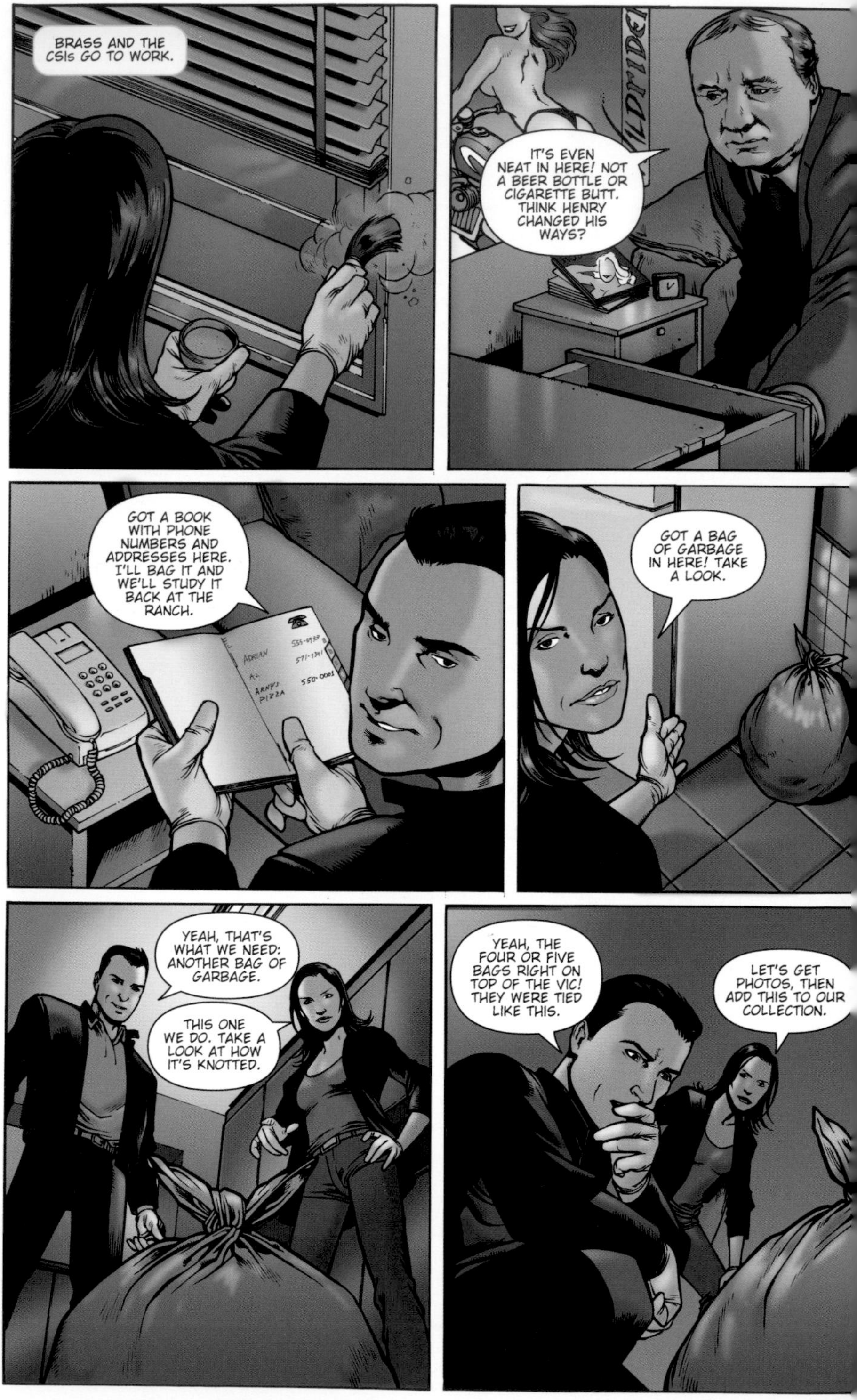

BRASS AND THE CSIs GO TO WORK.
IT'S EVEN NEAT IN HERE! NOT A BEER BOTTLE OR CIGARETTE BUTT. THINK HENRY CHANGED HIS WAYS?
GOT A BOOK WITH PHONE NUMBERS AND ADDRESSES HERE. I'LL BAG IT AND WE'LL STUDY IT BACK AT THE RANCH.
ADRIAN 555-0938
AL 571-1341
ARNY'S PIZZA 550-0001
GOT A BAG OF GARBAGE IN HERE! TAKE A LOOK.
YEAH, THAT'S WHAT WE NEED: ANOTHER BAG OF GARBAGE.
THIS ONE WE DO. TAKE A LOOK AT HOW IT'S KNOTTED.
YEAH, THE FOUR OR FIVE BAGS RIGHT ON TOP OF THE VIC! THEY WERE TIED LIKE THIS.
LET'S GET PHOTOS, THEN ADD THIS TO OUR COLLECTION.

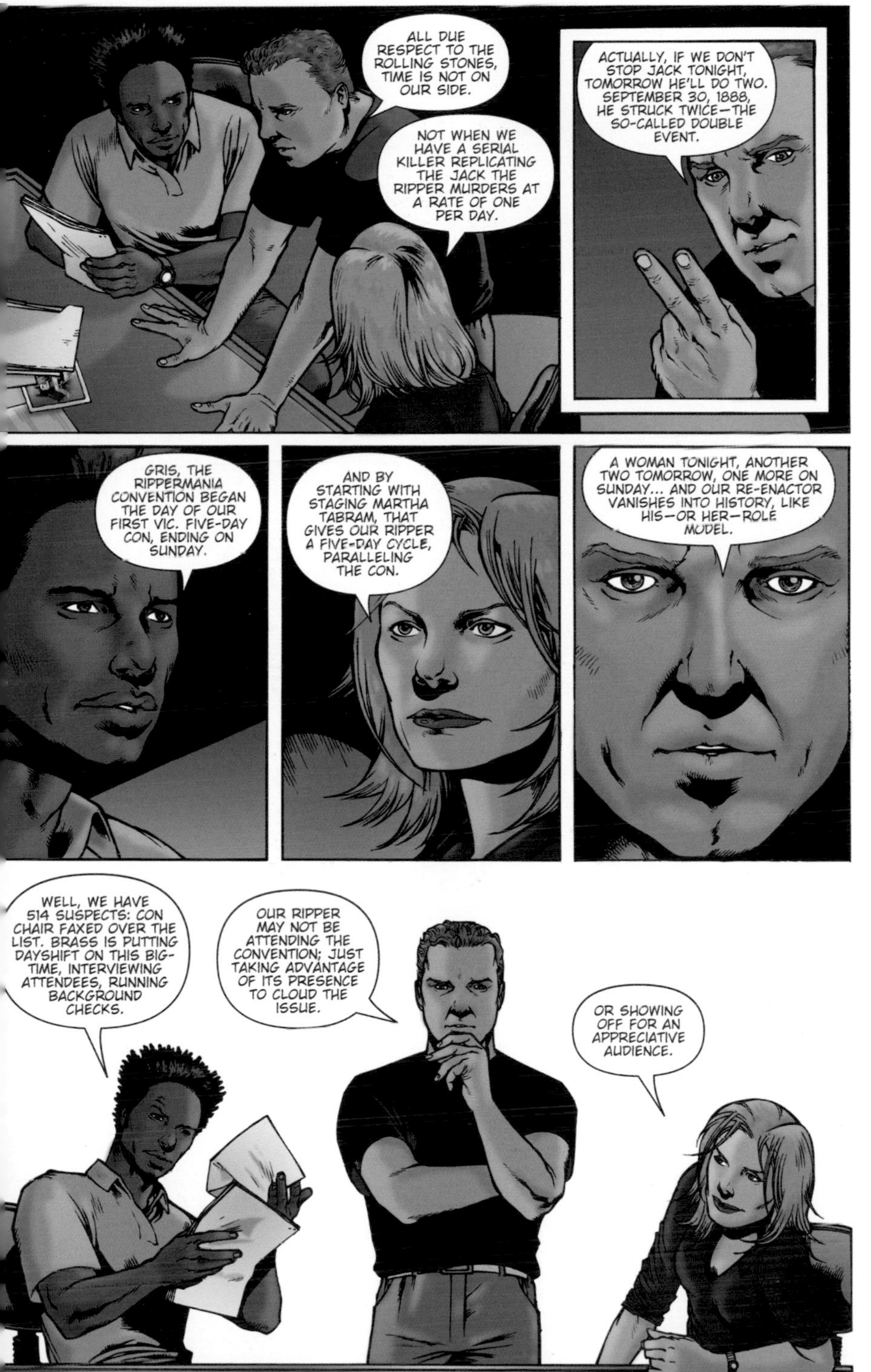
ALL DUE RESPECT TO THE ROLLING STONES, TIME IS NOT ON OUR SIDE.
NOT WHEN WE HAVE A SERIAL KILLER REPLICATING THE JACK THE RIPPER MURDERS AT A RATE OF ONE PER DAY.
ACTUALLY, IF WE DON'T STOP JACK TONIGHT, TOMORROW HE'LL DO TWO. SEPTEMBER 30, 1888, HE STRUCK TWICE—THE SO-CALLED DOUBLE EVENT.
GRIS, THE RIPPERMANIA CONVENTION BEGAN THE DAY OF OUR FIRST VIC. FIVE-DAY CON, ENDING ON SUNDAY.
AND BY STARTING WITH STAGING MARTHA TABRAM, THAT GIVES OUR RIPPER A FIVE-DAY CYCLE, PARALLELING THE CON.
A WOMAN TONIGHT, ANOTHER TWO TOMORROW, ONE MORE ON SUNDAY... AND OUR RE-ENACTOR VANISHES INTO HISTORY, LIKE HIS—OR HER—ROLE MODEL.
WELL, WE HAVE 514 SUSPECTS: CON CHAIR FAXED OVER THE LIST. BRASS IS PUTTING DAYSHIFT ON THIS BIG-TIME, INTERVIEWING ATTENDEES, RUNNING BACKGROUND CHECKS.
OUR RIPPER MAY NOT BE ATTENDING THE CONVENTION; JUST TAKING ADVANTAGE OF ITS PRESENCE TO CLOUD THE ISSUE.
OR SHOWING OFF FOR AN APPRECIATIVE AUDIENCE.

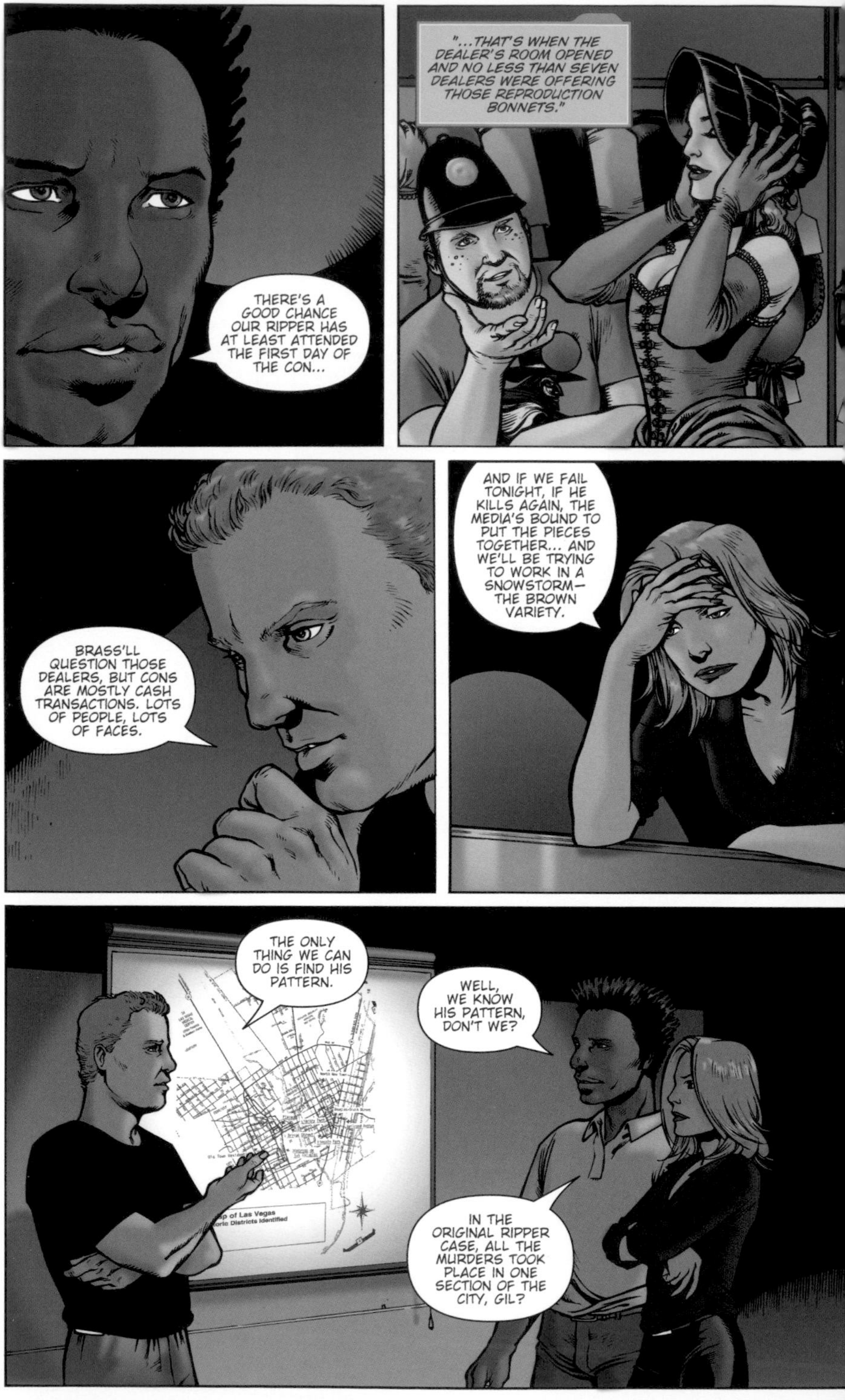
THERE'S A GOOD CHANCE OUR RIPPER HAS AT LEAST ATTENDED THE FIRST DAY OF THE CON...
"...THAT'S WHEN THE DEALER'S ROOM OPENED AND NO LESS THAN SEVEN DEALERS WERE OFFERING THOSE REPRODUCTION BONNETS."
BRASS'LL QUESTION THOSE DEALERS, BUT CONS ARE MOSTLY CASH TRANSACTIONS. LOTS OF PEOPLE, LOTS OF FACES.
AND IF WE FAIL TONIGHT, IF HE KILLS AGAIN, THE MEDIA'S BOUND TO PUT THE PIECES TOGETHER... AND WE'LL BE TRYING TO WORK IN A SNOWSTORM— THE BROWN VARIETY.
THE ONLY THING WE CAN DO IS FIND HIS PATTERN.
WELL, WE KNOW HIS PATTERN, DON'T WE?
IN THE ORIGINAL RIPPER CASE, ALL THE MURDERS TOOK PLACE IN ONE SECTION OF THE CITY, GIL?

"YES, WHITECHAPEL, IN LONDON'S EAST END—A RUNNING SORE ON THE SKIN OF THE CITY, AN AREA RIDDLED WITH POVERTY, HOMELESSNESS, AND PROSTITUTION.

"OUR FIRST MURDER TOOK PLACE ON GEORGE PLACE, WHICH MIRRORED GEORGE YARD, WHERE MARTHA TABRAM'S BODY WAS FOUND.

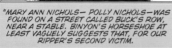

"MARY ANN NICHOLS— POLLY NICHOLS—WAS FOUND ON A STREET CALLED BUCK'S ROW, NEAR A STABLE. BINYON'S HORSESHOE AT LEAST VAGUELY SUGGESTS THAT, FOR OUR RIPPER'S SECOND VICTIM.

"WE KNOW FROM DOC ROBBINS'S AUTOPSY THAT OUR SECOND VICTIM'S THROAT WAS SLIT TO THE SPINAL COLUMN WITH A STURDY BLADE. HER ABDOMEN WAS OPENED, HER INTESTINES EXPOSED, BUT NO ORGANS WERE MISSING.

"THE MURDER OUR RIPPER MAY BE RE-ENACTING TONIGHT TOOK PLACE ON HANBURY STREET.

"A PROSTITUTE WAS SEEN BARGAINING WITH A PROSPECTIVE CLIENT."

WILL YOU?

YES.

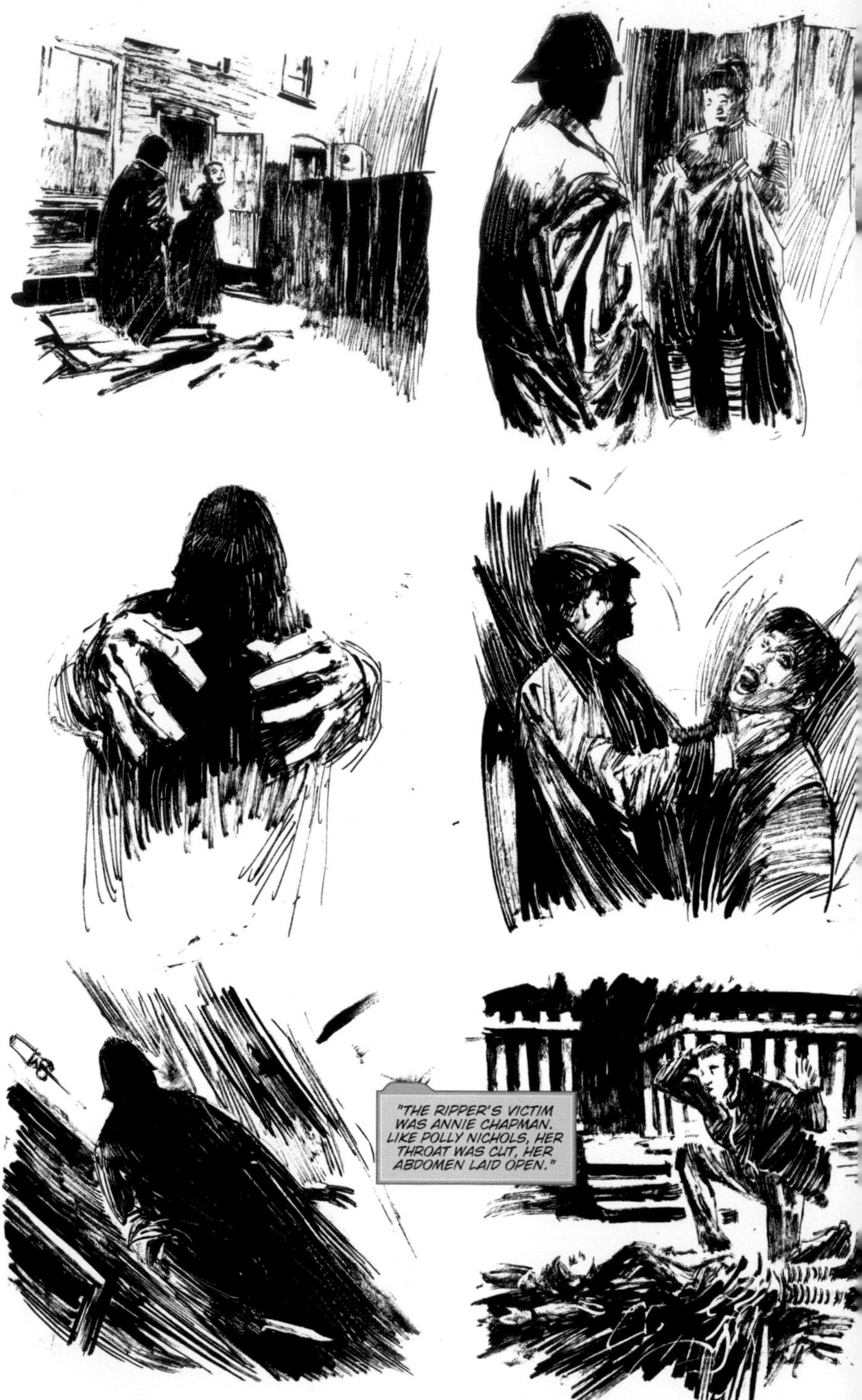
"THE RIPPER'S VICTIM WAS ANNIE CHAPMAN. LIKE POLLY NICHOLS, HER THROAT WAS CUT, HER ABDOMEN LAID OPEN."

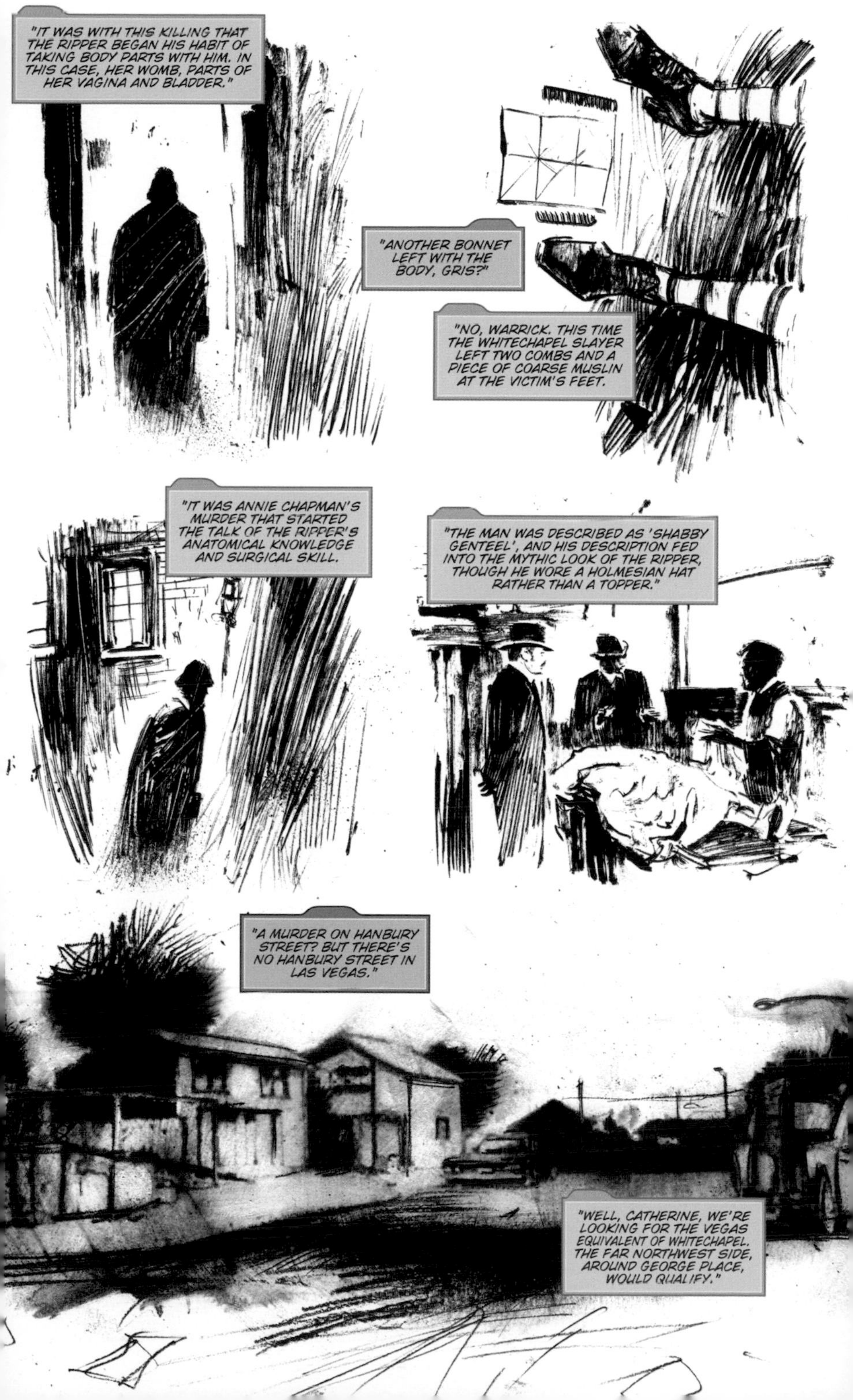
"IT WAS WITH THIS KILLING THAT THE RIPPER BEGAN HIS HABIT OF TAKING BODY PARTS WITH HIM. IN THIS CASE, HER WOMB, PARTS OF HER VAGINA AND BLADDER."
"ANOTHER BONNET LEFT WITH THE BODY, GRIS?"
"NO, WARRICK. THIS TIME THE WHITECHAPEL SLAYER LEFT TWO COMBS AND A PIECE OF COARSE MUSLIN AT THE VICTIM'S FEET.
"IT WAS ANNIE CHAPMAN'S MURDER THAT STARTED THE TALK OF THE RIPPER'S ANATOMICAL KNOWLEDGE AND SURGICAL SKILL.
"THE MAN WAS DESCRIBED AS 'SHABBY GENTEEL', AND HIS DESCRIPTION FED INTO THE MYTHIC LOOK OF THE RIPPER, THOUGH HE WORE A HOLMESIAN HAT RATHER THAN A TOPPER."
"A MURDER ON HANBURY STREET? BUT THERE'S NO HANBURY STREET IN LAS VEGAS."
"WELL, CATHERINE, WE'RE LOOKING FOR THE VEGAS EQUIVALENT OF WHITECHAPEL. THE FAR NORTHWEST SIDE, AROUND GEORGE PLACE, WOULD QUALIFY."

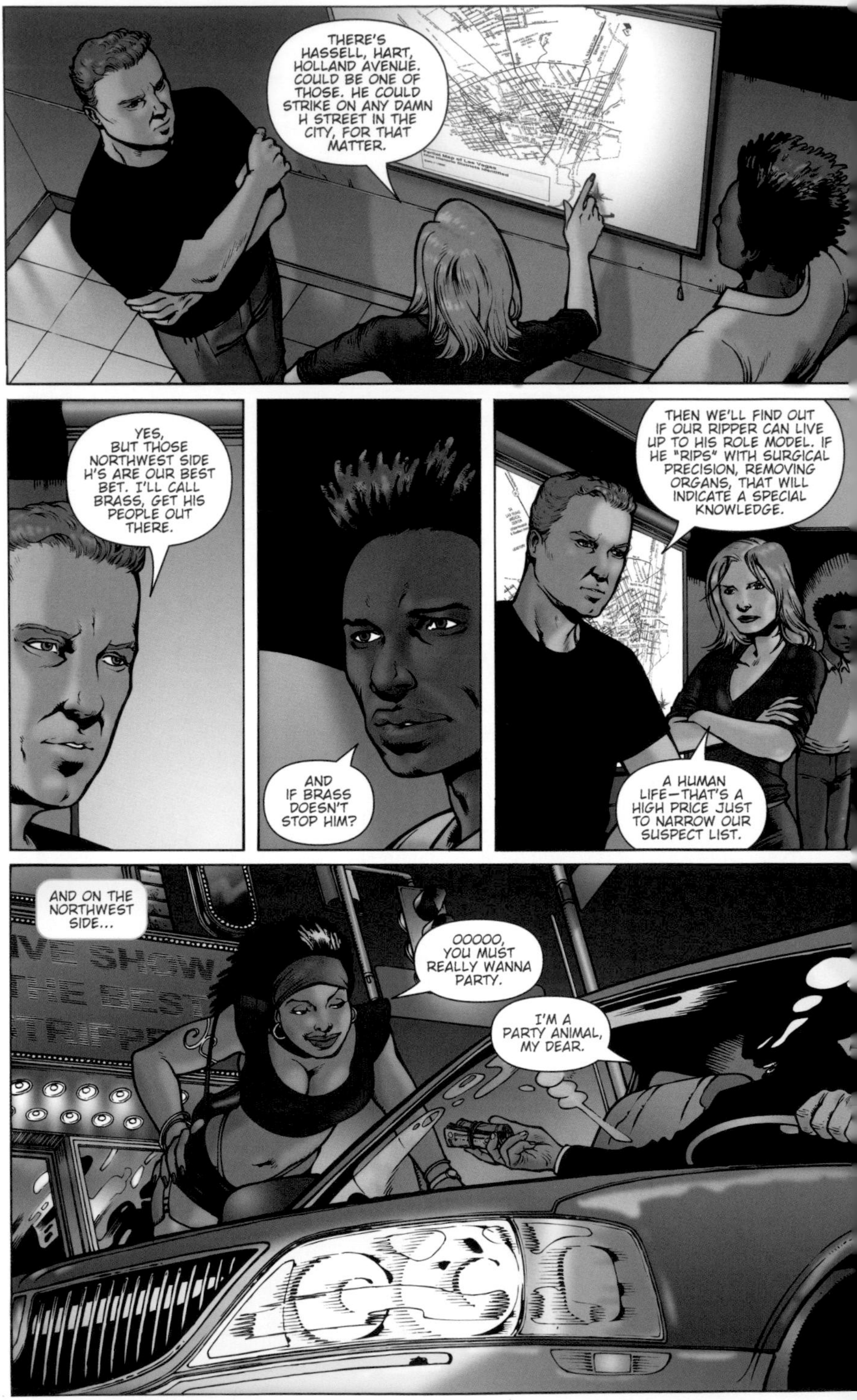
THERE'S HASSELL, HART, HOLLAND AVENUE. COULD BE ONE OF THOSE. HE COULD STRIKE ON ANY DAMN H STREET IN THE CITY, FOR THAT MATTER.
YES, BUT THOSE NORTHWEST SIDE H'S ARE OUR BEST BET. I'LL CALL BRASS, GET HIS PEOPLE OUT THERE.
AND IF BRASS DOESN'T STOP HIM?
THEN WE'LL FIND OUT IF OUR RIPPER CAN LIVE UP TO HIS ROLE MODEL. IF HE "RIPS" WITH SURGICAL PRECISION, REMOVING ORGANS, THAT WILL INDICATE A SPECIAL KNOWLEDGE.
A HUMAN LIFE—THAT'S A HIGH PRICE JUST TO NARROW OUR SUSPECT LIST.
AND ON THE NORTHWEST SIDE...
OOOOO, YOU MUST REALLY WANNA PARTY.
I'M A PARTY ANIMAL, MY DEAR.

chapter three

New Jack City

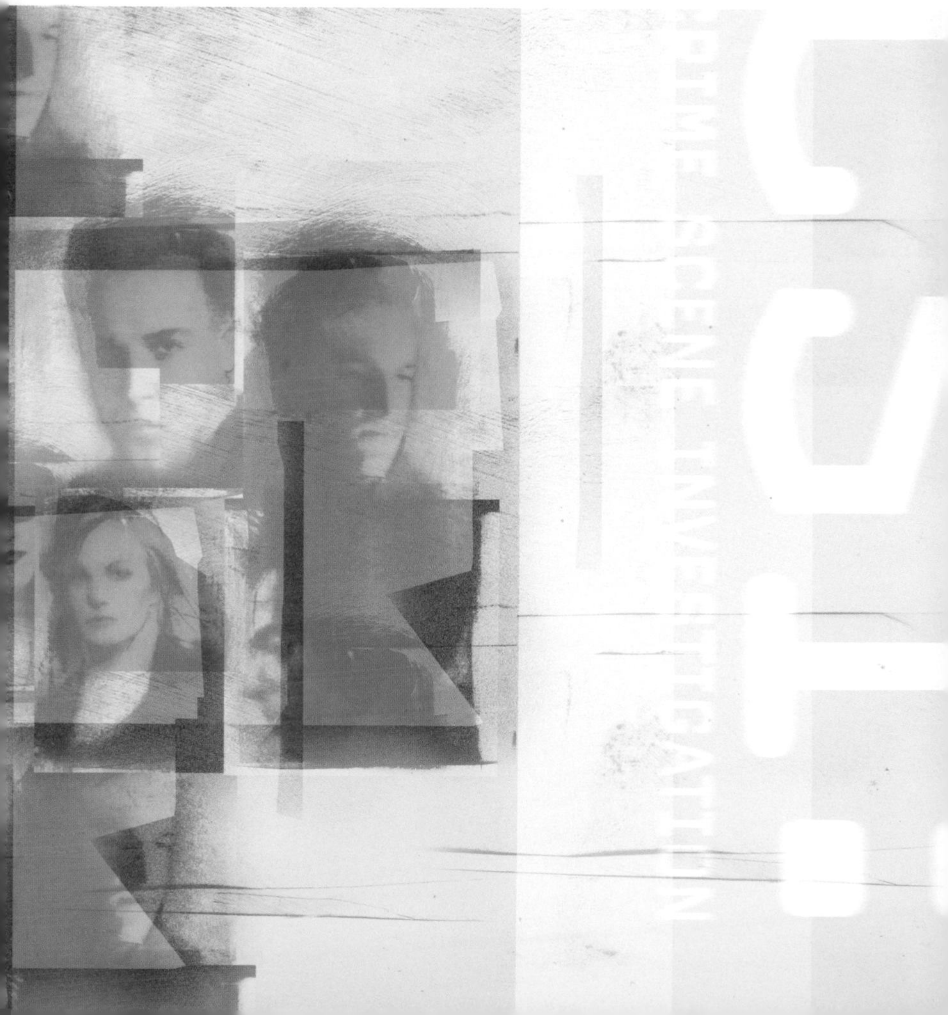

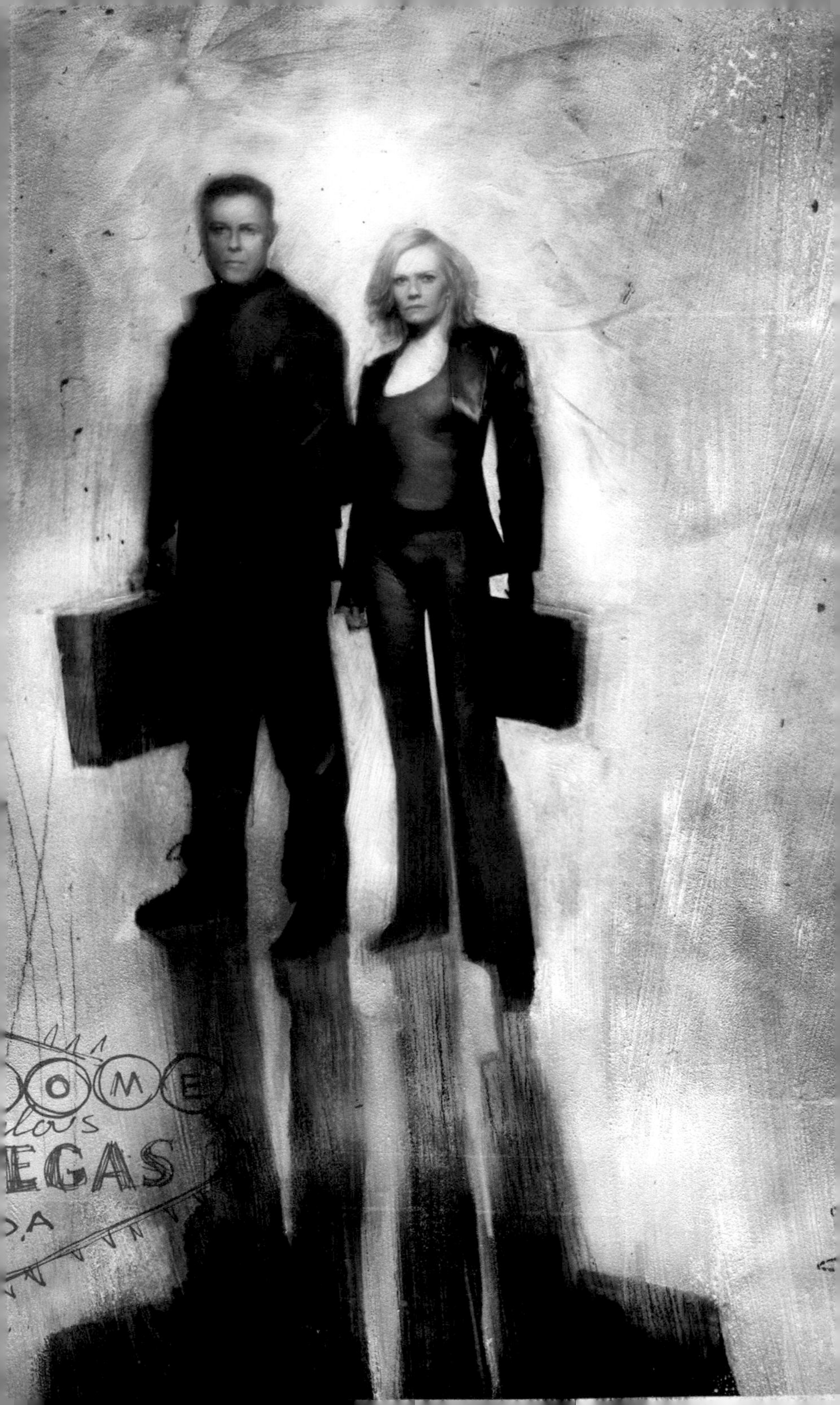

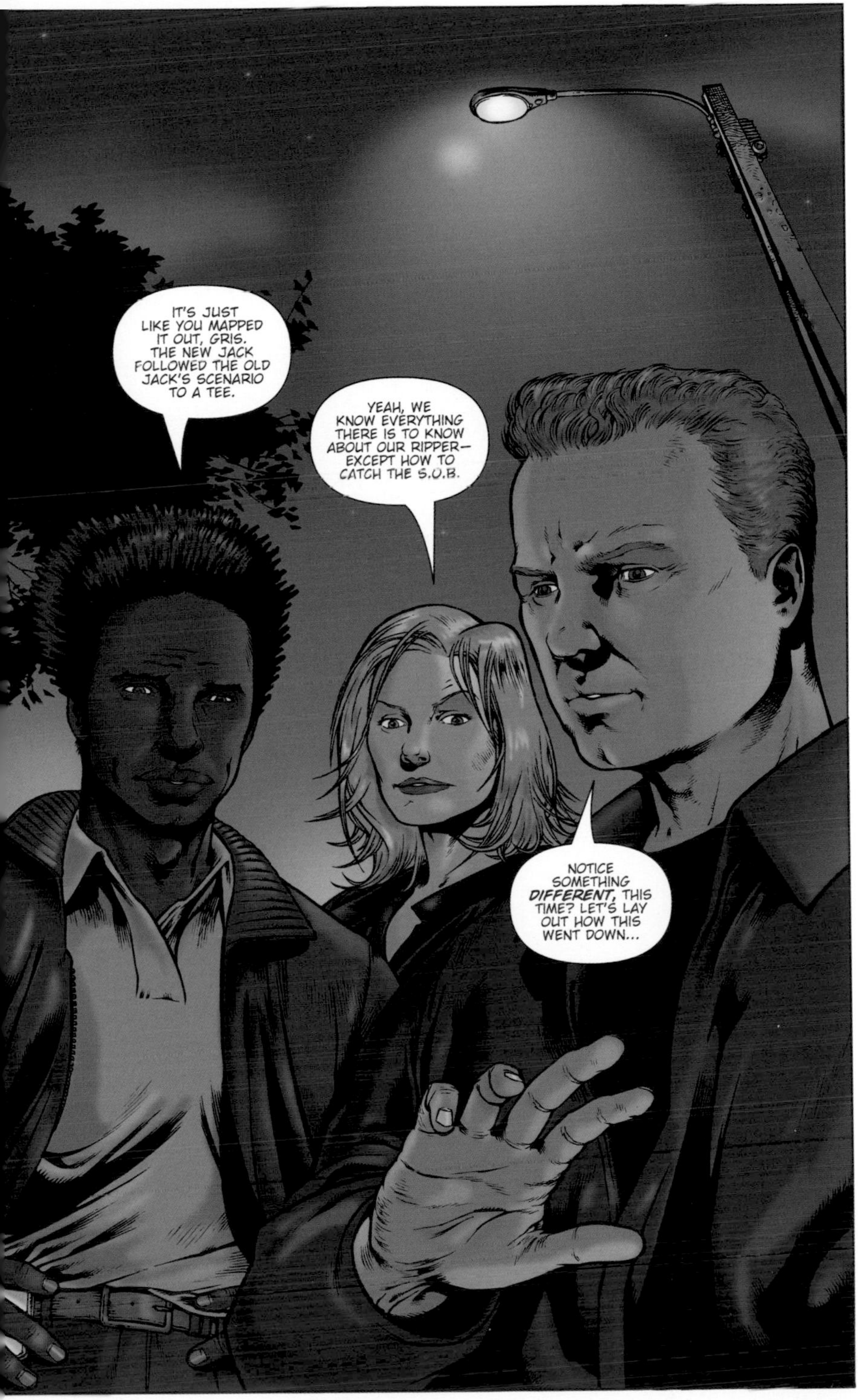
IT'S JUST LIKE YOU MAPPED IT OUT, GRIS. THE NEW JACK FOLLOWED THE OLD JACK'S SCENARIO TO A TEE.
YEAH, WE KNOW EVERYTHING THERE IS TO KNOW ABOUT OUR RIPPER— EXCEPT HOW TO CATCH THE S.O.B.
NOTICE SOMETHING ***DIFFERENT,*** THIS TIME? LET'S LAY OUT HOW THIS WENT DOWN...

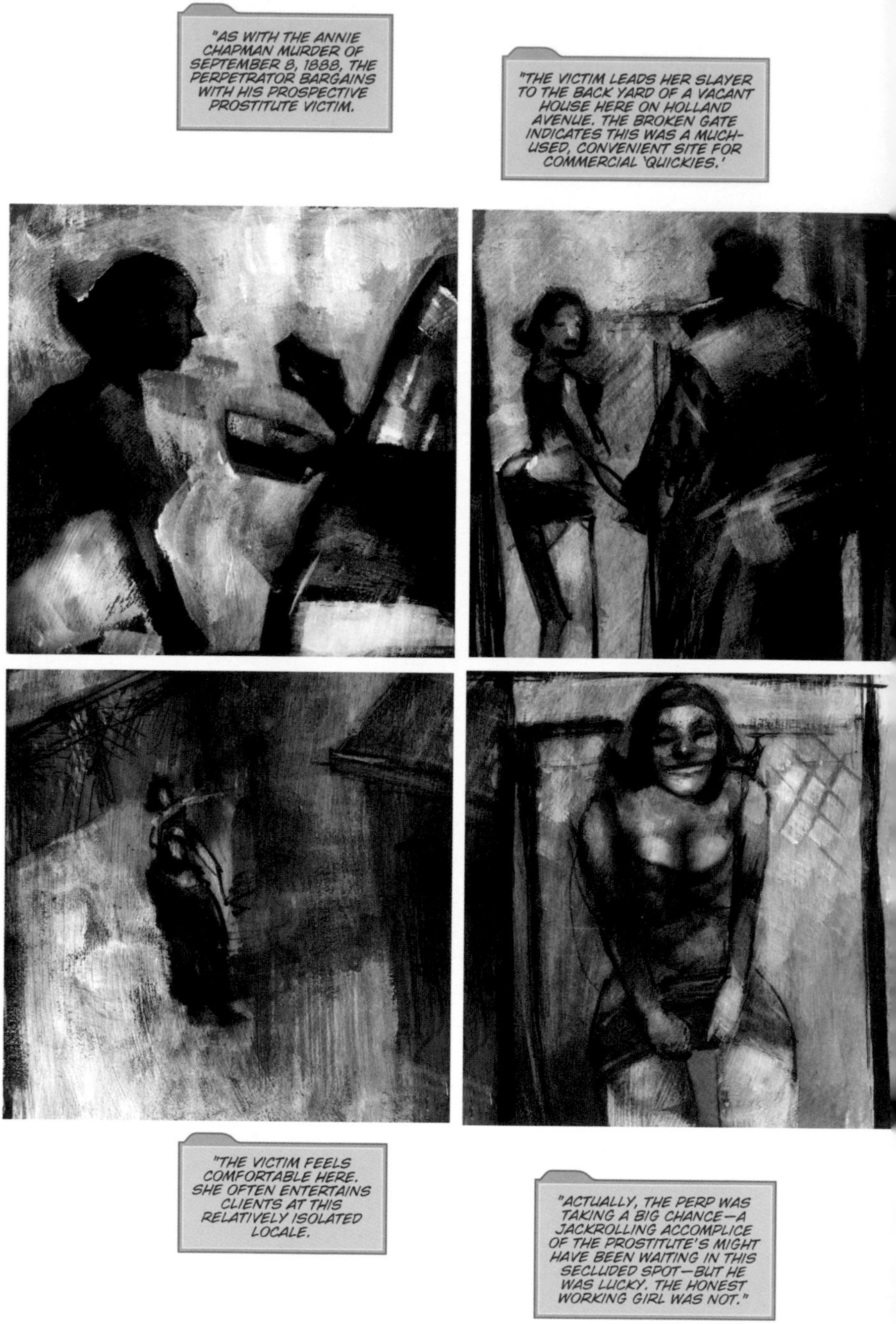
"AS WITH THE ANNIE CHAPMAN MURDER OF SEPTEMBER 8, 1888, THE PERPETRATOR BARGAINS WITH HIS PROSPECTIVE PROSTITUTE VICTIM.
"THE VICTIM LEADS HER SLAYER TO THE BACK YARD OF A VACANT HOUSE HERE ON HOLLAND AVENUE. THE BROKEN GATE INDICATES THIS WAS A MUCH-USED, CONVENIENT SITE FOR COMMERCIAL 'QUICKIES.'
"THE VICTIM FEELS COMFORTABLE HERE. SHE OFTEN ENTERTAINS CLIENTS AT THIS RELATIVELY ISOLATED LOCALE.
"ACTUALLY, THE PERP WAS TAKING A BIG CHANCE—A JACKROLLING ACCOMPLICE OF THE PROSTITUTE'S MIGHT HAVE BEEN WAITING IN THIS SECLUDED SPOT—BUT HE WAS LUCKY. THE HONEST WORKING GIRL WAS NOT."

"A JOHN INTO ROUGH SEX IS NO SURPRISE TO A HOOKER IN VEGAS; BUT OUR VICTIM WASN'T COUNTING ON ANYTHING THIS ROUGH.

"IT'S DIFFICULT TO SEE, BUT I THINK YOU CAN MAKE OUT THE LIGATURE MARKS. THIS VICTIM, LIKE ANNIE, WAS STRANGLED FIRST.

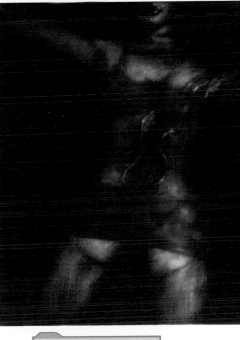

"AND THEN—WITH THE PRIVACY THIS BACKYARD PROVIDED—HE REALLY WENT TO WORK. DOC ROBBINS WILL TELL US WHETHER THE 'NEW JACK' HAS THE SURGICAL SKILLS OF HIS ROLE MODEL.

"BUT I THINK WE CAN ALL AGREE THAT HE'S A MATCH FOR THE ORIGINAL—IN BROAD STROKES, ANYWAY."

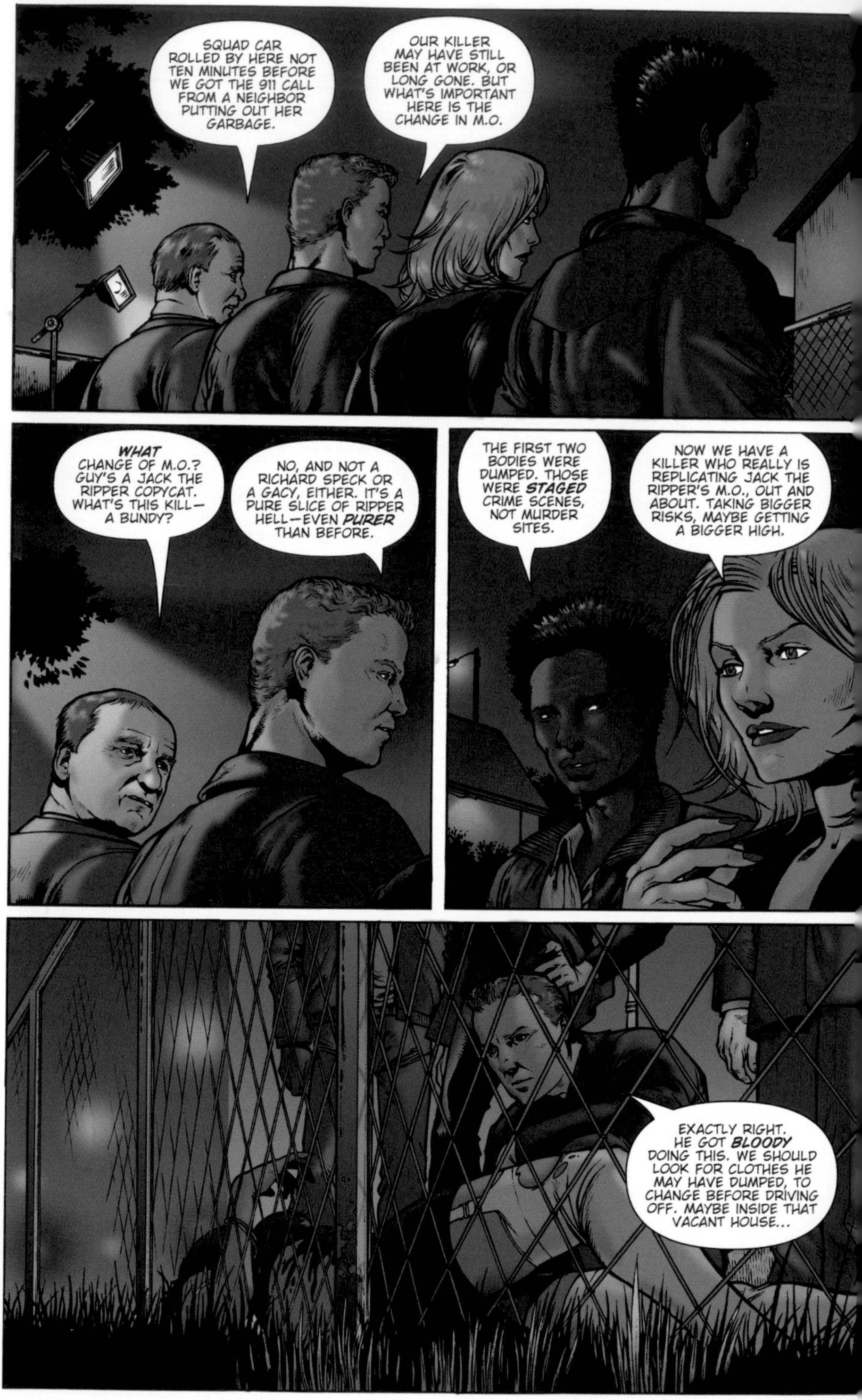
SQUAD CAR ROLLED BY HERE NOT TEN MINUTES BEFORE WE GOT THE 911 CALL FROM A NEIGHBOR PUTTING OUT HER GARBAGE.
OUR KILLER MAY HAVE STILL BEEN AT WORK, OR LONG GONE. BUT WHAT'S IMPORTANT HERE IS THE CHANGE IN M.O.
WHAT CHANGE OF M.O.? GUY'S A JACK THE RIPPER COPYCAT. WHAT'S THIS KILL— A BUNDY?
NO, AND NOT A RICHARD SPECK OR A GACY, EITHER. IT'S A PURE SLICE OF RIPPER HELL—EVEN PURER THAN BEFORE.
THE FIRST TWO BODIES WERE DUMPED. THOSE WERE STAGED CRIME SCENES, NOT MURDER SITES.
NOW WE HAVE A KILLER WHO REALLY IS REPLICATING JACK THE RIPPER'S M.O., OUT AND ABOUT. TAKING BIGGER RISKS, MAYBE GETTING A BIGGER HIGH.
EXACTLY RIGHT. HE GOT BLOODY DOING THIS. WE SHOULD LOOK FOR CLOTHES HE MAY HAVE DUMPED, TO CHANGE BEFORE DRIVING OFF. MAYBE INSIDE THAT VACANT HOUSE...

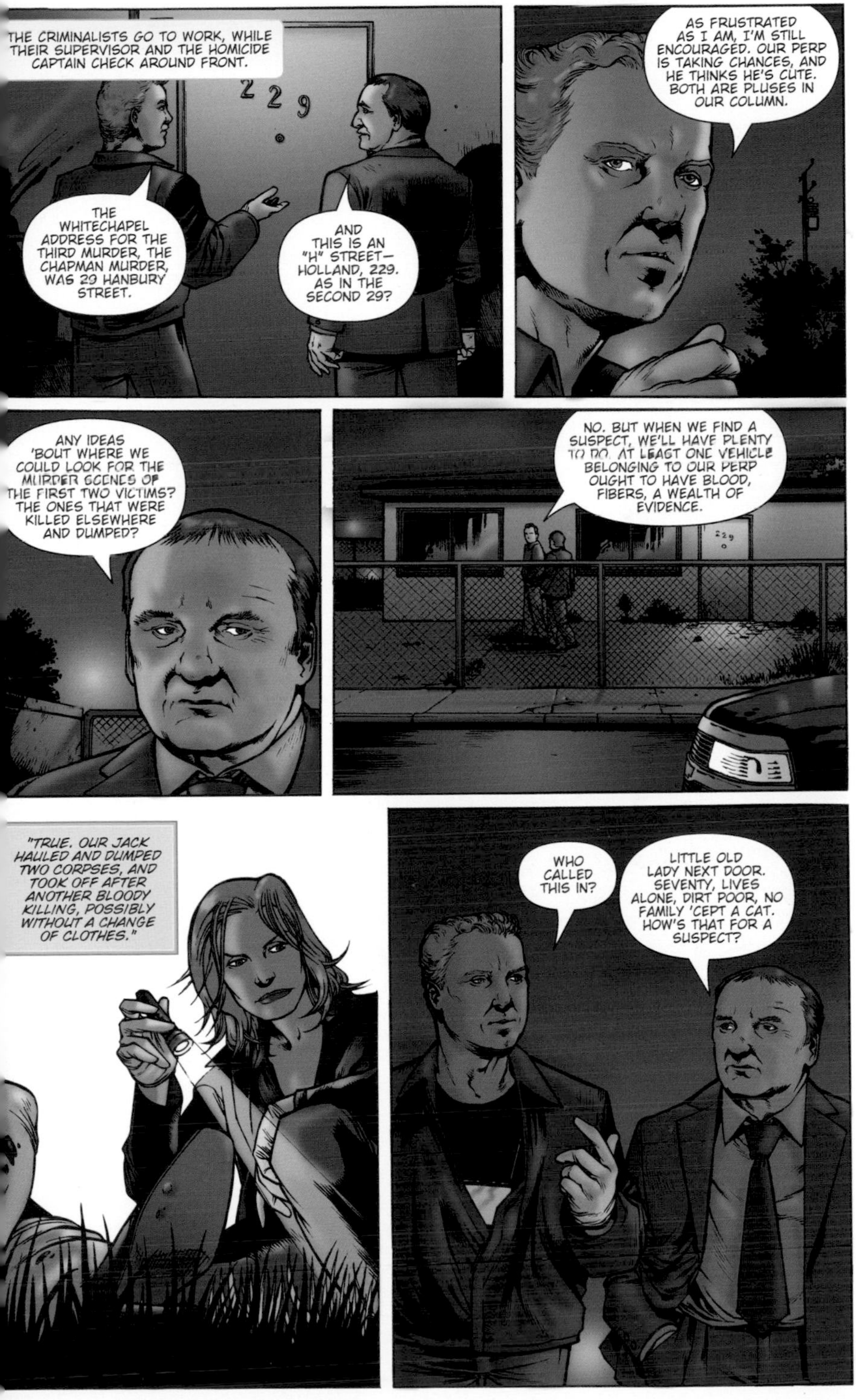
THE CRIMINALISTS GO TO WORK, WHILE THEIR SUPERVISOR AND THE HOMICIDE CAPTAIN CHECK AROUND FRONT.
229
THE WHITECHAPEL ADDRESS FOR THE THIRD MURDER, THE CHAPMAN MURDER, WAS 29 HANBURY STREET.
AND THIS IS AN "H" STREET— HOLLAND, 229. AS IN THE SECOND 29?
AS FRUSTRATED AS I AM, I'M STILL ENCOURAGED. OUR PERP IS TAKING CHANCES, AND HE THINKS HE'S CUTE. BOTH ARE PLUSES IN OUR COLUMN.
ANY IDEAS 'BOUT WHERE WE COULD LOOK FOR THE MURDER SCENES OF THE FIRST TWO VICTIMS? THE ONES THAT WERE KILLED ELSEWHERE AND DUMPED?
NO. BUT WHEN WE FIND A SUSPECT, WE'LL HAVE PLENTY TO DO. AT LEAST ONE VEHICLE BELONGING TO OUR PERP OUGHT TO HAVE BLOOD, FIBERS, A WEALTH OF EVIDENCE.
"TRUE. OUR JACK HAULED AND DUMPED TWO CORPSES, AND TOOK OFF AFTER ANOTHER BLOODY KILLING, POSSIBLY WITHOUT A CHANGE OF CLOTHES."
WHO CALLED THIS IN?
LITTLE OLD LADY NEXT DOOR. SEVENTY, LIVES ALONE, DIRT POOR, NO FAMILY 'CEPT A CAT. HOW'S THAT FOR A SUSPECT?

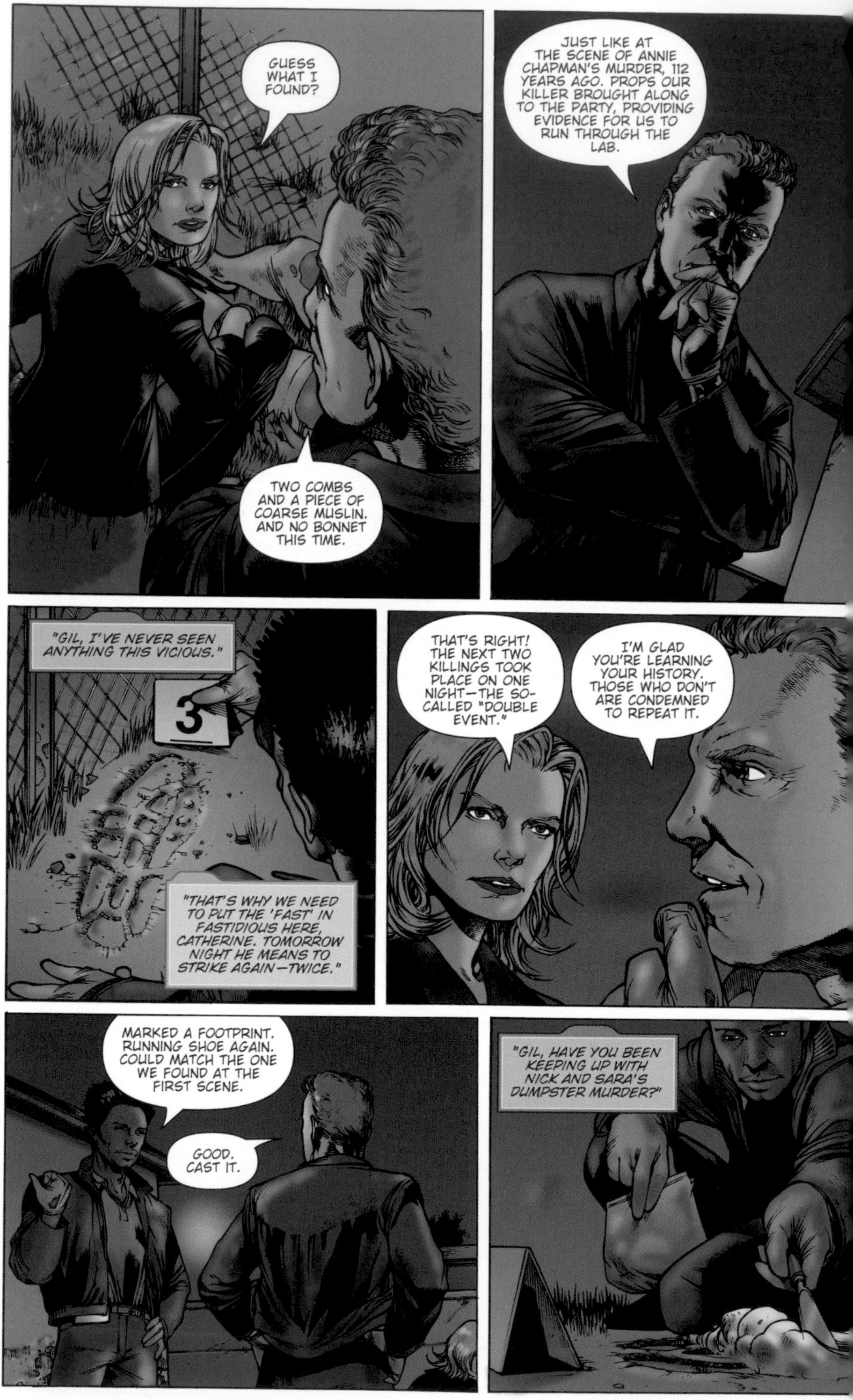
GUESS WHAT I FOUND?
TWO COMBS AND A PIECE OF COARSE MUSLIN. AND NO BONNET THIS TIME.
JUST LIKE AT THE SCENE OF ANNIE CHAPMAN'S MURDER, 112 YEARS AGO. PROPS OUR KILLER BROUGHT ALONG TO THE PARTY, PROVIDING EVIDENCE FOR US TO RUN THROUGH THE LAB.
"GIL, I'VE NEVER SEEN ANYTHING THIS VICIOUS."
3
"THAT'S WHY WE NEED TO PUT THE 'FAST' IN FASTIDIOUS HERE, CATHERINE. TOMORROW NIGHT HE MEANS TO STRIKE AGAIN—TWICE."
THAT'S RIGHT! THE NEXT TWO KILLINGS TOOK PLACE ON ONE NIGHT—THE SO-CALLED "DOUBLE EVENT."
I'M GLAD YOU'RE LEARNING YOUR HISTORY. THOSE WHO DON'T ARE CONDEMNED TO REPEAT IT.
MARKED A FOOTPRINT. RUNNING SHOE AGAIN. COULD MATCH THE ONE WE FOUND AT THE FIRST SCENE.
GOOD. CAST IT.
"GIL, HAVE YOU BEEN KEEPING UP WITH NICK AND SARA'S DUMPSTER MURDER?"

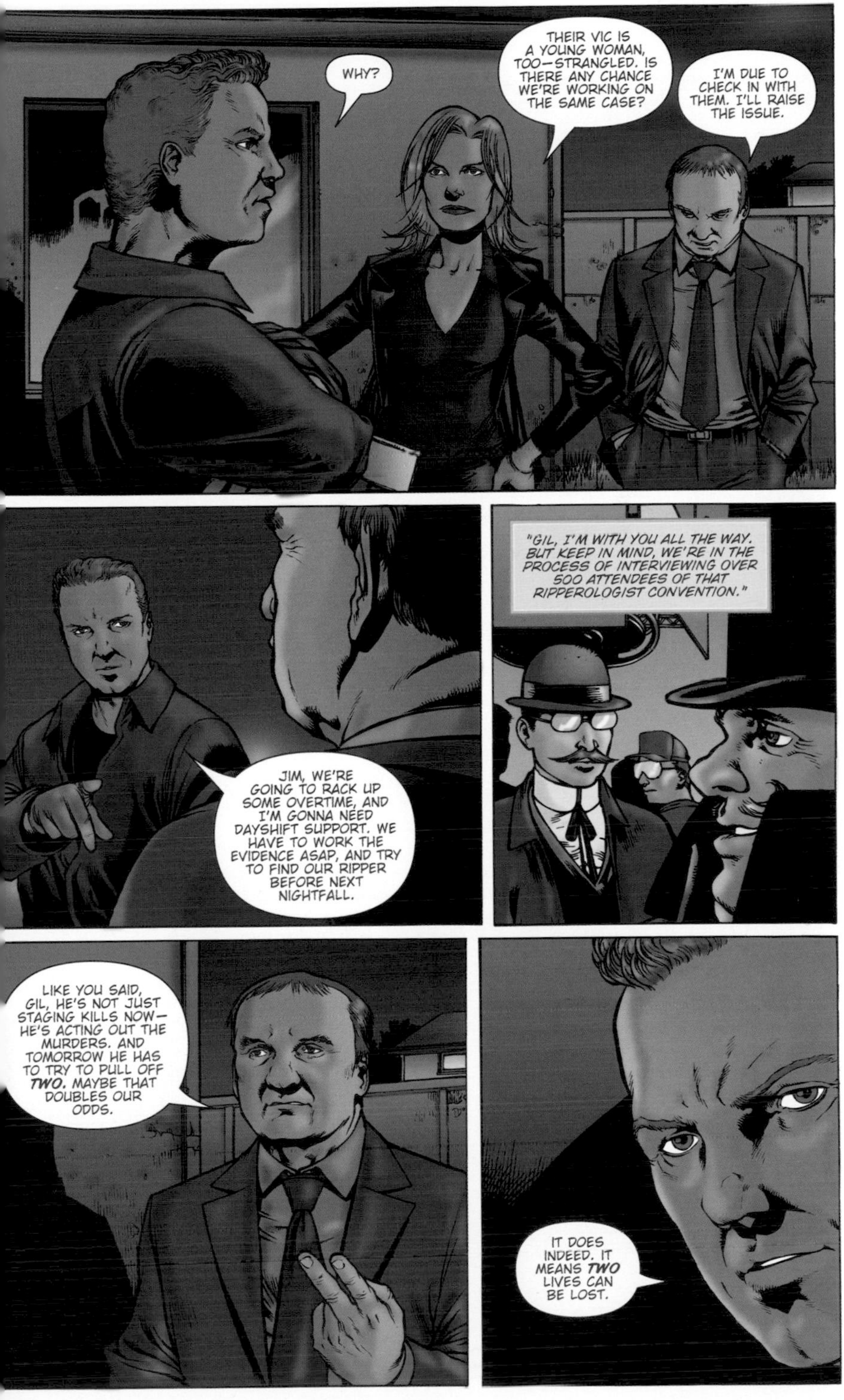
WHY?
THEIR VIC IS A YOUNG WOMAN, TOO—STRANGLED. IS THERE ANY CHANCE WE'RE WORKING ON THE SAME CASE?
I'M DUE TO CHECK IN WITH THEM. I'LL RAISE THE ISSUE.
JIM, WE'RE GOING TO RACK UP SOME OVERTIME, AND I'M GONNA NEED DAYSHIFT SUPPORT. WE HAVE TO WORK THE EVIDENCE ASAP, AND TRY TO FIND OUR RIPPER BEFORE NEXT NIGHTFALL.
"GIL, I'M WITH YOU ALL THE WAY. BUT KEEP IN MIND, WE'RE IN THE PROCESS OF INTERVIEWING OVER 500 ATTENDEES OF THAT RIPPEROLOGIST CONVENTION."
LIKE YOU SAID, GIL, HE'S NOT JUST STAGING KILLS NOW—HE'S ACTING OUT THE MURDERS. AND TOMORROW HE HAS TO TRY TO PULL OFF TWO. MAYBE THAT DOUBLES OUR ODDS.
IT DOES INDEED. IT MEANS TWO LIVES CAN BE LOST.

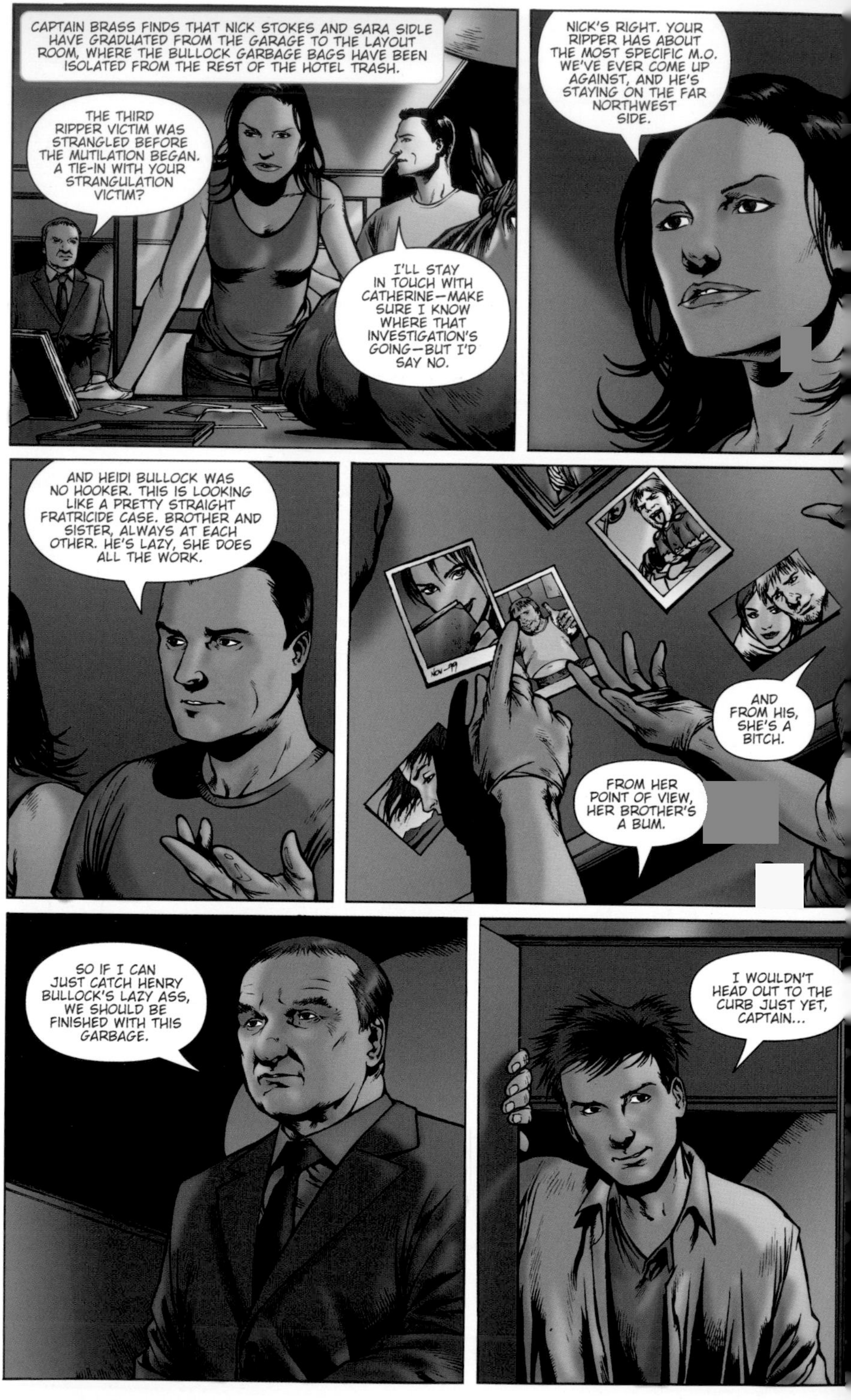

CAPTAIN BRASS FINDS THAT NICK STOKES AND SARA SIDLE HAVE GRADUATED FROM THE GARAGE TO THE LAYOUT ROOM, WHERE THE BULLOCK GARBAGE BAGS HAVE BEEN ISOLATED FROM THE REST OF THE HOTEL TRASH.
THE THIRD RIPPER VICTIM WAS STRANGLED BEFORE THE MUTILATION BEGAN. A TIE-IN WITH YOUR STRANGULATION VICTIM?
I'LL STAY IN TOUCH WITH CATHERINE—MAKE SURE I KNOW WHERE THAT INVESTIGATION'S GOING—BUT I'D SAY NO.
NICK'S RIGHT. YOUR RIPPER HAS ABOUT THE MOST SPECIFIC M.O. WE'VE EVER COME UP AGAINST, AND HE'S STAYING ON THE FAR NORTHWEST SIDE.
AND HEIDI BULLOCK WAS NO HOOKER. THIS IS LOOKING LIKE A PRETTY STRAIGHT FRATRICIDE CASE. BROTHER AND SISTER, ALWAYS AT EACH OTHER. HE'S LAZY, SHE DOES ALL THE WORK.
NOV-99
FROM HER POINT OF VIEW, HER BROTHER'S A BUM.
AND FROM HIS, SHE'S A BITCH.
SO IF I CAN JUST CATCH HENRY BULLOCK'S LAZY ASS, WE SHOULD BE FINISHED WITH THIS GARBAGE.
I WOULDN'T HEAD OUT TO THE CURB JUST YET, CAPTAIN...

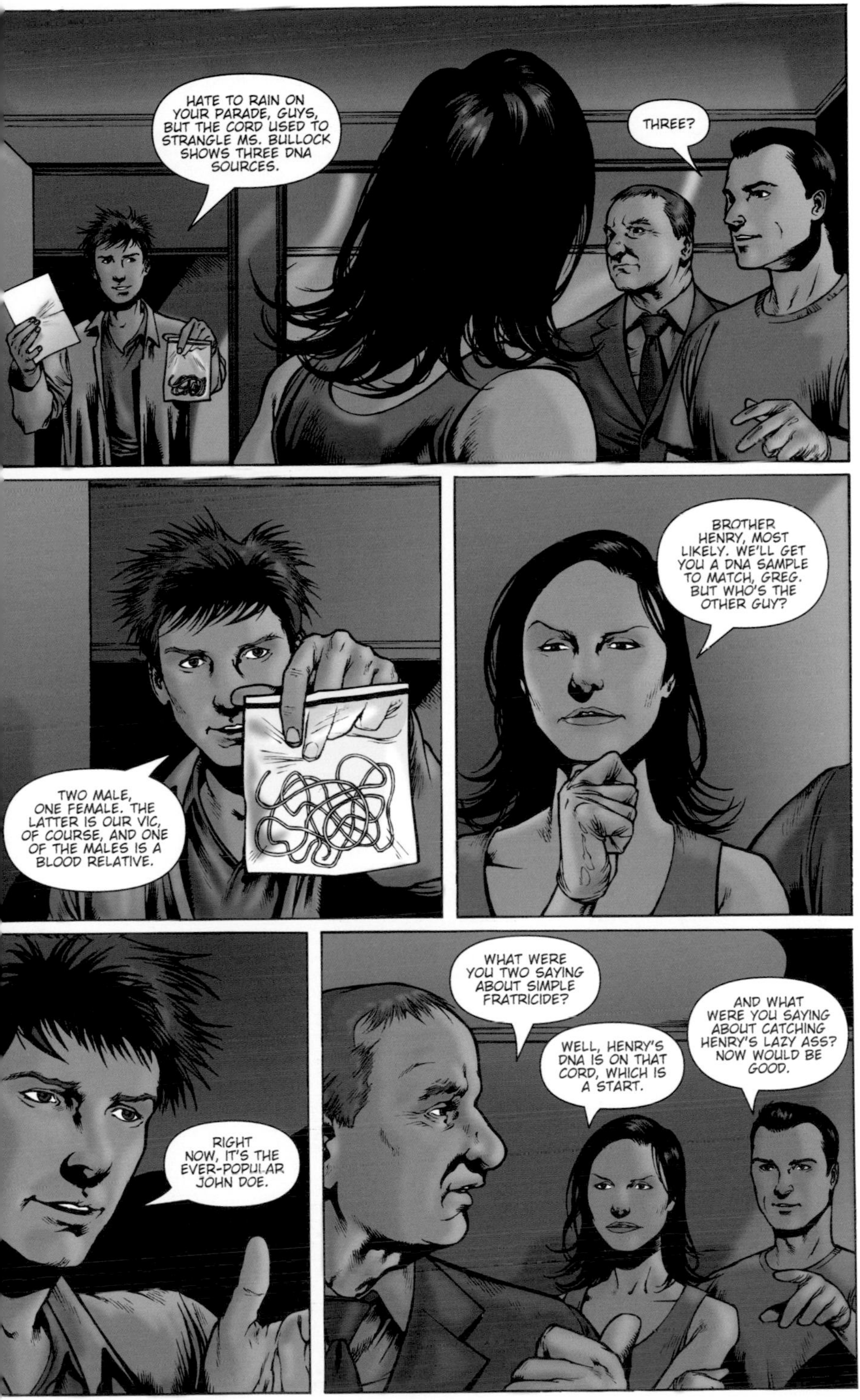
HATE TO RAIN ON YOUR PARADE, GUYS, BUT THE CORD USED TO STRANGLE MS. BULLOCK SHOWS THREE DNA SOURCES.
THREE?
TWO MALE, ONE FEMALE. THE LATTER IS OUR VIC, OF COURSE, AND ONE OF THE MALES IS A BLOOD RELATIVE.
BROTHER HENRY, MOST LIKELY. WE'LL GET YOU A DNA SAMPLE TO MATCH, GREG. BUT WHO'S THE OTHER GUY?
RIGHT NOW, IT'S THE EVER-POPULAR JOHN DOE.
WHAT WERE YOU TWO SAYING ABOUT SIMPLE FRATRICIDE?
WELL, HENRY'S DNA IS ON THAT CORD, WHICH IS A START.
AND WHAT WERE YOU SAYING ABOUT CATCHING HENRY'S LAZY ASS? NOW WOULD BE GOOD.

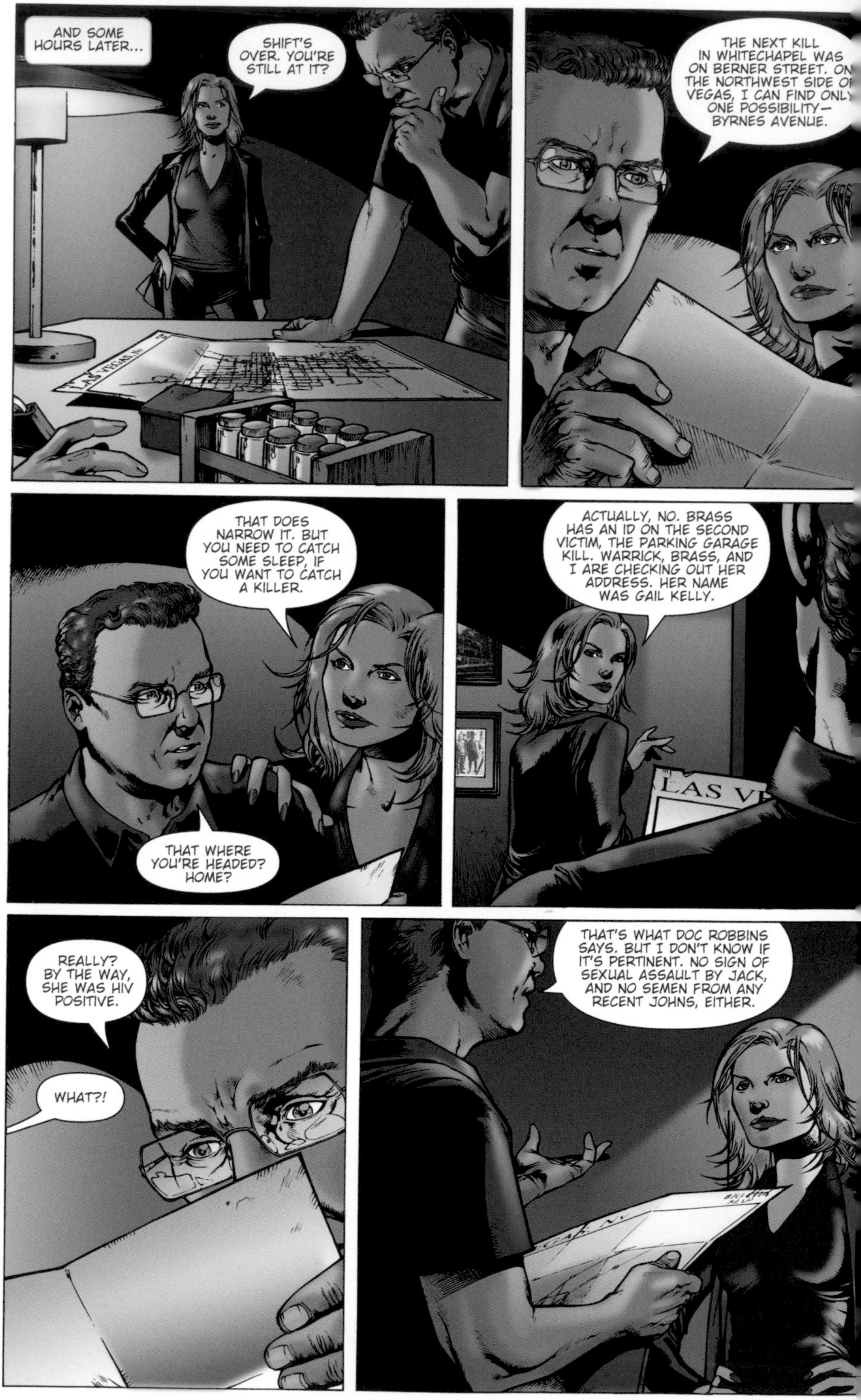
AND SOME HOURS LATER...
SHIFT'S OVER. YOU'RE STILL AT IT?
LAS VEGAS NV
THE NEXT KILL IN WHITECHAPEL WAS ON BERNER STREET. ON THE NORTHWEST SIDE OF VEGAS, I CAN FIND ONLY ONE POSSIBILITY— BYRNES AVENUE.
THAT DOES NARROW IT. BUT YOU NEED TO CATCH SOME SLEEP, IF YOU WANT TO CATCH A KILLER.
THAT WHERE YOU'RE HEADED? HOME?
ACTUALLY, NO. BRASS HAS AN ID ON THE SECOND VICTIM, THE PARKING GARAGE KILL. WARRICK, BRASS, AND I ARE CHECKING OUT HER ADDRESS. HER NAME WAS GAIL KELLY.
LAS V
REALLY? BY THE WAY, SHE WAS HIV POSITIVE.
WHAT?!
THAT'S WHAT DOC ROBBINS SAYS. BUT I DON'T KNOW IF IT'S PERTINENT. NO SIGN OF SEXUAL ASSAULT BY JACK, AND NO SEMEN FROM ANY RECENT JOHNS, EITHER.

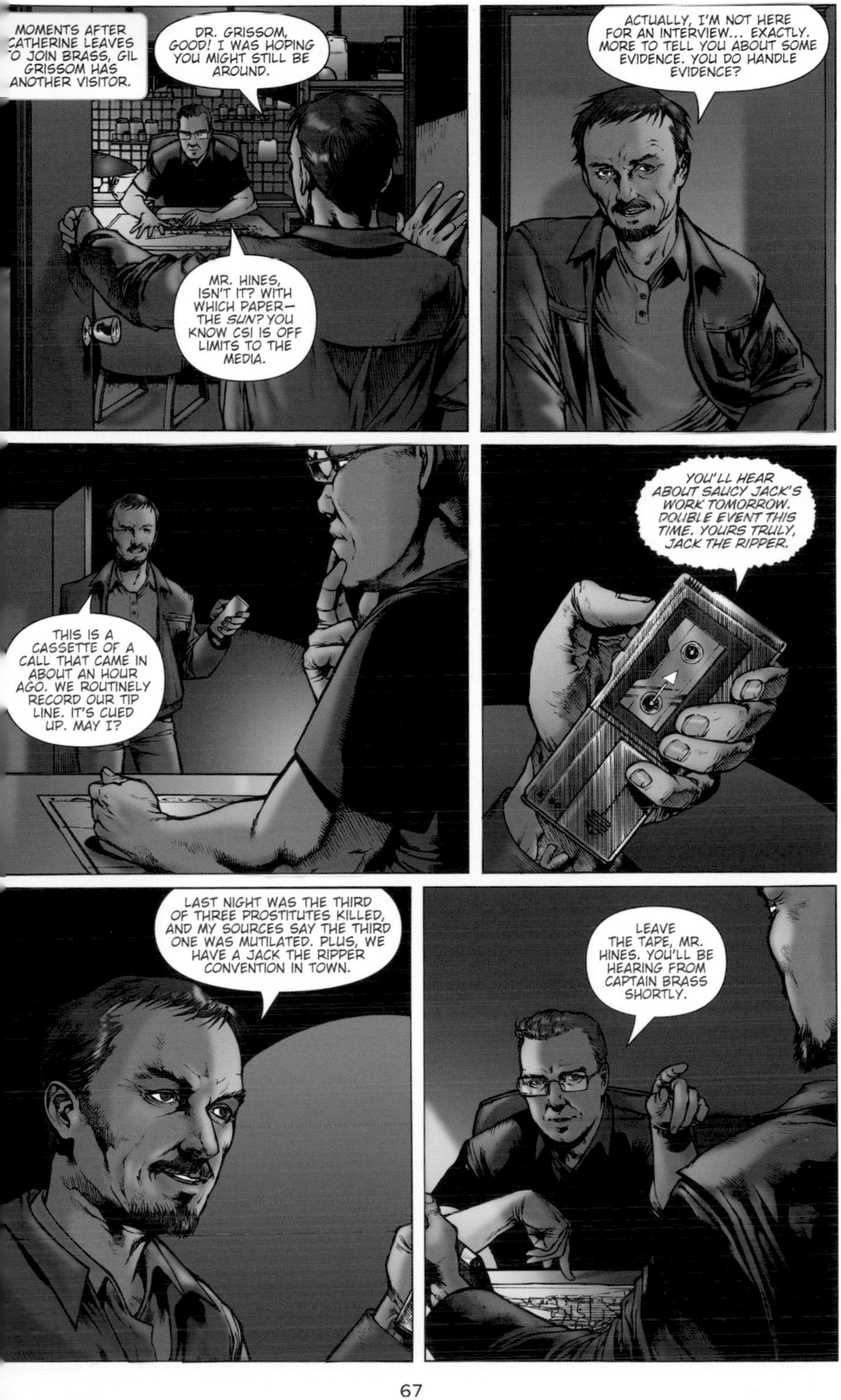

MOMENTS AFTER CATHERINE LEAVES TO JOIN BRASS, GIL GRISSOM HAS ANOTHER VISITOR.
DR. GRISSOM, GOOD! I WAS HOPING YOU MIGHT STILL BE AROUND.
MR. HINES, ISN'T IT? WITH WHICH PAPER— THE SUN? YOU KNOW CSI IS OFF LIMITS TO THE MEDIA.
ACTUALLY, I'M NOT HERE FOR AN INTERVIEW... EXACTLY. MORE TO TELL YOU ABOUT SOME EVIDENCE. YOU DO HANDLE EVIDENCE?
THIS IS A CASSETTE OF A CALL THAT CAME IN ABOUT AN HOUR AGO. WE ROUTINELY RECORD OUR TIP LINE. IT'S CUED UP. MAY I?
YOU'LL HEAR ABOUT SAUCY JACK'S WORK TOMORROW. DOUBLE EVENT THIS TIME. YOURS TRULY, JACK THE RIPPER.
LAST NIGHT WAS THE THIRD OF THREE PROSTITUTES KILLED, AND MY SOURCES SAY THE THIRD ONE WAS MUTILATED. PLUS, WE HAVE A JACK THE RIPPER CONVENTION IN TOWN.
LEAVE THE TAPE, MR. HINES. YOU'LL BE HEARING FROM CAPTAIN BRASS SHORTLY.

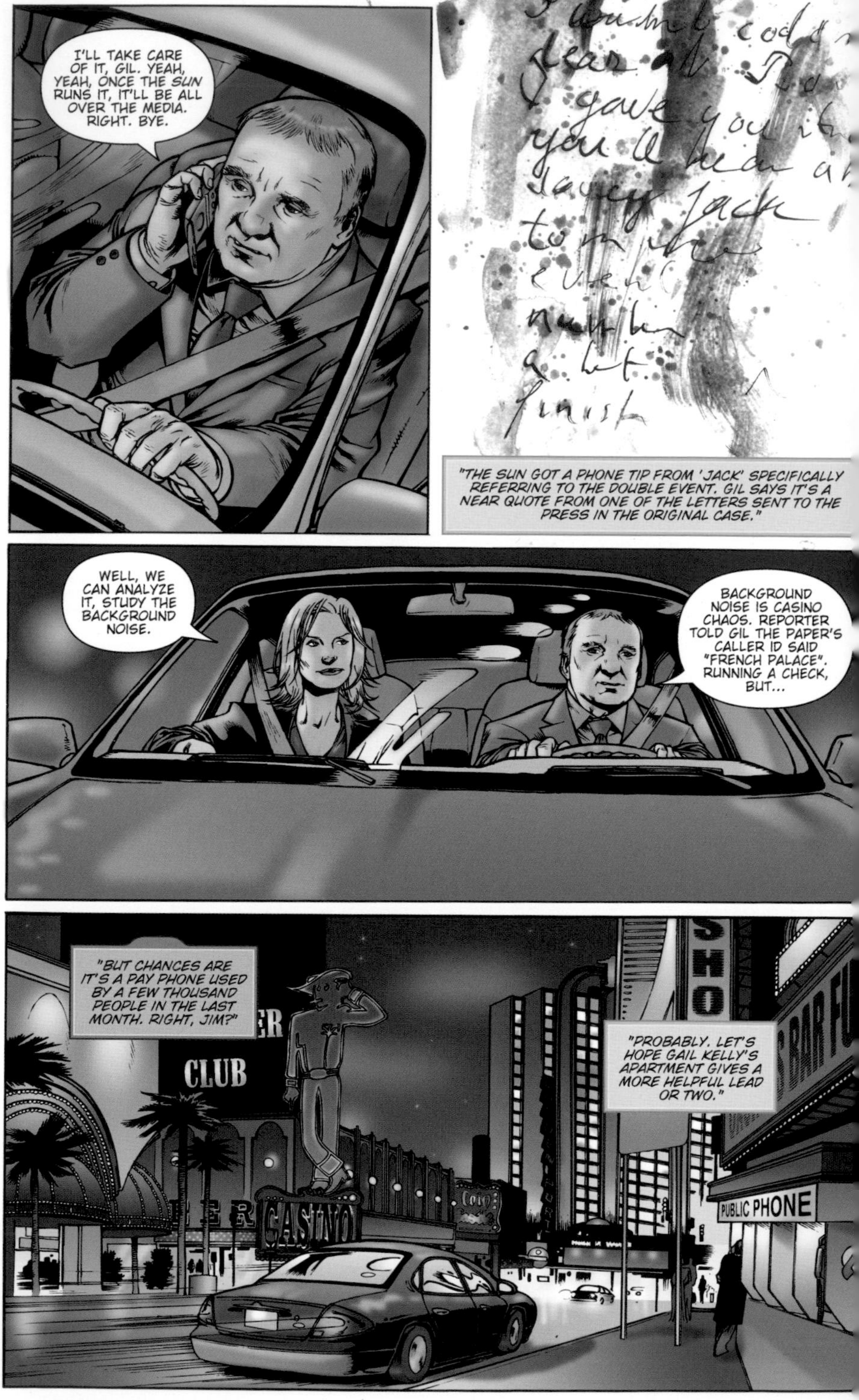
I'LL TAKE CARE OF IT, GIL. YEAH, YEAH, ONCE THE *SUN* RUNS IT, IT'LL BE ALL OVER THE MEDIA. RIGHT. BYE.
"THE SUN GOT A PHONE TIP FROM 'JACK' SPECIFICALLY REFERRING TO THE DOUBLE EVENT. GIL SAYS IT'S A NEAR QUOTE FROM ONE OF THE LETTERS SENT TO THE PRESS IN THE ORIGINAL CASE."
WELL, WE CAN ANALYZE IT, STUDY THE BACKGROUND NOISE.
BACKGROUND NOISE IS CASINO CHAOS. REPORTER TOLD GIL THE PAPER'S CALLER ID SAID "FRENCH PALACE". RUNNING A CHECK, BUT...
"BUT CHANCES ARE IT'S A PAY PHONE USED BY A FEW THOUSAND PEOPLE IN THE LAST MONTH. RIGHT, JIM?"
CLUB
CASINO
"PROBABLY. LET'S HOPE GAIL KELLY'S APARTMENT GIVES A MORE HELPFUL LEAD OR TWO."
PUBLIC PHONE

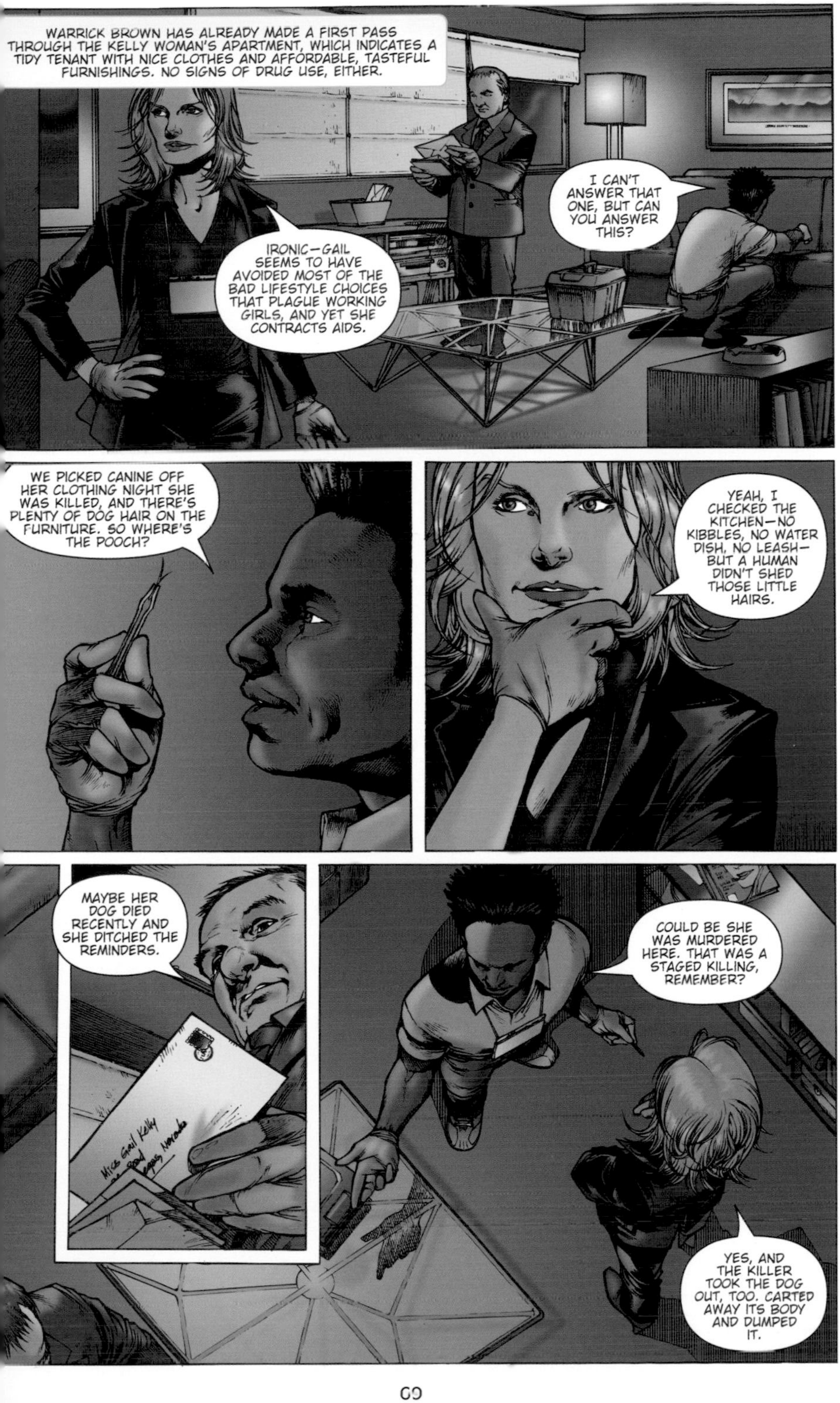
WARRICK BROWN HAS ALREADY MADE A FIRST PASS THROUGH THE KELLY WOMAN'S APARTMENT, WHICH INDICATES A TIDY TENANT WITH NICE CLOTHES AND AFFORDABLE, TASTEFUL FURNISHINGS. NO SIGNS OF DRUG USE, EITHER.
IRONIC—GAIL SEEMS TO HAVE AVOIDED MOST OF THE BAD LIFESTYLE CHOICES THAT PLAGUE WORKING GIRLS, AND YET SHE CONTRACTS AIDS.
I CAN'T ANSWER THAT ONE, BUT CAN YOU ANSWER THIS?
WE PICKED CANINE OFF HER CLOTHING NIGHT SHE WAS KILLED, AND THERE'S PLENTY OF DOG HAIR ON THE FURNITURE. SO WHERE'S THE POOCH?
YEAH, I CHECKED THE KITCHEN—NO KIBBLES, NO WATER DISH, NO LEASH—BUT A HUMAN DIDN'T SHED THOSE LITTLE HAIRS.
MAYBE HER DOG DIED RECENTLY AND SHE DITCHED THE REMINDERS.
COULD BE SHE WAS MURDERED HERE. THAT WAS A STAGED KILLING, REMEMBER?
YES, AND THE KILLER TOOK THE DOG OUT, TOO. CARTED AWAY ITS BODY AND DUMPED IT.

I'VE GOT A PHONE BILL HERE. I'M GOING OUT TO CALL IT IN SO WE CAN RUN HER RECORDS.

IF THIS WAS THE ACTUAL MURDER SITE, WE'LL KNOW SOON ENOUGH.

HEY, CATH! CHECK THIS OUT!

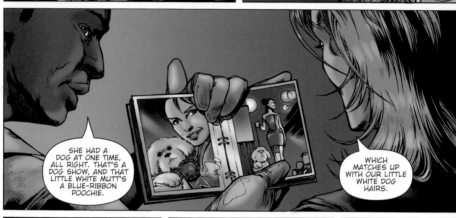

SHE HAD A DOG AT ONE TIME, ALL RIGHT. THAT'S A DOG SHOW, AND THAT LITTLE WHITE MUTT'S A BLUE-RIBBON POOCHIE.

WHICH MATCHES UP WITH OUR LITTLE WHITE DOG HAIRS.

I'M GONNA TRY THE BATHROOM. SINCE THERE'S NO OBVIOUS SIGN OF A MESS ANYWHERE ELSE IN THE APARTMENT, MAYBE JACK DISEMBOWELED THE VIC IN HER TUB.

BUT THE LEUCO-CRYSTAL VIOLET TREATMENT TURNS UP NO SIGN OF BLOOD.

DO YOU DO WINDOWS?

VERY FUNNY. I DON'T THINK THIS APARTMENT WAS THE MURDER SCENE. I'LL CHECK THE DRAIN.

FINE, BUT FIRST LOOK WHAT I FOUND IN A DRAWER—A CONTRACT FOR GAIL KELLY TO SHOW DOGS FOR A MRS. EMILY MAYFIELD.

CONTRACT

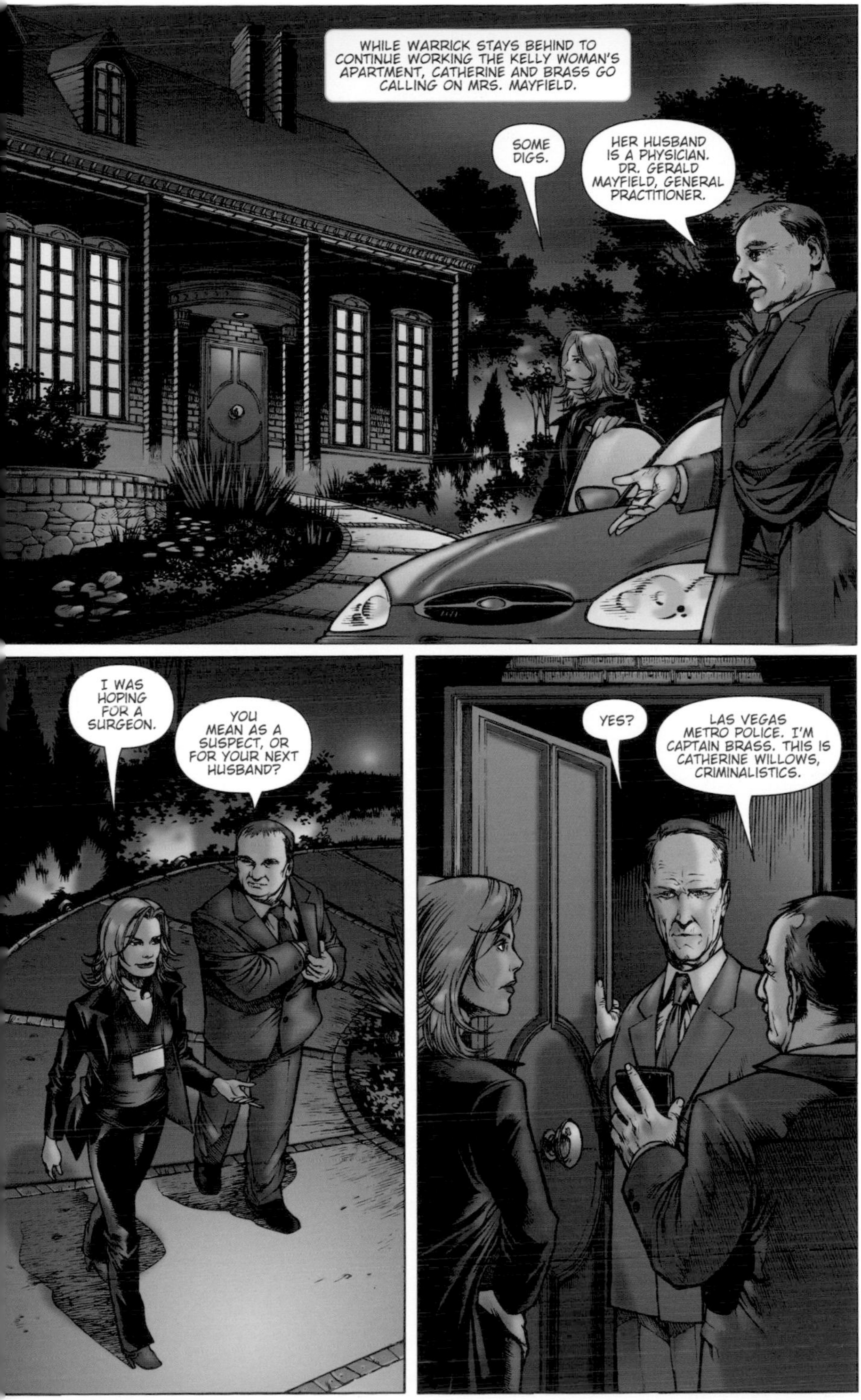
WHILE WARRICK STAYS BEHIND TO CONTINUE WORKING THE KELLY WOMAN'S APARTMENT, CATHERINE AND BRASS GO CALLING ON MRS. MAYFIELD.
SOME DIGS.
HER HUSBAND IS A PHYSICIAN. DR. GERALD MAYFIELD, GENERAL PRACTITIONER.
I WAS HOPING FOR A SURGEON.
YOU MEAN AS A SUSPECT, OR FOR YOUR NEXT HUSBAND?
YES?
LAS VEGAS METRO POLICE. I'M CAPTAIN BRASS. THIS IS CATHERINE WILLOWS, CRIMINALISTICS.

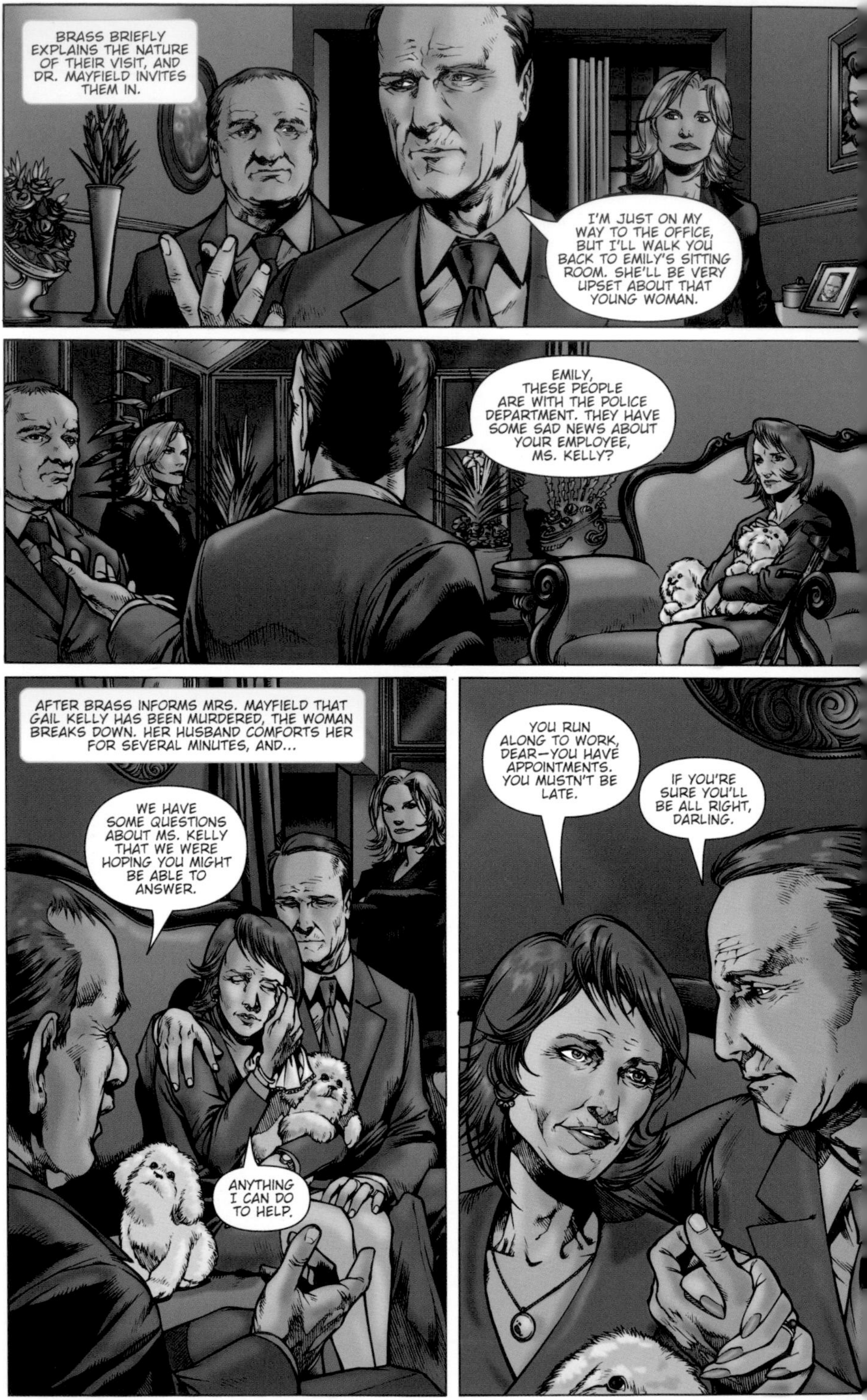
BRASS BRIEFLY EXPLAINS THE NATURE OF THEIR VISIT, AND DR. MAYFIELD INVITES THEM IN.
I'M JUST ON MY WAY TO THE OFFICE, BUT I'LL WALK YOU BACK TO EMILY'S SITTING ROOM. SHE'LL BE VERY UPSET ABOUT THAT YOUNG WOMAN.
EMILY, THESE PEOPLE ARE WITH THE POLICE DEPARTMENT. THEY HAVE SOME SAD NEWS ABOUT YOUR EMPLOYEE, MS. KELLY?
AFTER BRASS INFORMS MRS. MAYFIELD THAT GAIL KELLY HAS BEEN MURDERED, THE WOMAN BREAKS DOWN. HER HUSBAND COMFORTS HER FOR SEVERAL MINUTES, AND...
WE HAVE SOME QUESTIONS ABOUT MS. KELLY THAT WE WERE HOPING YOU MIGHT BE ABLE TO ANSWER.
ANYTHING I CAN DO TO HELP.
YOU RUN ALONG TO WORK, DEAR—YOU HAVE APPOINTMENTS. YOU MUSTN'T BE LATE.
IF YOU'RE SURE YOU'LL BE ALL RIGHT, DARLING.

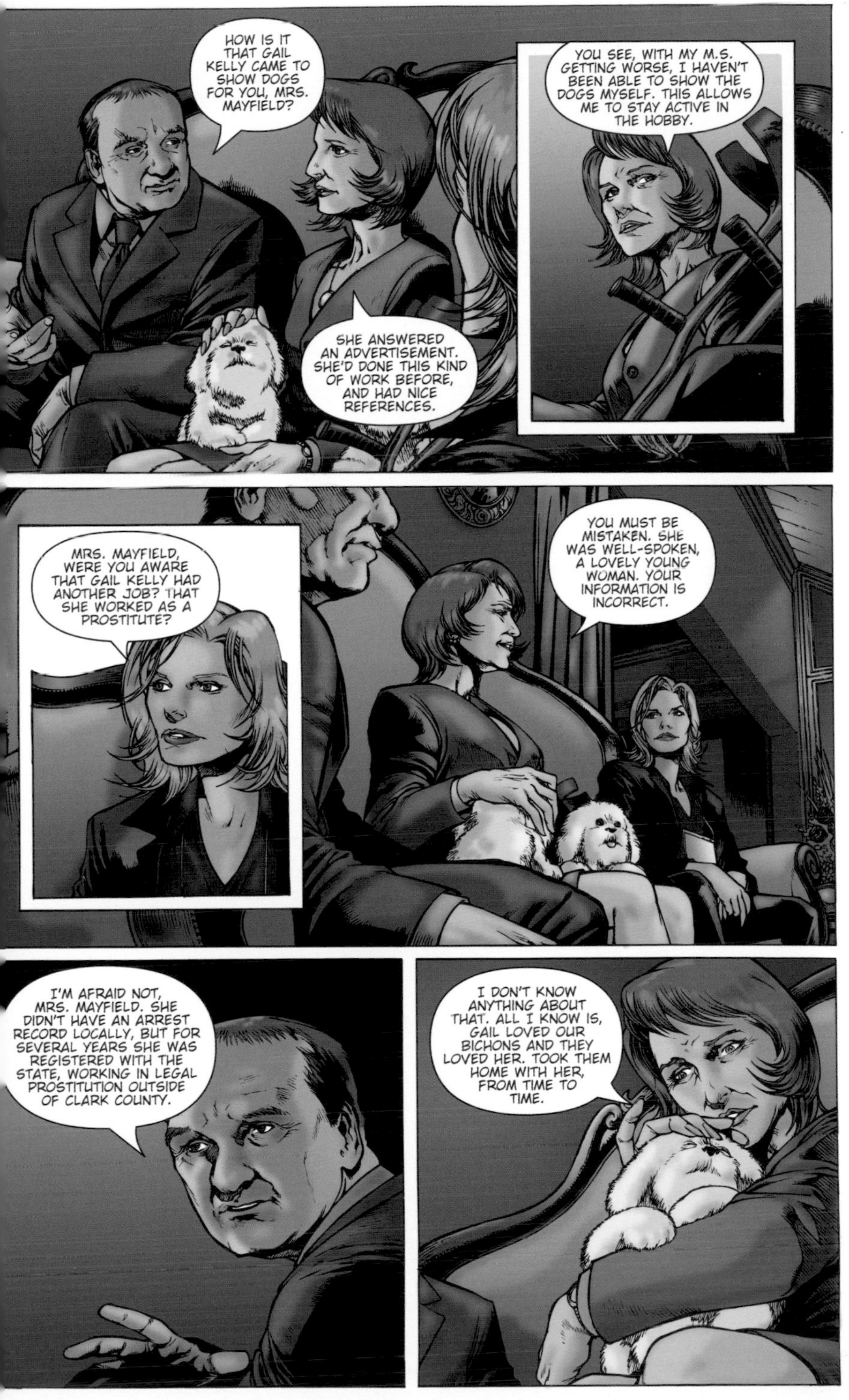
HOW IS IT THAT GAIL KELLY CAME TO SHOW DOGS FOR YOU, MRS. MAYFIELD?
SHE ANSWERED AN ADVERTISEMENT. SHE'D DONE THIS KIND OF WORK BEFORE, AND HAD NICE REFERENCES.
YOU SEE, WITH MY M.S. GETTING WORSE, I HAVEN'T BEEN ABLE TO SHOW THE DOGS MYSELF. THIS ALLOWS ME TO STAY ACTIVE IN THE HOBBY.
MRS. MAYFIELD, WERE YOU AWARE THAT GAIL KELLY HAD ANOTHER JOB? THAT SHE WORKED AS A PROSTITUTE?
YOU MUST BE MISTAKEN. SHE WAS WELL-SPOKEN, A LOVELY YOUNG WOMAN. YOUR INFORMATION IS INCORRECT.
I'M AFRAID NOT, MRS. MAYFIELD. SHE DIDN'T HAVE AN ARREST RECORD LOCALLY, BUT FOR SEVERAL YEARS SHE WAS REGISTERED WITH THE STATE, WORKING IN LEGAL PROSTITUTION OUTSIDE OF CLARK COUNTY.
I DON'T KNOW ANYTHING ABOUT THAT. ALL I KNOW IS, GAIL LOVED OUR BICHONS AND THEY LOVED HER. TOOK THEM HOME WITH HER, FROM TIME TO TIME.

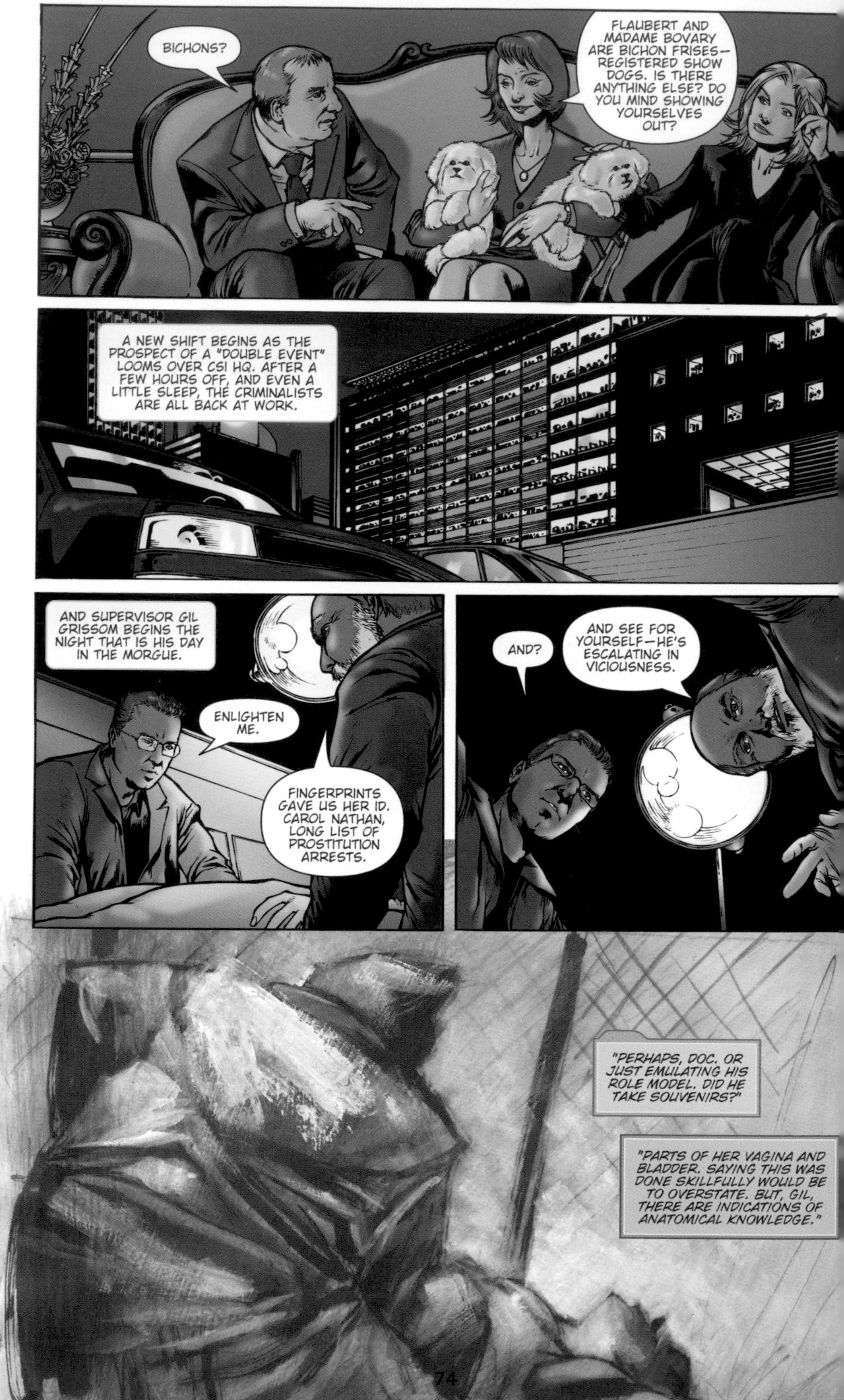
BICHONS?
FLAUBERT AND MADAME BOVARY ARE BICHON FRISES—REGISTERED SHOW DOGS. IS THERE ANYTHING ELSE? DO YOU MIND SHOWING YOURSELVES OUT?
A NEW SHIFT BEGINS AS THE PROSPECT OF A "DOUBLE EVENT" LOOMS OVER CSI HQ. AFTER A FEW HOURS OFF, AND EVEN A LITTLE SLEEP, THE CRIMINALISTS ARE ALL BACK AT WORK.
AND SUPERVISOR GIL GRISSOM BEGINS THE NIGHT THAT IS HIS DAY IN THE MORGUE.
ENLIGHTEN ME.
FINGERPRINTS GAVE US HER ID. CAROL NATHAN, LONG LIST OF PROSTITUTION ARRESTS.
AND?
AND SEE FOR YOURSELF—HE'S ESCALATING IN VICIOUSNESS.
"PERHAPS, DOC. OR JUST EMULATING HIS ROLE MODEL. DID HE TAKE SOUVENIRS?"
"PARTS OF HER VAGINA AND BLADDER. SAYING THIS WAS DONE SKILLFULLY WOULD BE TO OVERSTATE. BUT, GIL, THERE ARE INDICATIONS OF ANATOMICAL KNOWLEDGE."

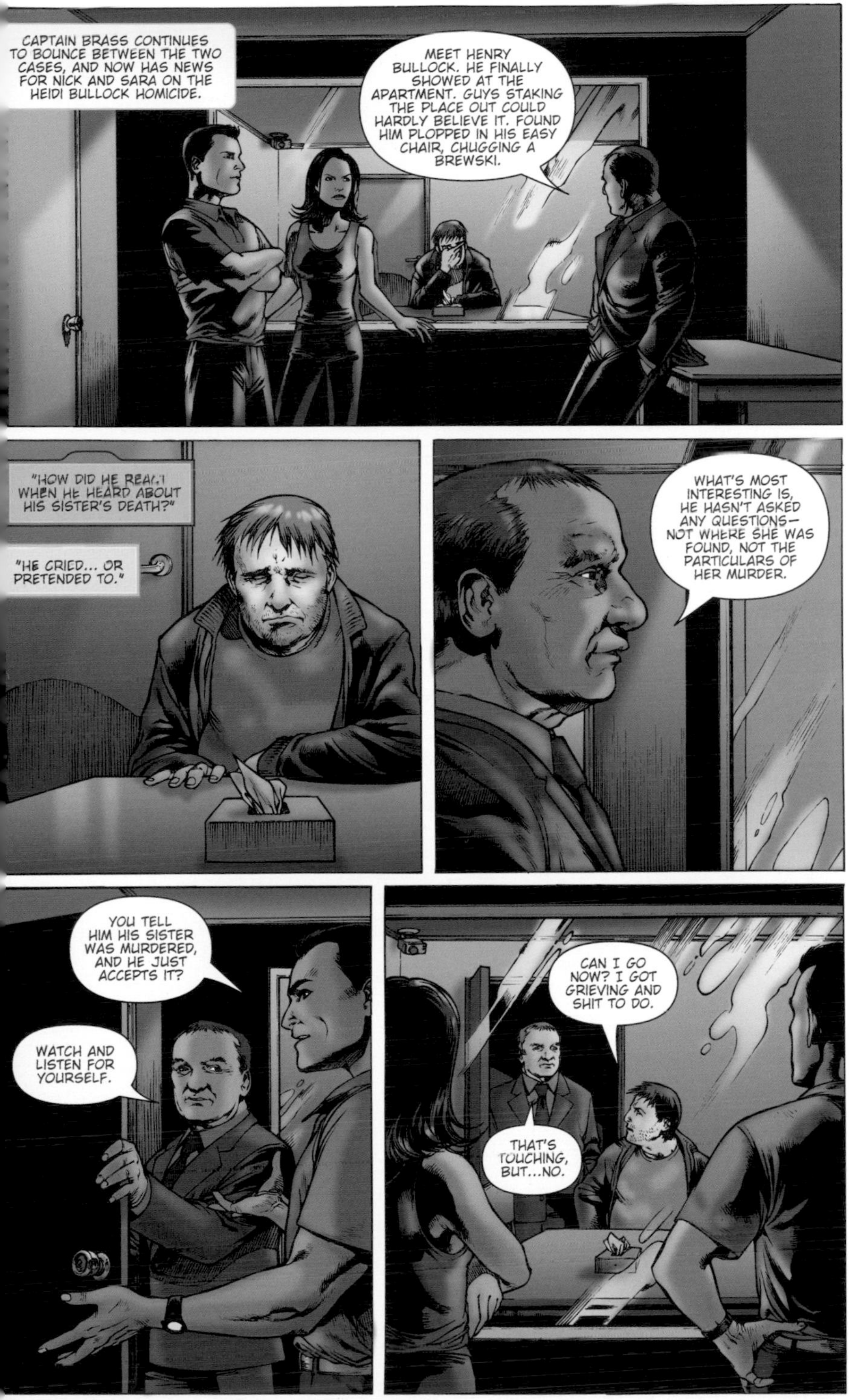
CAPTAIN BRASS CONTINUES TO BOUNCE BETWEEN THE TWO CASES, AND NOW HAS NEWS FOR NICK AND SARA ON THE HEIDI BULLOCK HOMICIDE.
MEET HENRY BULLOCK. HE FINALLY SHOWED AT THE APARTMENT. GUYS STAKING THE PLACE OUT COULD HARDLY BELIEVE IT. FOUND HIM PLOPPED IN HIS EASY CHAIR, CHUGGING A BREWSKI.
"HOW DID HE REACT WHEN HE HEARD ABOUT HIS SISTER'S DEATH?"
"HE CRIED... OR PRETENDED TO."
WHAT'S MOST INTERESTING IS, HE HASN'T ASKED ANY QUESTIONS— NOT WHERE SHE WAS FOUND, NOT THE PARTICULARS OF HER MURDER.
YOU TELL HIM HIS SISTER WAS MURDERED, AND HE JUST ACCEPTS IT?
WATCH AND LISTEN FOR YOURSELF.
CAN I GO NOW? I GOT GRIEVING AND SHIT TO DO.
THAT'S TOUCHING, BUT...NO.

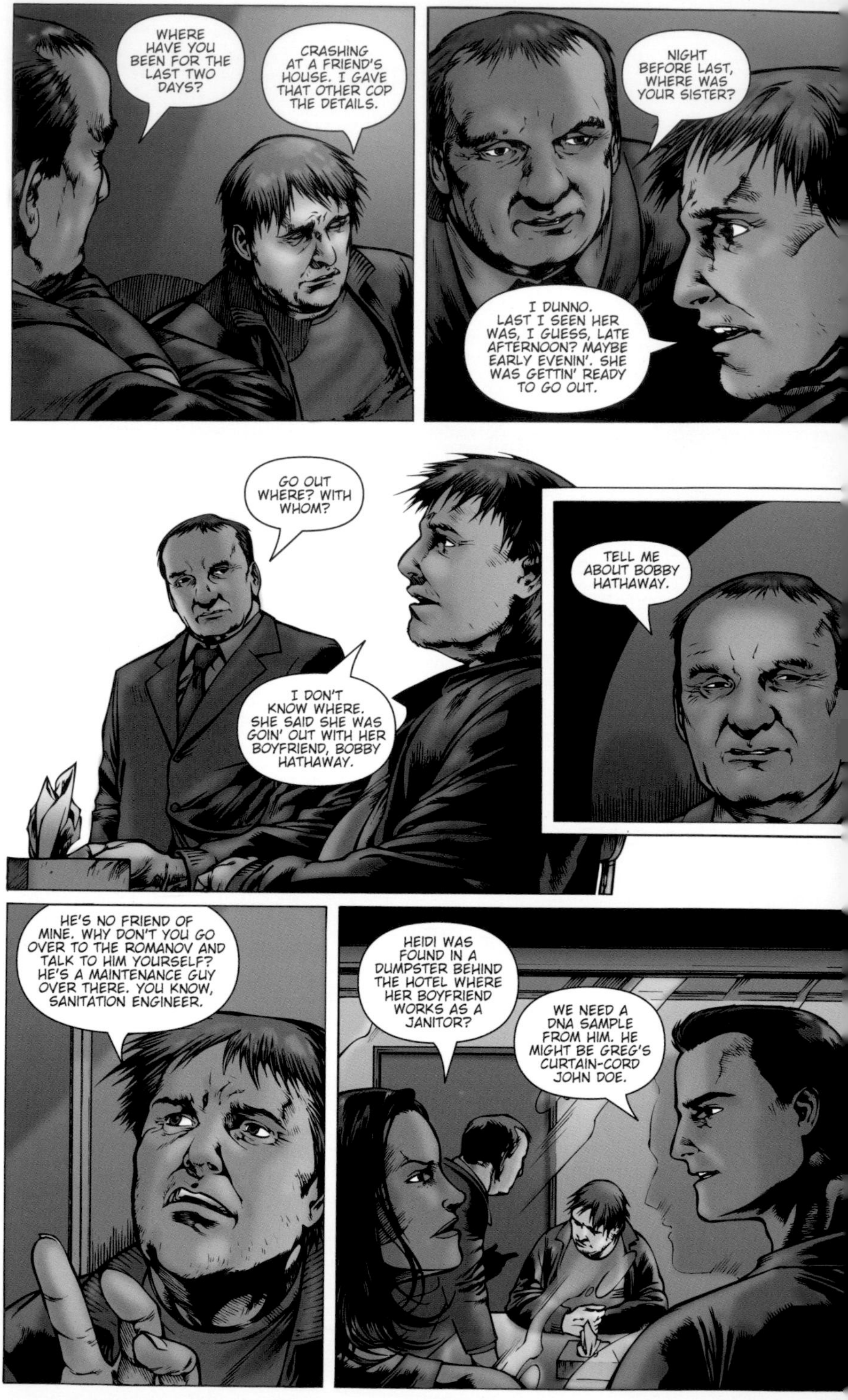

WHERE HAVE YOU BEEN FOR THE LAST TWO DAYS?
CRASHING AT A FRIEND'S HOUSE. I GAVE THAT OTHER COP THE DETAILS.
NIGHT BEFORE LAST, WHERE WAS YOUR SISTER?
I DUNNO. LAST I SEEN HER WAS, I GUESS, LATE AFTERNOON? MAYBE EARLY EVENIN'. SHE WAS GETTIN' READY TO GO OUT.
GO OUT WHERE? WITH WHOM?
I DON'T KNOW WHERE. SHE SAID SHE WAS GOIN' OUT WITH HER BOYFRIEND, BOBBY HATHAWAY.
TELL ME ABOUT BOBBY HATHAWAY.
HE'S NO FRIEND OF MINE. WHY DON'T YOU GO OVER TO THE ROMANOV AND TALK TO HIM YOURSELF? HE'S A MAINTENANCE GUY OVER THERE. YOU KNOW, SANITATION ENGINEER.
HEIDI WAS FOUND IN A DUMPSTER BEHIND THE HOTEL WHERE HER BOYFRIEND WORKS AS A JANITOR?
WE NEED A DNA SAMPLE FROM HIM. HE MIGHT BE GREG'S CURTAIN-CORD JOHN DOE.

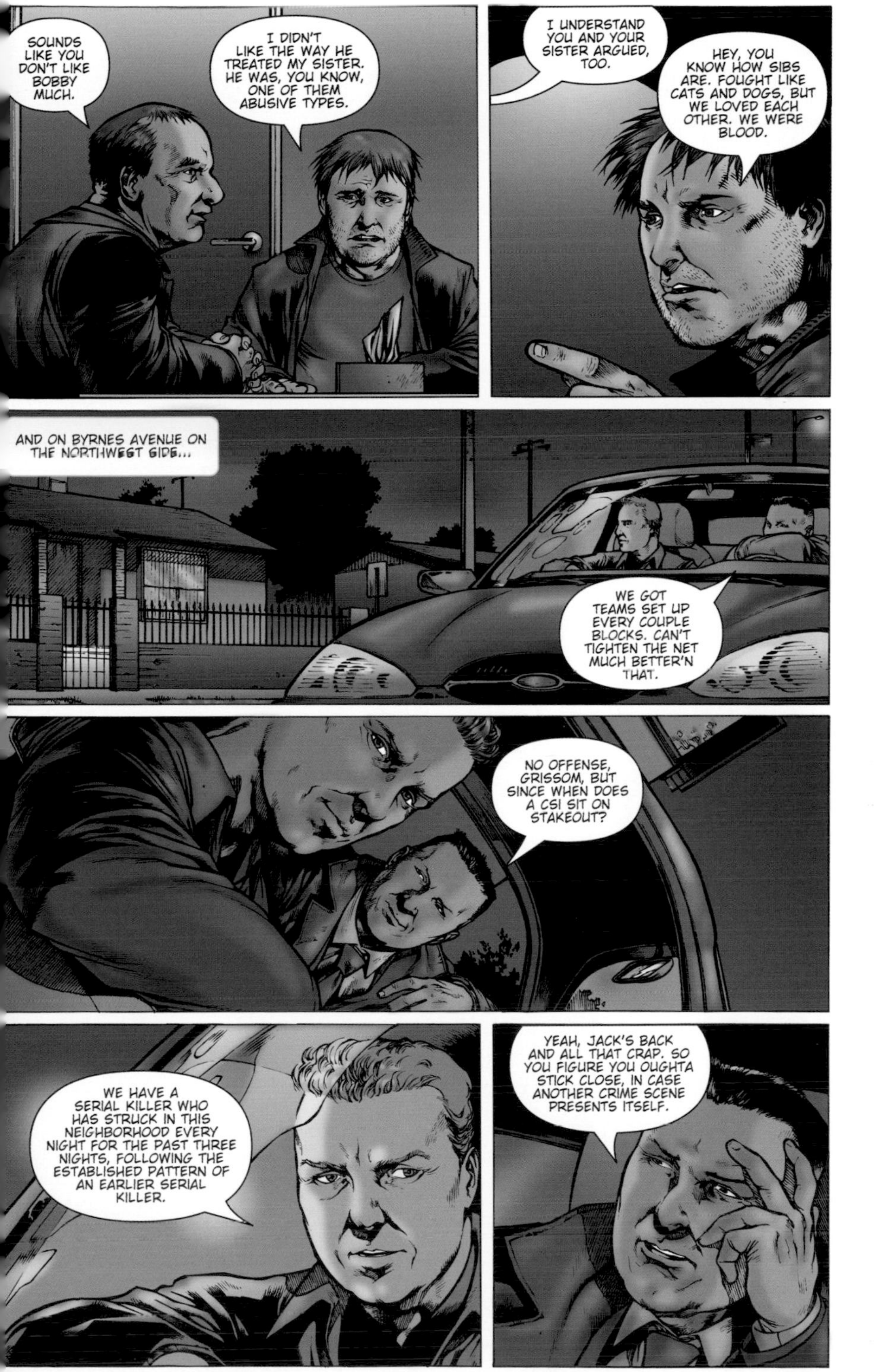
SOUNDS LIKE YOU DON'T LIKE BOBBY MUCH.
I DIDN'T LIKE THE WAY HE TREATED MY SISTER. HE WAS, YOU KNOW, ONE OF THEM ABUSIVE TYPES.
I UNDERSTAND YOU AND YOUR SISTER ARGUED, TOO.
HEY, YOU KNOW HOW SIBS ARE. FOUGHT LIKE CATS AND DOGS, BUT WE LOVED EACH OTHER. WE WERE BLOOD.
AND ON BYRNES AVENUE ON THE NORTHWEST SIDE...
WE GOT TEAMS SET UP EVERY COUPLE BLOCKS. CAN'T TIGHTEN THE NET MUCH BETTER'N THAT.
NO OFFENSE, GRISSOM, BUT SINCE WHEN DOES A CSI SIT ON STAKEOUT?
WE HAVE A SERIAL KILLER WHO HAS STRUCK IN THIS NEIGHBORHOOD EVERY NIGHT FOR THE PAST THREE NIGHTS, FOLLOWING THE ESTABLISHED PATTERN OF AN EARLIER SERIAL KILLER.
YEAH, JACK'S BACK AND ALL THAT CRAP. SO YOU FIGURE YOU OUGHTA STICK CLOSE, IN CASE ANOTHER CRIME SCENE PRESENTS ITSELF.

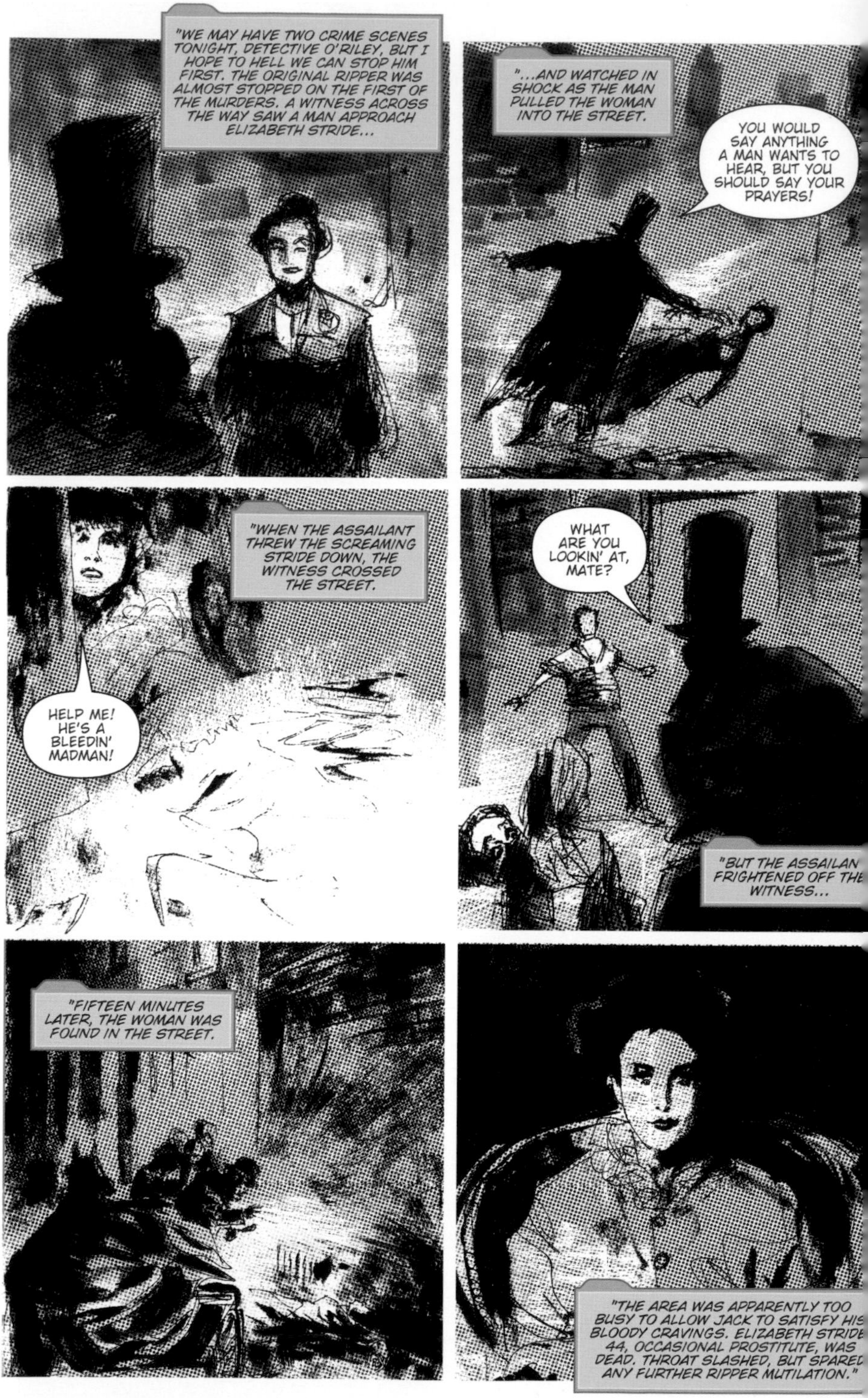
"WE MAY HAVE TWO CRIME SCENES TONIGHT, DETECTIVE O'RILEY, BUT I HOPE TO HELL WE CAN STOP HIM FIRST. THE ORIGINAL RIPPER WAS ALMOST STOPPED ON THE FIRST OF THE MURDERS. A WITNESS ACROSS THE WAY SAW A MAN APPROACH ELIZABETH STRIDE...
"...AND WATCHED IN SHOCK AS THE MAN PULLED THE WOMAN INTO THE STREET.
YOU WOULD SAY ANYTHING A MAN WANTS TO HEAR, BUT YOU SHOULD SAY YOUR PRAYERS!
"WHEN THE ASSAILANT THREW THE SCREAMING STRIDE DOWN, THE WITNESS CROSSED THE STREET.
HELP ME! HE'S A BLEEDIN' MADMAN!
WHAT ARE YOU LOOKIN' AT, MATE?
"BUT THE ASSAILAN FRIGHTENED OFF THE WITNESS...
"FIFTEEN MINUTES LATER, THE WOMAN WAS FOUND IN THE STREET.
"THE AREA WAS APPARENTLY TOO BUSY TO ALLOW JACK TO SATISFY HIS BLOODY CRAVINGS. ELIZABETH STRIDE 44, OCCASIONAL PROSTITUTE, WAS DEAD. THROAT SLASHED, BUT SPARED ANY FURTHER RIPPER MUTILATION."

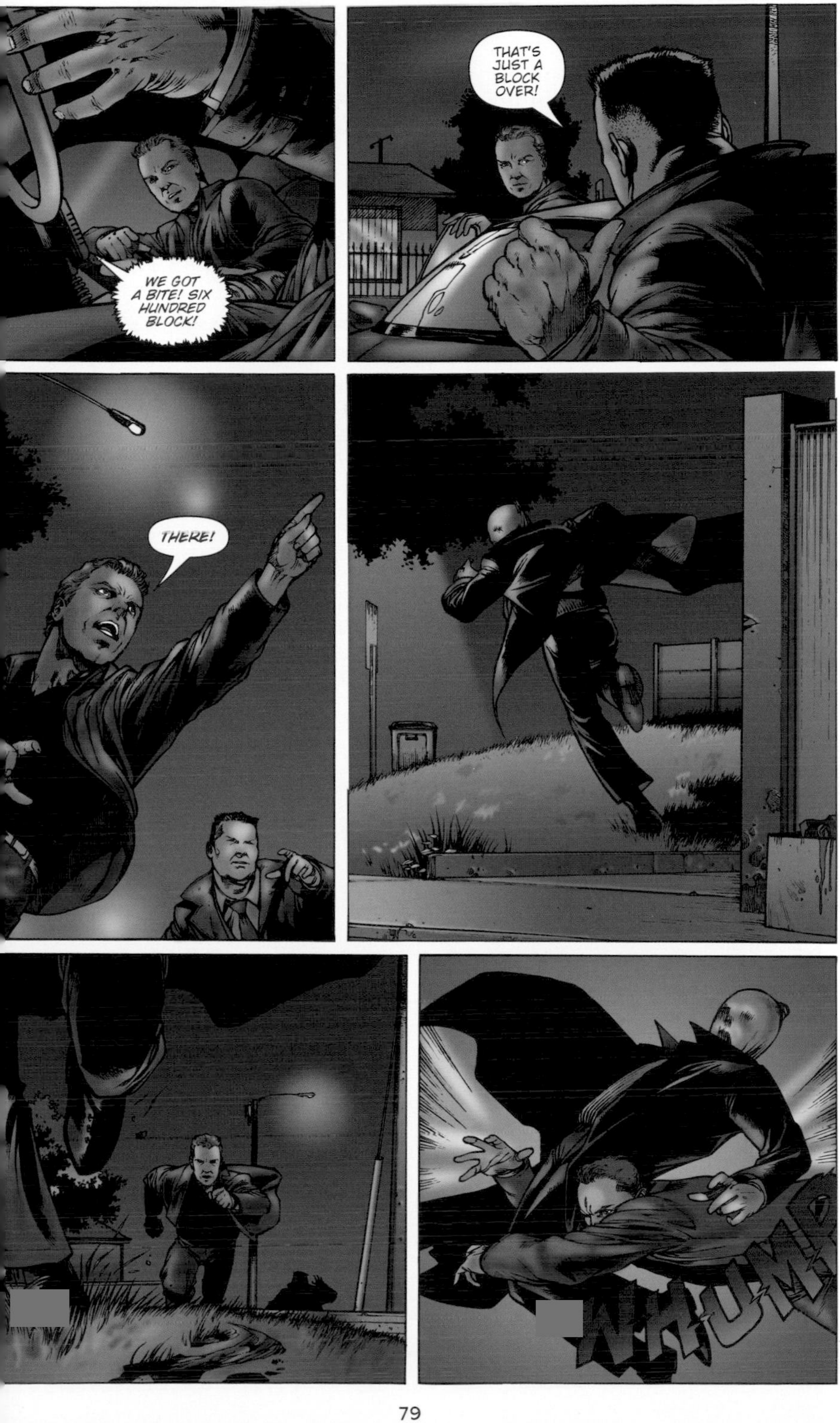
WE GOT A BITE! SIX HUNDRED BLOCK!
THAT'S JUST A BLOCK OVER!
THERE!
WHUMP

HE'S CUTTING THROUGH TO THE ALLEY! HEAD HIM OFF!

BUT THE NEIGHBORHOOD IS A MAZE OF HOUSES AND BACKYARDS AND ALLEYS. THE SUSPECT SLIPS THE NET.

YOU'RE ALL RIGHT?

DON'T TOUCH ME— I'M EVIDENCE! HOW'S OUR POLICEWOMAN?

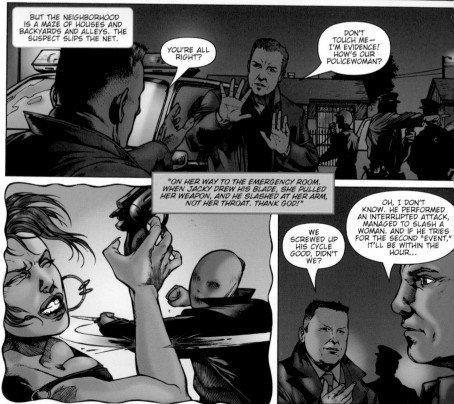

"ON HER WAY TO THE EMERGENCY ROOM. WHEN JACKY DREW HIS BLADE, SHE PULLED HER WEAPON, AND HE SLASHED AT HER ARM, NOT HER THROAT. THANK GOD!"

WE SCREWED UP HIS CYCLE GOOD, DIDN'T WE?

OH, I DON'T KNOW. HE PERFORMED AN INTERRUPTED ATTACK, MANAGED TO SLASH A WOMAN. AND IF HE TRIES FOR THE SECOND "EVENT," IT'LL BE WITHIN THE HOUR...

chapter four

Don't Know Jack

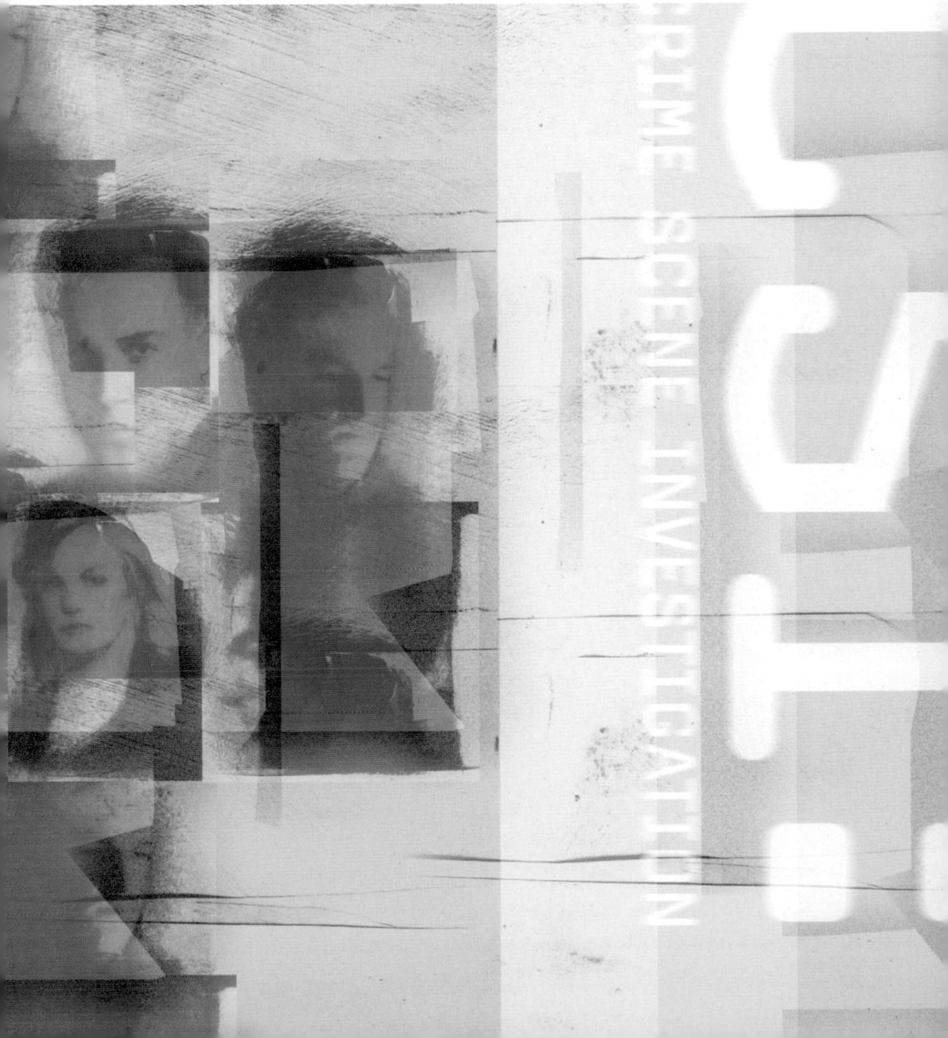
CRIME SCENE INVESTIGATION

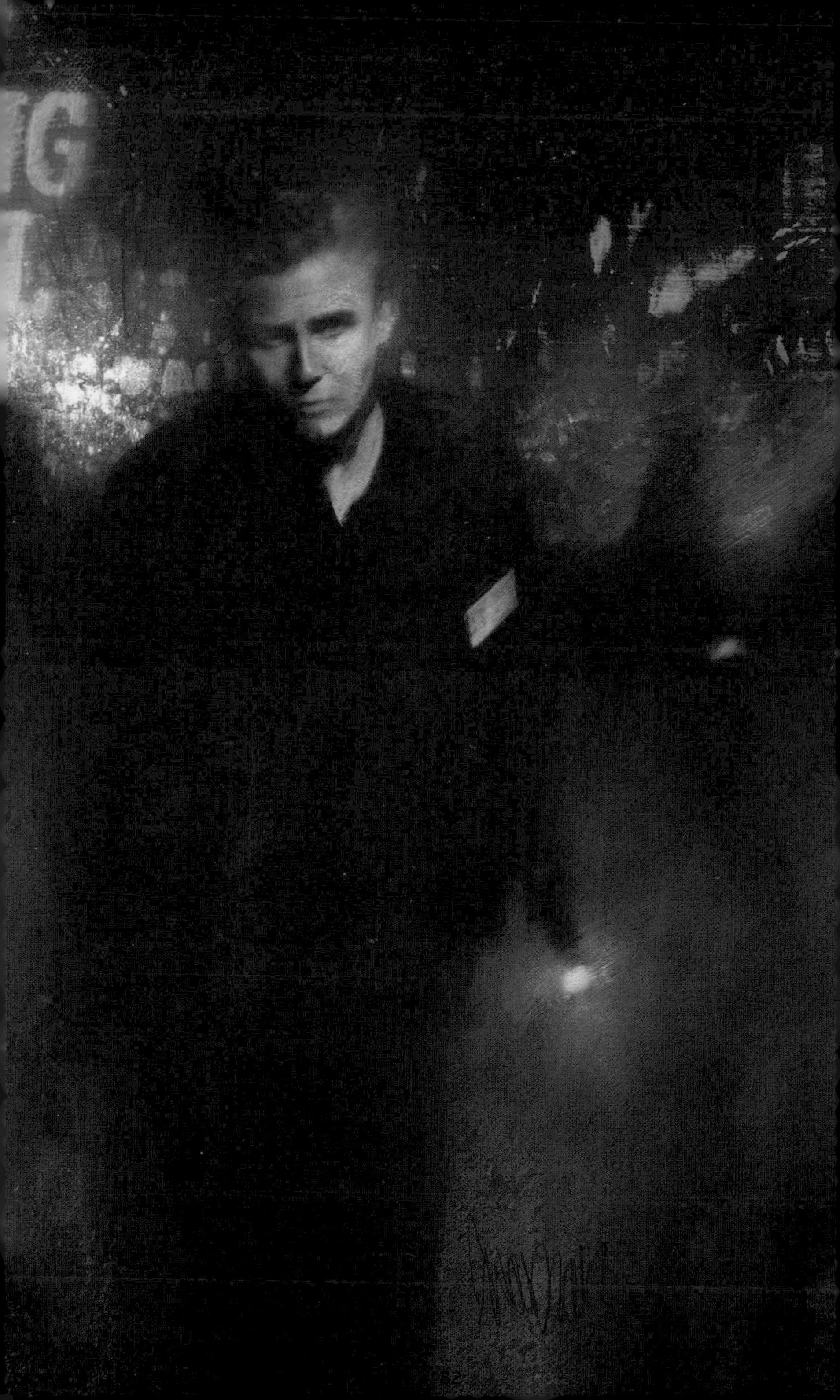

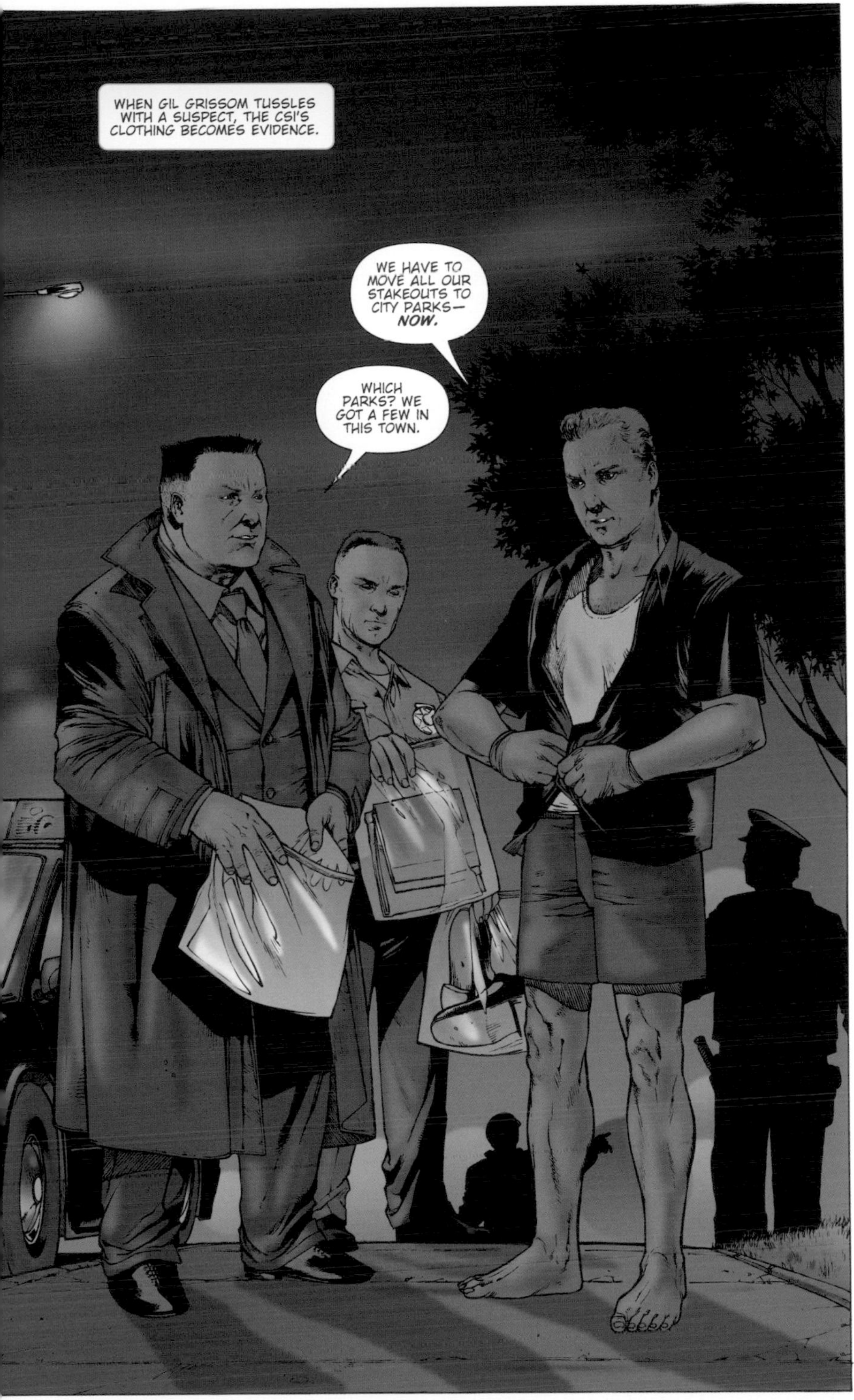
WHEN GIL GRISSOM TUSSLES WITH A SUSPECT, THE CSI'S CLOTHING BECOMES EVIDENCE.
WE HAVE TO MOVE ALL OUR STAKEOUTS TO CITY PARKS— *NOW.*
WHICH PARKS? WE GOT A FEW IN THIS TOWN.

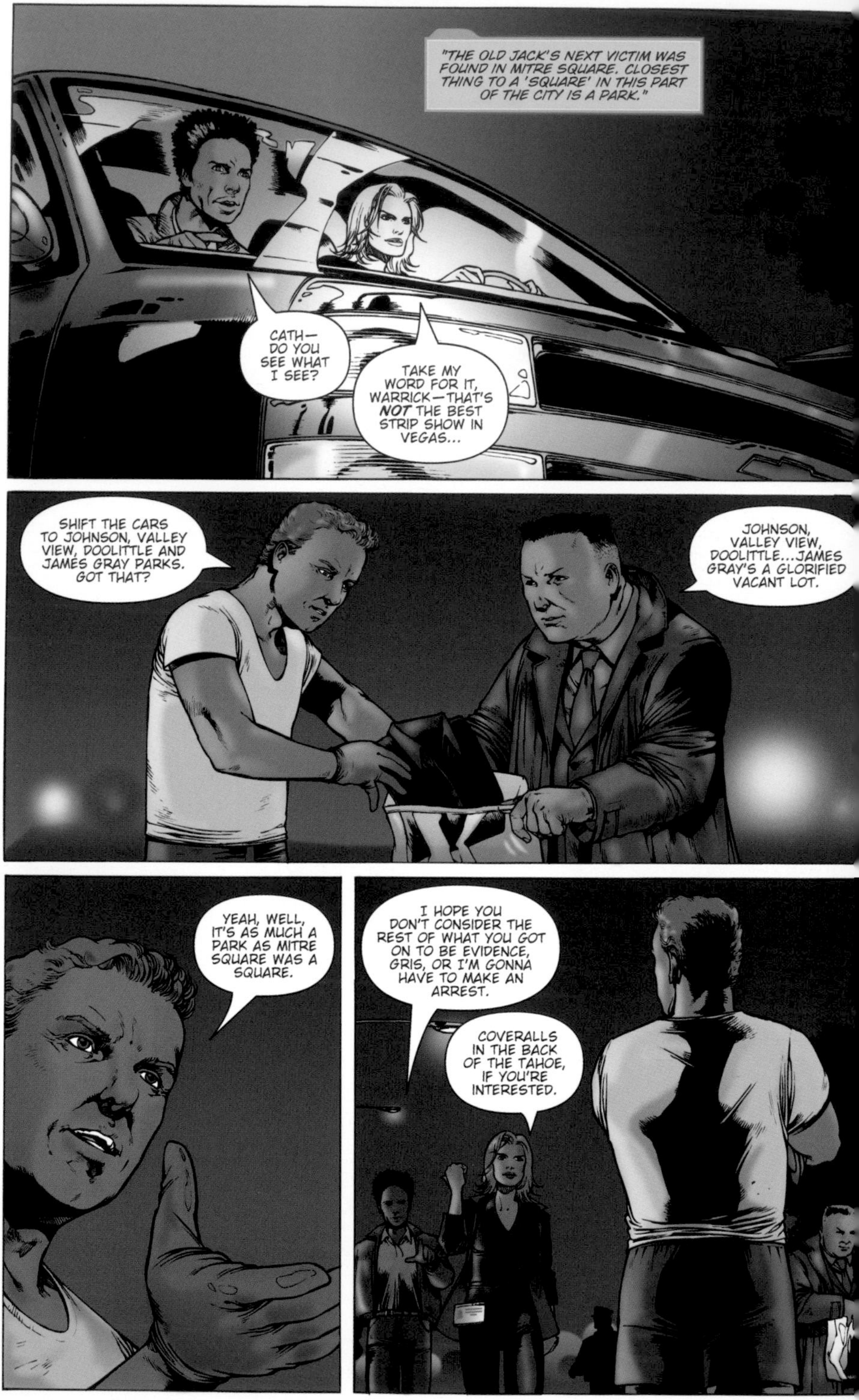
"THE OLD JACK'S NEXT VICTIM WAS FOUND IN MITRE SQUARE. CLOSEST THING TO A 'SQUARE' IN THIS PART OF THE CITY IS A PARK."
CATH— DO YOU SEE WHAT I SEE?
TAKE MY WORD FOR IT, WARRICK—THAT'S *NOT* THE BEST STRIP SHOW IN VEGAS...
SHIFT THE CARS TO JOHNSON, VALLEY VIEW, DOOLITTLE AND JAMES GRAY PARKS. GOT THAT?
JOHNSON, VALLEY VIEW, DOOLITTLE...JAMES GRAY'S A GLORIFIED VACANT LOT.
YEAH, WELL, IT'S AS MUCH A PARK AS MITRE SQUARE WAS A SQUARE.
I HOPE YOU DON'T CONSIDER THE REST OF WHAT YOU GOT ON TO BE EVIDENCE, GRIS, OR I'M GONNA HAVE TO MAKE AN ARREST.
COVERALLS IN THE BACK OF THE TAHOE, IF YOU'RE INTERESTED.

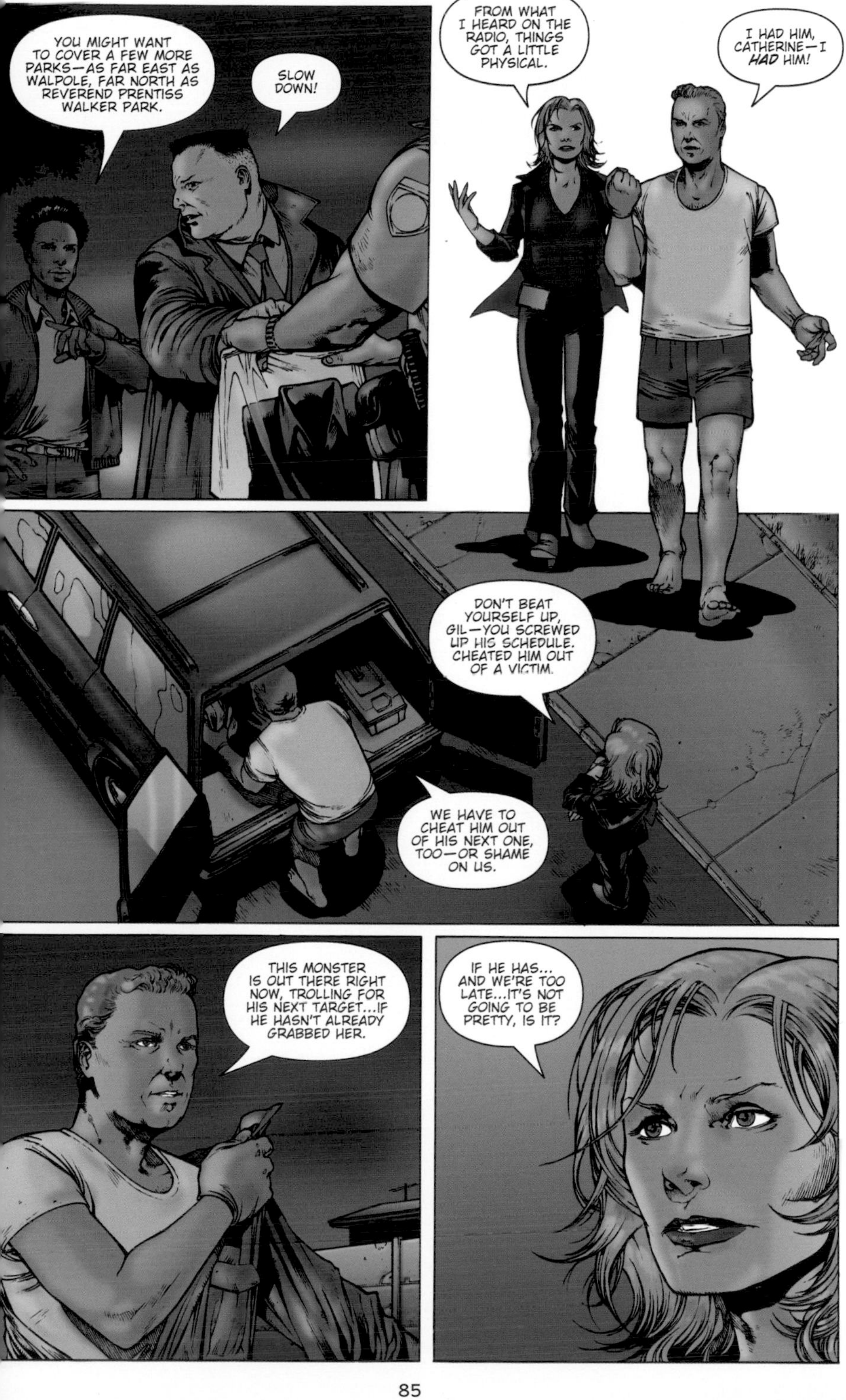

YOU MIGHT WANT TO COVER A FEW MORE PARKS—AS FAR EAST AS WALPOLE, FAR NORTH AS REVEREND PRENTISS WALKER PARK.
SLOW DOWN!
FROM WHAT I HEARD ON THE RADIO, THINGS GOT A LITTLE PHYSICAL.
I HAD HIM, CATHERINE—I *HAD* HIM!
DON'T BEAT YOURSELF UP, GIL—YOU SCREWED UP HIS SCHEDULE. CHEATED HIM OUT OF A VICTIM.
WE HAVE TO CHEAT HIM OUT OF HIS NEXT ONE, TOO—OR SHAME ON US.
THIS MONSTER IS OUT THERE RIGHT NOW, TROLLING FOR HIS NEXT TARGET...IF HE HASN'T ALREADY GRABBED HER.
IF HE HAS... AND WE'RE TOO LATE...IT'S NOT GOING TO BE PRETTY, IS IT?

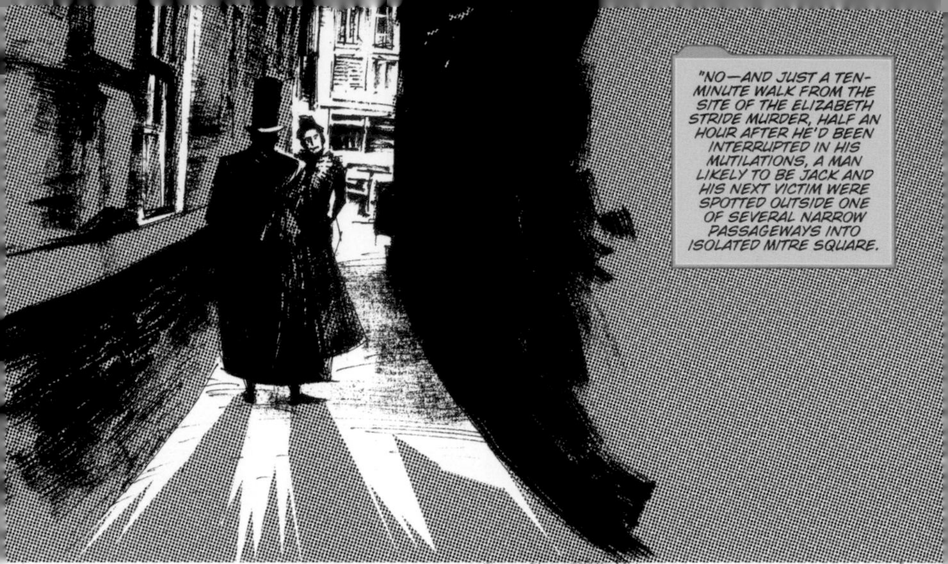
"NO—AND JUST A TEN-MINUTE WALK FROM THE SITE OF THE ELIZABETH STRIDE MURDER, HALF AN HOUR AFTER HE'D BEEN INTERRUPTED IN HIS MUTILATIONS, A MAN LIKELY TO BE JACK AND HIS NEXT VICTIM WERE SPOTTED OUTSIDE ONE OF SEVERAL NARROW PASSAGEWAYS INTO ISOLATED MITRE SQUARE.

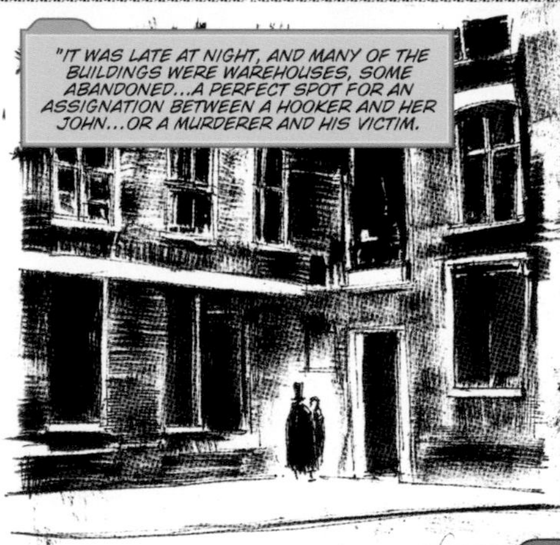
"IT WAS LATE AT NIGHT, AND MANY OF THE BUILDINGS WERE WAREHOUSES, SOME ABANDONED...A PERFECT SPOT FOR AN ASSIGNATION BETWEEN A HOOKER AND HER JOHN...OR A MURDERER AND HIS VICTIM.

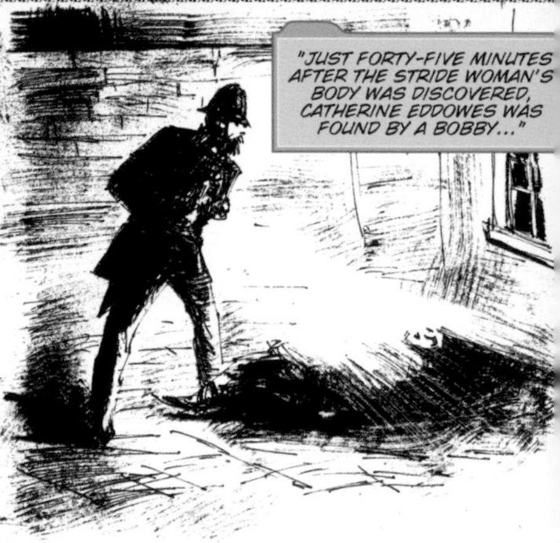
"JUST FORTY-FIVE MINUTES AFTER THE STRIDE WOMAN'S BODY WAS DISCOVERED, CATHERINE EDDOWES WAS FOUND BY A BOBBY..."

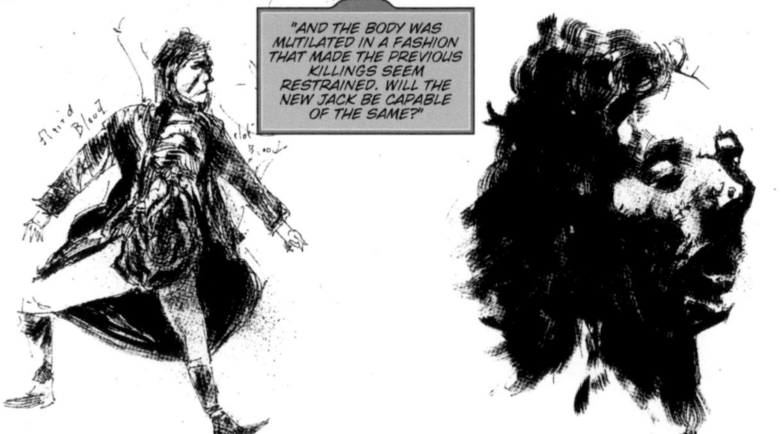
"AND THE BODY WAS MUTILATED IN A FASHION THAT MADE THE PREVIOUS KILLINGS SEEM RESTRAINED. WILL THE NEW JACK BE CAPABLE OF THE SAME?"

HE'S DONE HIS ROLE MODEL PROUD, SO FAR, AND YOU CAN BET HE ISN'T WASTING TIME.

SO WHERE DO WE START?

...DOOLITTLE, JAMES GRAY, WALPOLE...

WARRICK, TURN THE BACK OF THE TAHOE INTO A CRIME LAB—START RUNNING MY CLOTHES, NOW...

...CATHERINE AND I WILL WORK THE SCENE.

YOU GOT IT.

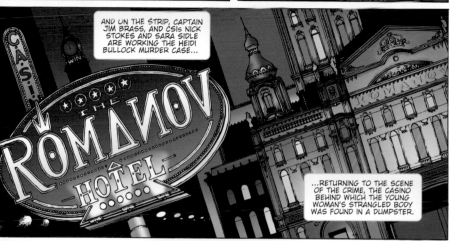

AND ON THE STRIP, CAPTAIN JIM BRASS, AND CSIs NICK STOKES AND SARA SIDLE ARE WORKING THE HEIDI BULLOCK MURDER CASE...

...RETURNING TO THE SCENE OF THE CRIME, THE CASINO BEHIND WHICH THE YOUNG WOMAN'S STRANGLED BODY WAS FOUND IN A DUMPSTER.

THE TRIO SEEKS NEITHER THE GLITTER OF THE CASINO NOR THE GLOOM OF THE ALLEY...

...RATHER, THE DECIDEDLY UNGLAMOROUS LOCKER ROOM FOR MALE EMPLOYEES, WHERE THEY QUESTION THE MURDER VICTIM'S BOYFRIEND, MAINTENANCE MAN BOBBY HATHAWAY.

I DIDN'T EVEN KNOW SHE WAS DEAD TILL YESTERDAY.

WE'D HAD A LITTLE ARGUMENT, AND SHE'D KINDA POUT WHEN SHE WAS PISSED AT ME. SO WHEN I GOT THE ANSWERING MACHINE, AND SHE DIDN'T PICK UP...HELL.

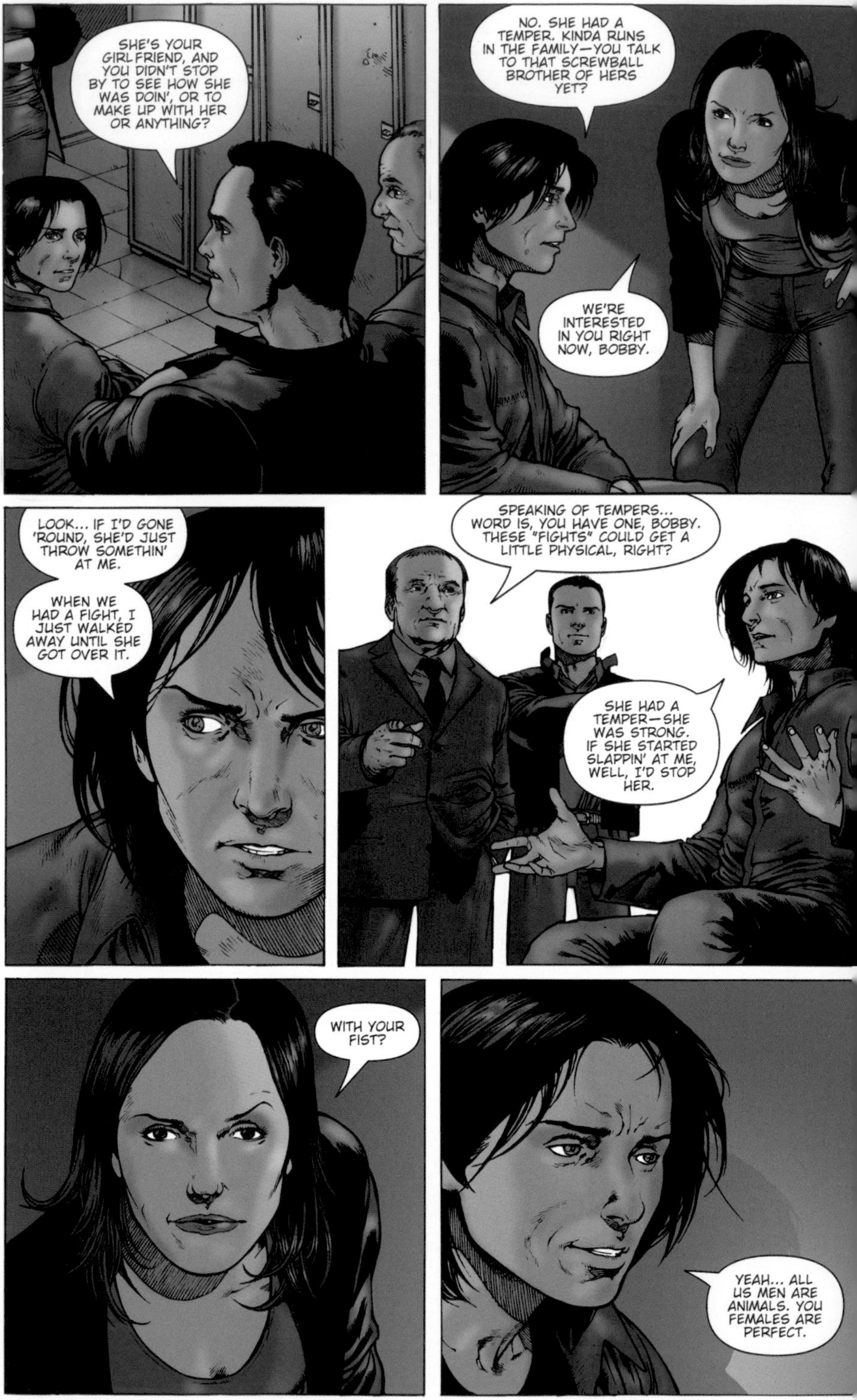
SHE'S YOUR GIRLFRIEND, AND YOU DIDN'T STOP BY TO SEE HOW SHE WAS DOIN', OR TO MAKE UP WITH HER OR ANYTHING?
NO. SHE HAD A TEMPER. KINDA RUNS IN THE FAMILY—YOU TALK TO THAT SCREWBALL BROTHER OF HERS YET?
WE'RE INTERESTED IN YOU RIGHT NOW, BOBBY.
LOOK... IF I'D GONE 'ROUND, SHE'D JUST THROW SOMETHIN' AT ME.
WHEN WE HAD A FIGHT, I JUST WALKED AWAY UNTIL SHE GOT OVER IT.
SPEAKING OF TEMPERS... WORD IS, YOU HAVE ONE, BOBBY. THESE "FIGHTS" COULD GET A LITTLE PHYSICAL, RIGHT?
SHE HAD A TEMPER—SHE WAS STRONG. IF SHE STARTED SLAPPIN' AT ME, WELL, I'D STOP HER.
WITH YOUR FIST?
YEAH... ALL US MEN ARE ANIMALS. YOU FEMALES ARE PERFECT.

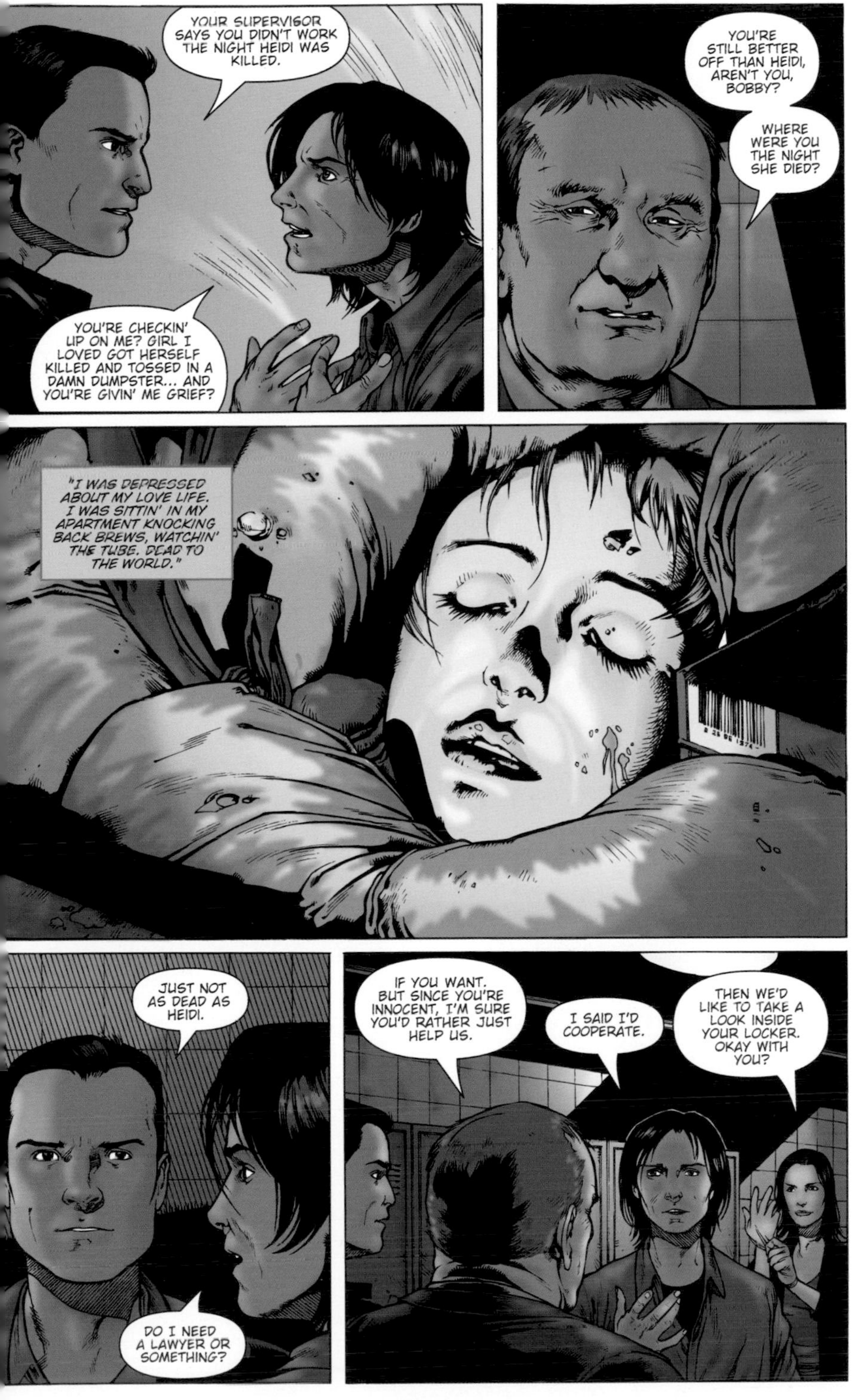
YOUR SUPERVISOR SAYS YOU DIDN'T WORK THE NIGHT HEIDI WAS KILLED.
YOU'RE CHECKIN' UP ON ME? GIRL I LOVED GOT HERSELF KILLED AND TOSSED IN A DAMN DUMPSTER... AND YOU'RE GIVIN' ME GRIEF?
YOU'RE STILL BETTER OFF THAN HEIDI, AREN'T YOU, BOBBY?
WHERE WERE YOU THE NIGHT SHE DIED?
"I WAS DEPRESSED ABOUT MY LOVE LIFE. I WAS SITTIN' IN MY APARTMENT KNOCKING BACK BREWS, WATCHIN' THE TUBE. DEAD TO THE WORLD."
JUST NOT AS DEAD AS HEIDI.
DO I NEED A LAWYER OR SOMETHING?
IF YOU WANT. BUT SINCE YOU'RE INNOCENT, I'M SURE YOU'D RATHER JUST HELP US.
I SAID I'D COOPERATE.
THEN WE'D LIKE TO TAKE A LOOK INSIDE YOUR LOCKER. OKAY WITH YOU?

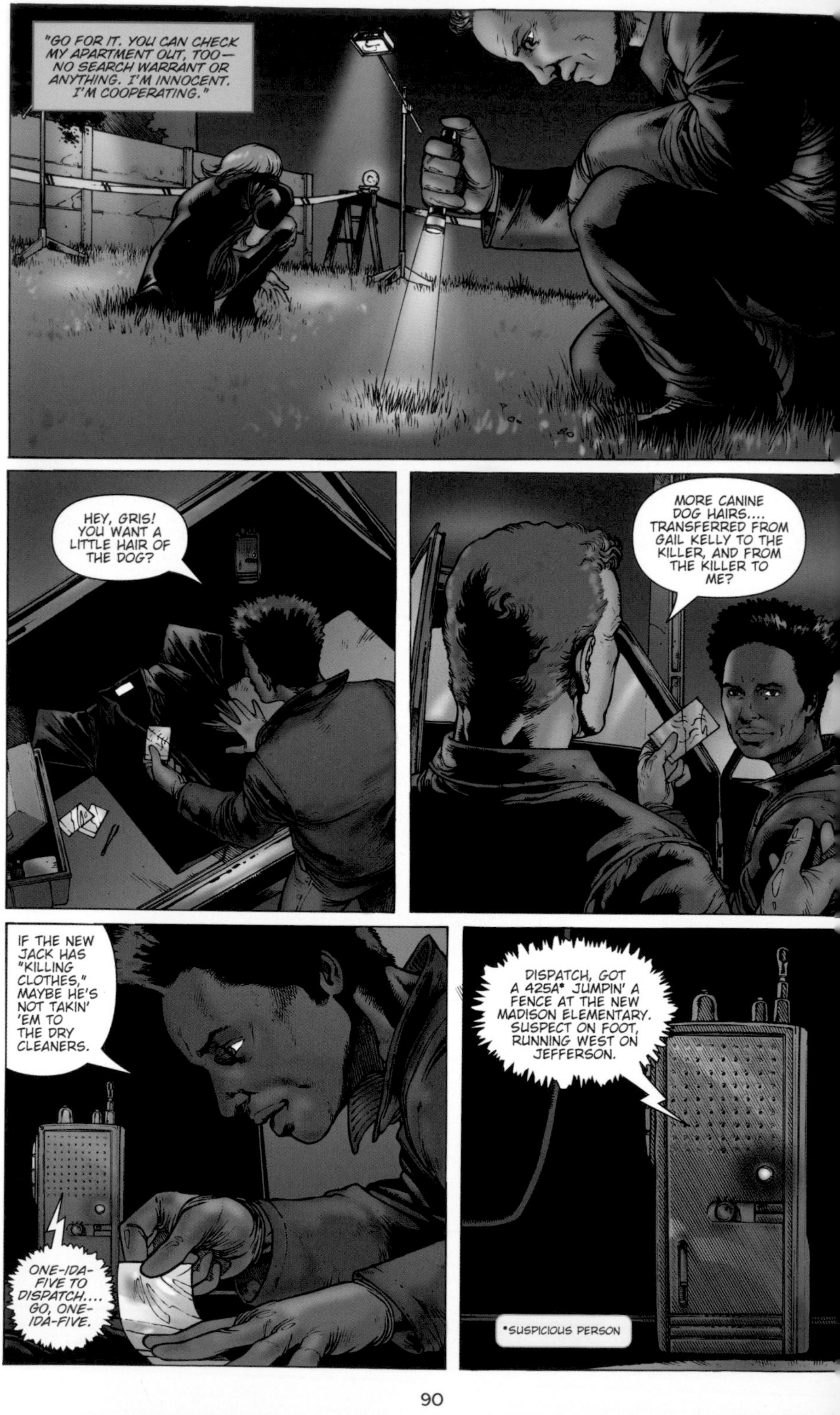

"GO FOR IT. YOU CAN CHECK MY APARTMENT OUT, TOO— NO SEARCH WARRANT OR ANYTHING. I'M INNOCENT. I'M COOPERATING."
HEY, GRIS! YOU WANT A LITTLE HAIR OF THE DOG?
MORE CANINE DOG HAIRS.... TRANSFERRED FROM GAIL KELLY TO THE KILLER, AND FROM THE KILLER TO ME?
IF THE NEW JACK HAS "KILLING CLOTHES," MAYBE HE'S NOT TAKIN' 'EM TO THE DRY CLEANERS.
ONE-IDA-FIVE TO DISPATCH.... GO, ONE-IDA-FIVE.
DISPATCH, GOT A 425A* JUMPIN' A FENCE AT THE NEW MADISON ELEMENTARY. SUSPECT ON FOOT, RUNNING WEST ON JEFFERSON.
*SUSPICIOUS PERSON

IS IT OUR MAN? IS IT JACK?
COME ON, COME ON... DESCRIBE THE SUCKER.
SUSPECT IS SIX FEET, DRESSED IN BLACK AND... HELL!
ONE-IDA-FIVE?
ONE-IDA-FIVE? COME IN, ONE-IDA-FIVE.
SORRY, DISPATCH, ONE-IDA-FIVE HERE—SUSPECT CUT BETWEEN TWO HOUSES AND I LOST HIM!
ONE-IDA-FIVE—GIL GRISSOM, CRIMINALISTICS.
YES, SIR?
LET THE SUSPECT GO—ALERT THE OTHER CARS, BUT YOU GET BACK TO THAT SCHOOL. I NEED YOU THERE. YOU MAY... FIND SOMETHING.

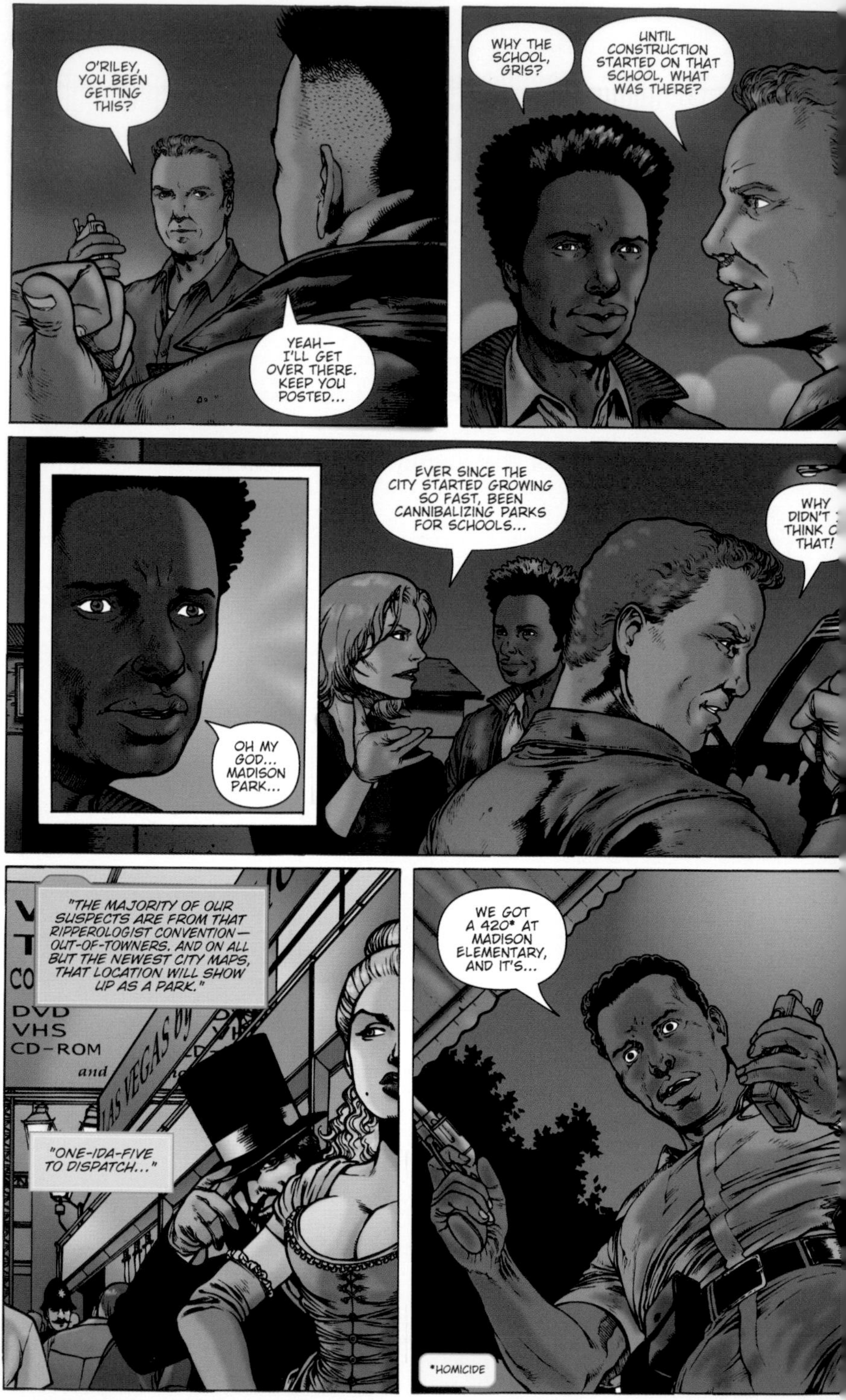
O'RILEY, YOU BEEN GETTING THIS?
YEAH— I'LL GET OVER THERE. KEEP YOU POSTED...
WHY THE SCHOOL, GRIS?
UNTIL CONSTRUCTION STARTED ON THAT SCHOOL, WHAT WAS THERE?
EVER SINCE THE CITY STARTED GROWING SO FAST, BEEN CANNIBALIZING PARKS FOR SCHOOLS...
WHY DIDN'T
THINK
THAT!
OH MY GOD... MADISON PARK...
"THE MAJORITY OF OUR SUSPECTS ARE FROM THAT RIPPEROLOGIST CONVENTION— OUT-OF-TOWNERS. AND ON ALL BUT THE NEWEST CITY MAPS, THAT LOCATION WILL SHOW UP AS A PARK."
DVD
VHS
CD-ROM
and
"ONE-IDA-FIVE TO DISPATCH..."
WE GOT A 420* AT MADISON ELEMENTARY, AND IT'S...
*HOMICIDE

MEANWHILE, THE OTHER CSIs ARE BACK AT HQ, WITH A PAIR OF SUSPECTS.

SO WE HAVE BOYFRIEND BOBBY HATHAWAY IN INTERVIEW ROOM #1...

...AND LOVING BROTHER HENRY BULLOCK IN INTERVIEW ROOM #2. WHAT ELSE DO WE HAVE?

NOTHING FROM THE LOCKER. WE STILL HAVE HATHAWAY'S APARTMENT TO WORK.

GARBAGE BAGS WITH ONLY HEIDI'S PRINTS.

"THE VENETIAN BLIND CORD GAVE UP DNA FROM HEIDI AND HENRY...

"...AND GREG JUST ADDED BOBBY HATHAWAY TO THE PARTY.

"PLUS WE HAVE BOBBY'S FINGERPRINTS OFF THE DUMPSTER."

SO YOU'RE SAYING YOU HAVE A MAINTENANCE MAN'S FINGERPRINTS ON A DUMPSTER HE ROUTINELY FILLS....

I DIDN'T SAY I WAS PROUD OF IT.

"THE BLIND CORD WASN'T [CU]T WITH A KNIFE—IT WAS SNAPPED, RIGHT?"

"RIGHT."

"WELL, THEN, MAYBE I CAN HAND YOU YOUR PERP, CAPTAIN."

AND AT AN UNFINISHED ELEMENTARY SCHOOL ON THE NORTHWEST SIDE OF THE CITY, GIL GRISSOM AND CREW HAVE BEEN TAUGHT A TERRIBLE LESSON....

I FAILED YOU.

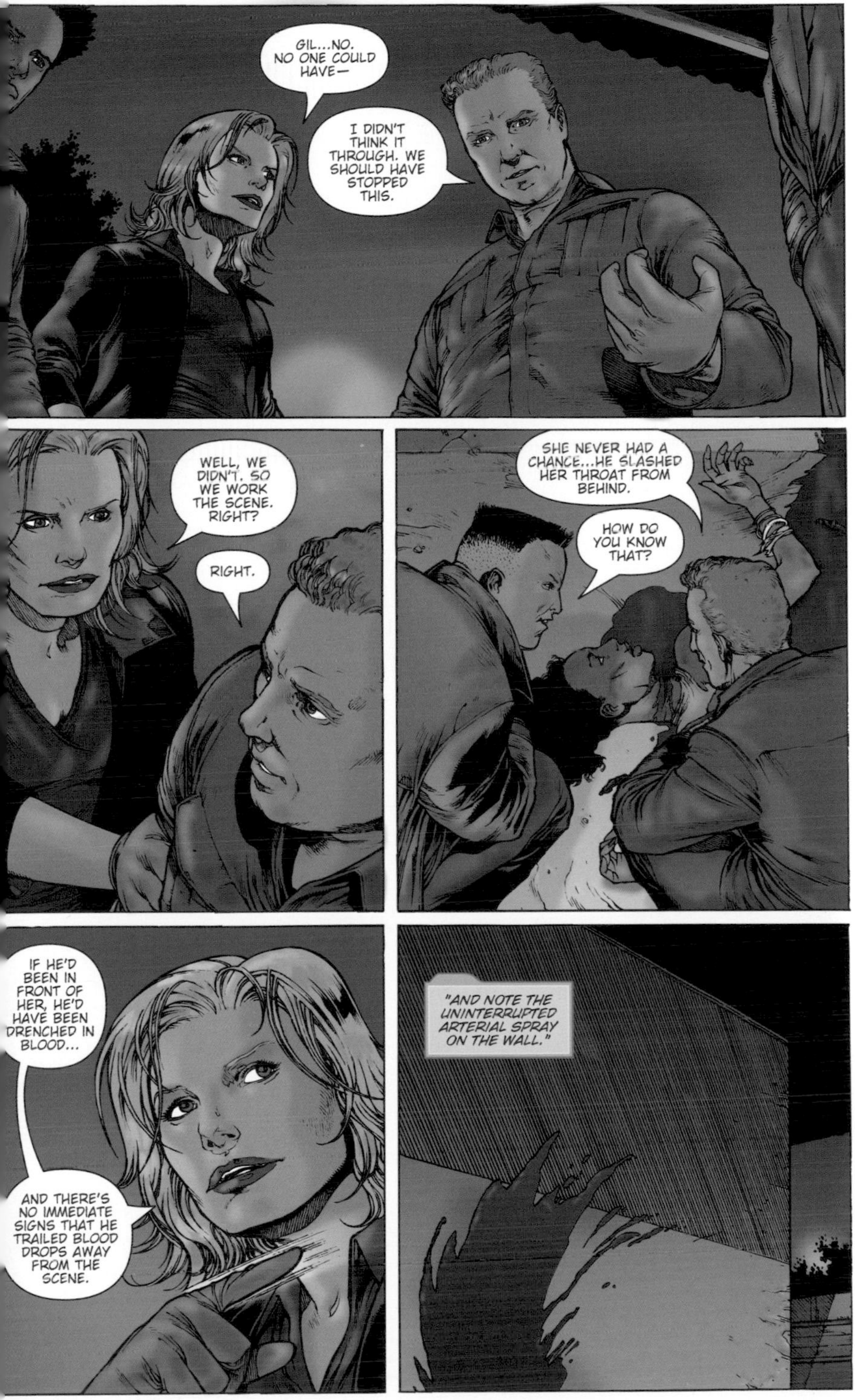

GIL...NO. NO ONE COULD HAVE—
I DIDN'T THINK IT THROUGH. WE SHOULD HAVE STOPPED THIS.
WELL, WE DIDN'T. SO WE WORK THE SCENE. RIGHT?
RIGHT.
SHE NEVER HAD A CHANCE...HE SLASHED HER THROAT FROM BEHIND.
HOW DO YOU KNOW THAT?
IF HE'D BEEN IN FRONT OF HER, HE'D HAVE BEEN DRENCHED IN BLOOD...
AND THERE'S NO IMMEDIATE SIGNS THAT HE TRAILED BLOOD DROPS AWAY FROM THE SCENE.
"AND NOTE THE UNINTERRUPTED ARTERIAL SPRAY ON THE WALL."

"HAD HE BEEN IN FRONT OF HER WHEN HE SLASHED HER...

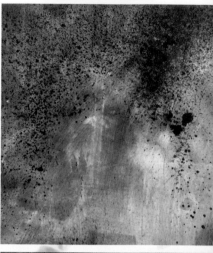

"...THERE WOULD BE AN INTERRUPTION ON THE WALL, WHERE HE STOOD, BLOCKING THE SPRAY.

"BUT IN FACT, HE STOOD BEHIND HER...

"...AND LEFT US THIS JACKSON POLLOCK.

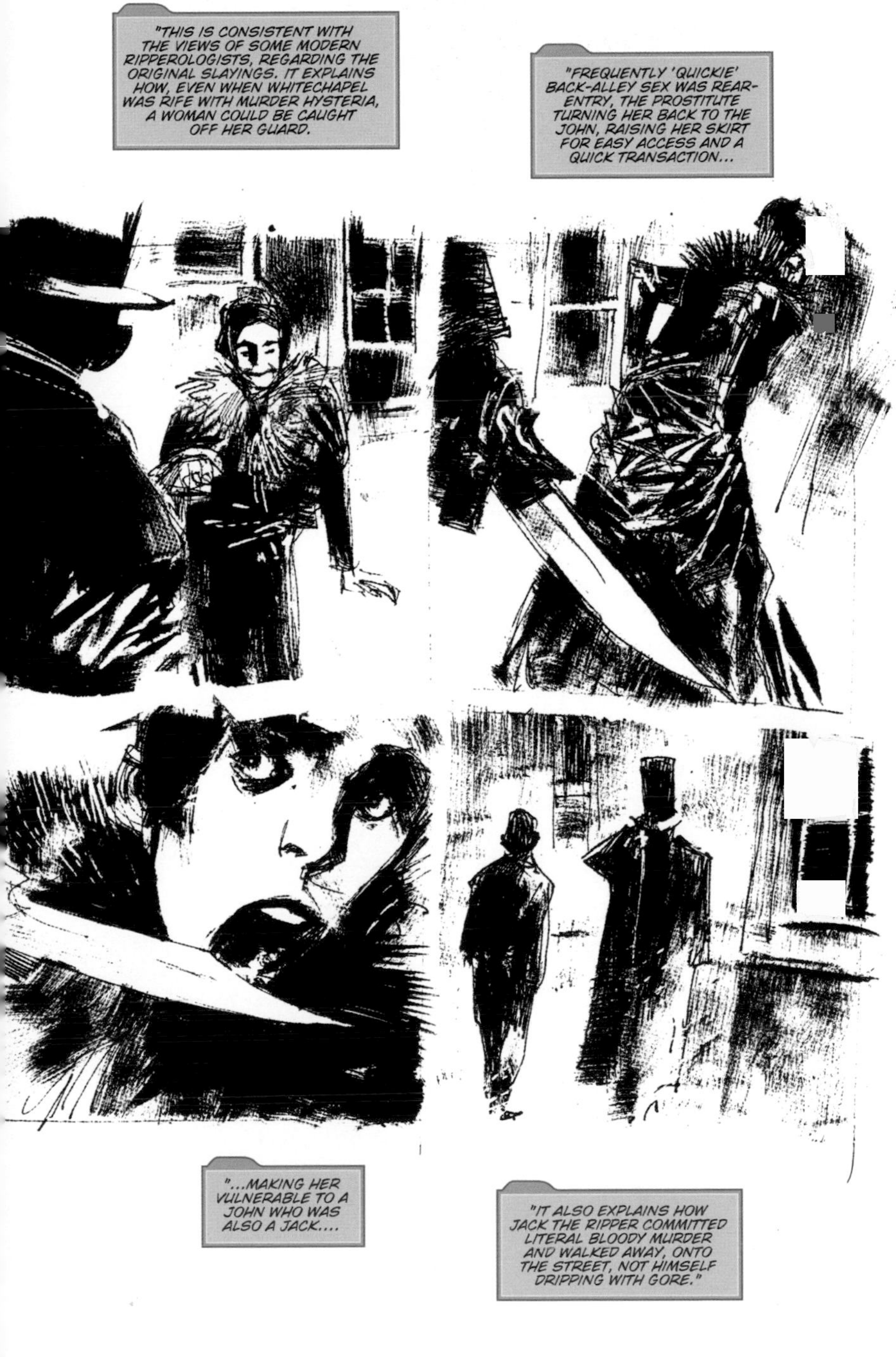
"THIS IS CONSISTENT WITH THE VIEWS OF SOME MODERN RIPPEROLOGISTS, REGARDING THE ORIGINAL SLAYINGS. IT EXPLAINS HOW, EVEN WHEN WHITECHAPEL WAS RIFE WITH MURDER HYSTERIA, A WOMAN COULD BE CAUGHT OFF HER GUARD.
"FREQUENTLY 'QUICKIE' BACK-ALLEY SEX WAS REAR-ENTRY, THE PROSTITUTE TURNING HER BACK TO THE JOHN, RAISING HER SKIRT FOR EASY ACCESS AND A QUICK TRANSACTION...
"...MAKING HER VULNERABLE TO A JOHN WHO WAS ALSO A JACK....
"IT ALSO EXPLAINS HOW JACK THE RIPPER COMMITTED LITERAL BLOODY MURDER AND WALKED AWAY, ONTO THE STREET, NOT HIMSELF DRIPPING WITH GORE."

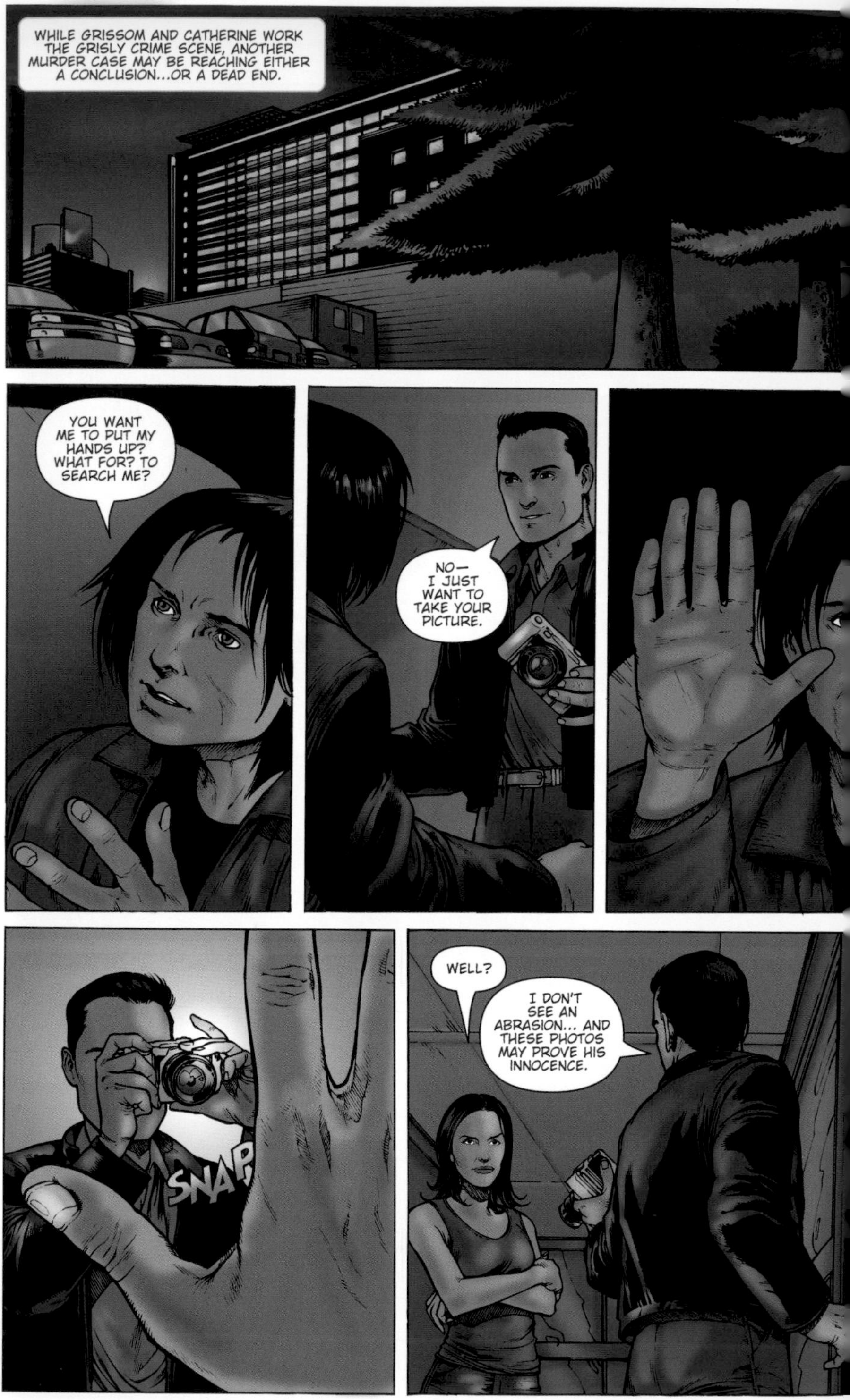
WHILE GRISSOM AND CATHERINE WORK THE GRISLY CRIME SCENE, ANOTHER MURDER CASE MAY BE REACHING EITHER A CONCLUSION...OR A DEAD END.
YOU WANT ME TO PUT MY HANDS UP? WHAT FOR? TO SEARCH ME?
NO— I JUST WANT TO TAKE YOUR PICTURE.
SNAP
WELL?
I DON'T SEE AN ABRASION... AND THESE PHOTOS MAY PROVE HIS INNOCENCE.

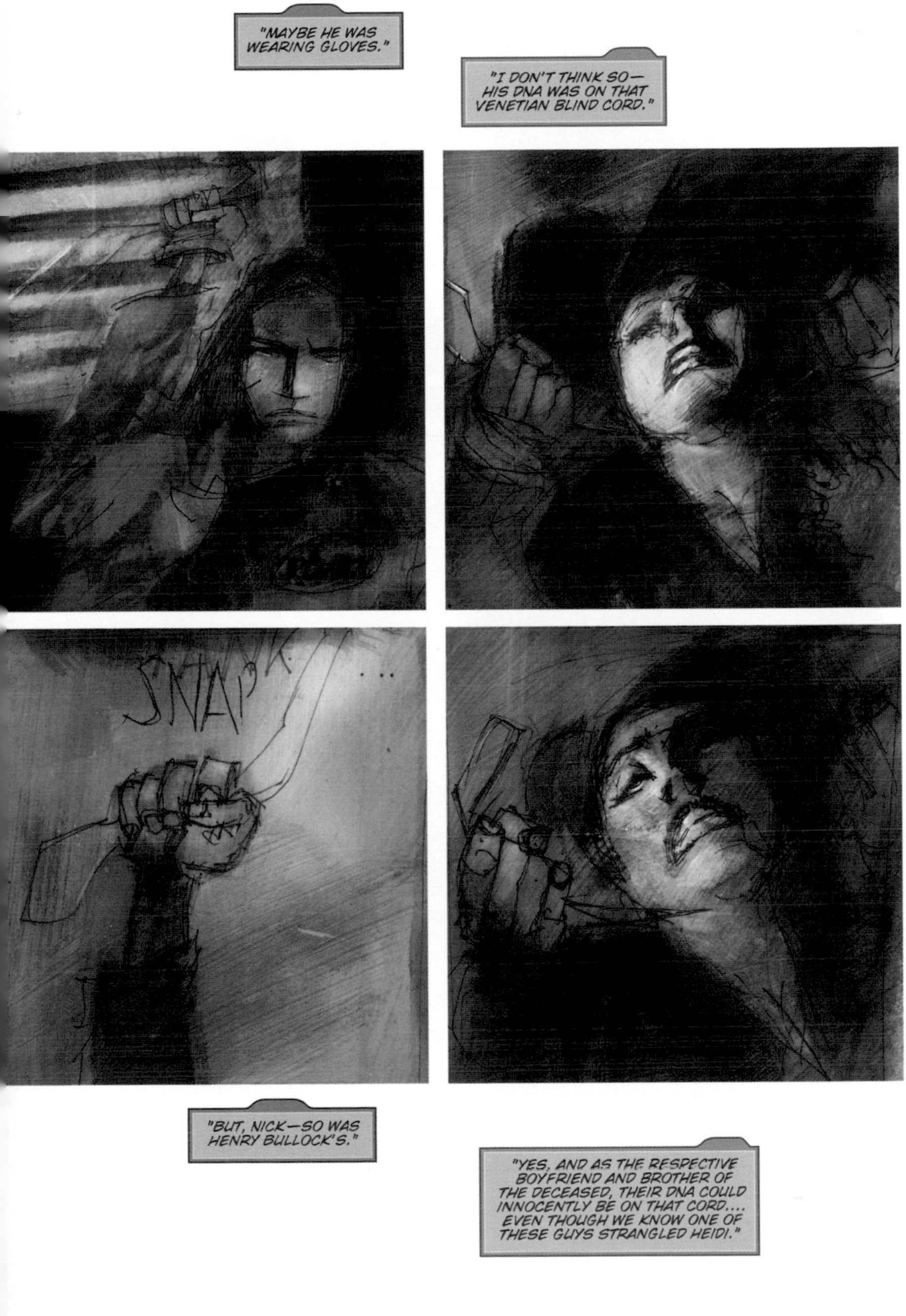
"MAYBE HE WAS WEARING GLOVES."
"I DON'T THINK SO— HIS DNA WAS ON THAT VENETIAN BLIND CORD."
SNAP
"BUT, NICK—SO WAS HENRY BULLOCK'S."
"YES, AND AS THE RESPECTIVE BOYFRIEND AND BROTHER OF THE DECEASED, THEIR DNA COULD INNOCENTLY BE ON THAT CORD.... EVEN THOUGH WE KNOW ONE OF THESE GUYS STRANGLED HEIDI."

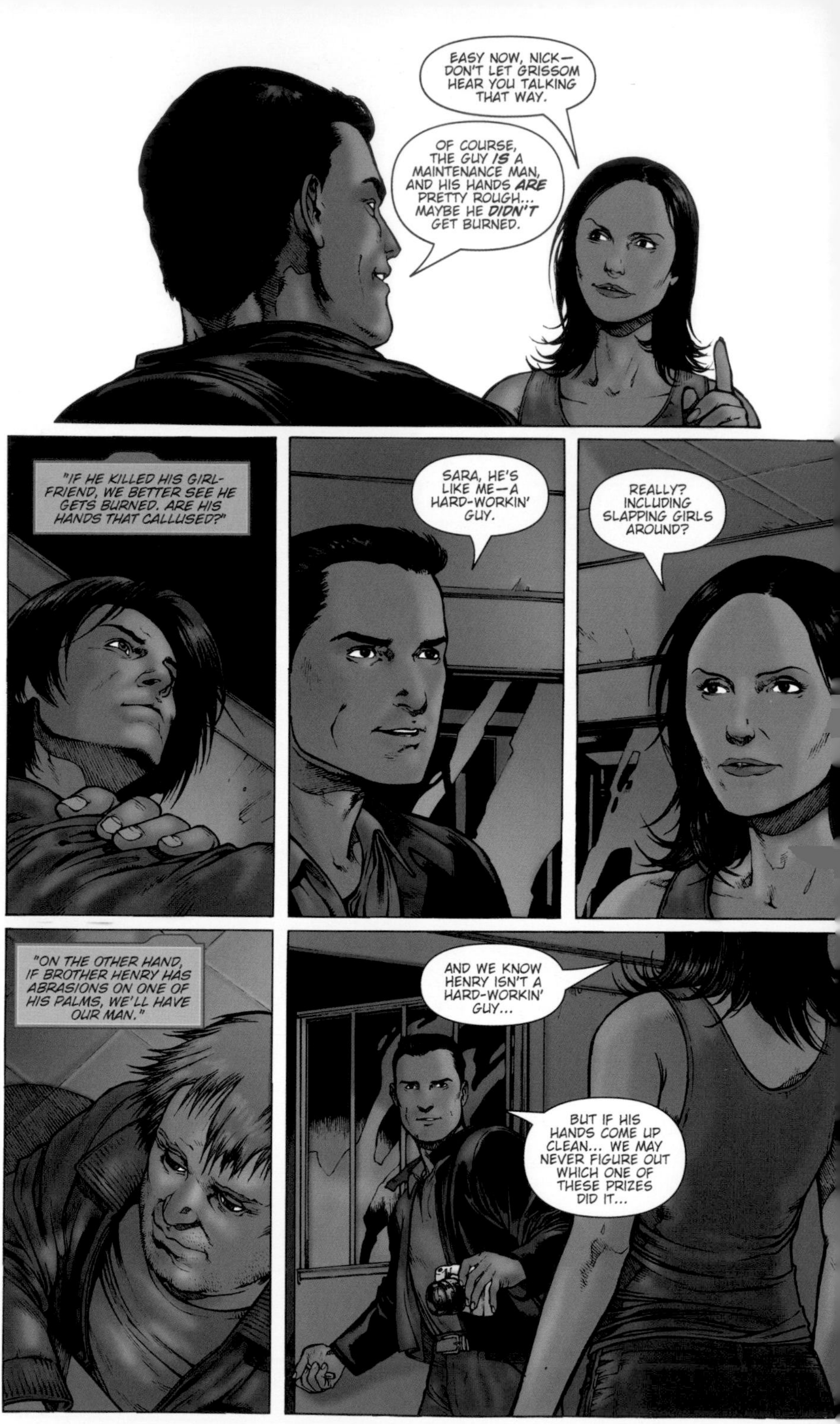
EASY NOW, NICK— DON'T LET GRISSOM HEAR YOU TALKING THAT WAY.
OF COURSE, THE GUY IS A MAINTENANCE MAN, AND HIS HANDS ARE PRETTY ROUGH... MAYBE HE DIDN'T GET BURNED.
"IF HE KILLED HIS GIRL-FRIEND, WE BETTER SEE HE GETS BURNED. ARE HIS HANDS THAT CALLUSED?"
SARA, HE'S LIKE ME—A HARD-WORKIN' GUY.
REALLY? INCLUDING SLAPPING GIRLS AROUND?
"ON THE OTHER HAND, IF BROTHER HENRY HAS ABRASIONS ON ONE OF HIS PALMS, WE'LL HAVE OUR MAN."
AND WE KNOW HENRY ISN'T A HARD-WORKIN' GUY...
BUT IF HIS HANDS COME UP CLEAN... WE MAY NEVER FIGURE OUT WHICH ONE OF THESE PRIZES DID IT...

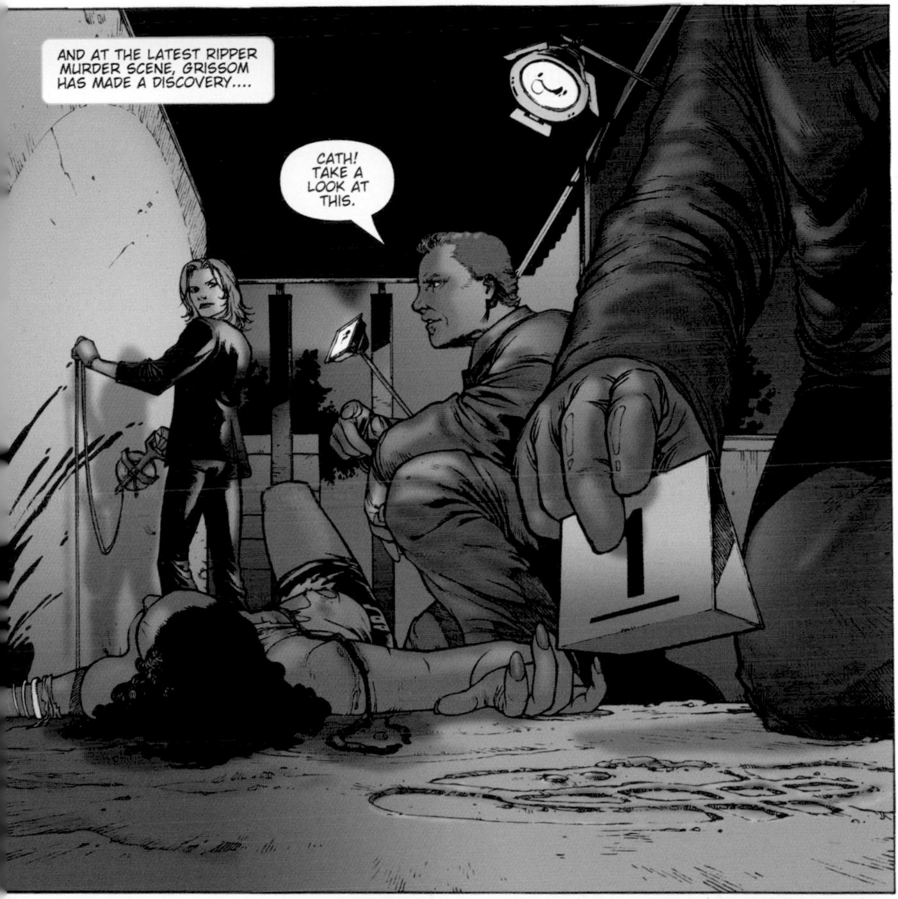
AND AT THE LATEST RIPPER MURDER SCENE, GRISSOM HAS MADE A DISCOVERY....
CATH! TAKE A LOOK AT THIS.
1

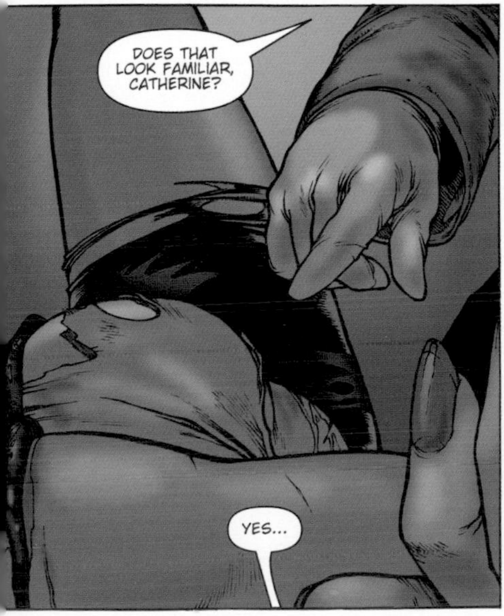
DOES THAT LOOK FAMILIAR, CATHERINE?
YES...

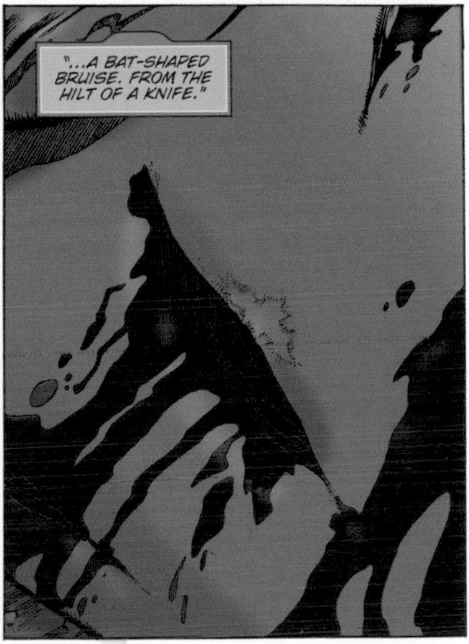
"...A BAT-SHAPED BRUISE. FROM THE HILT OF A KNIFE."

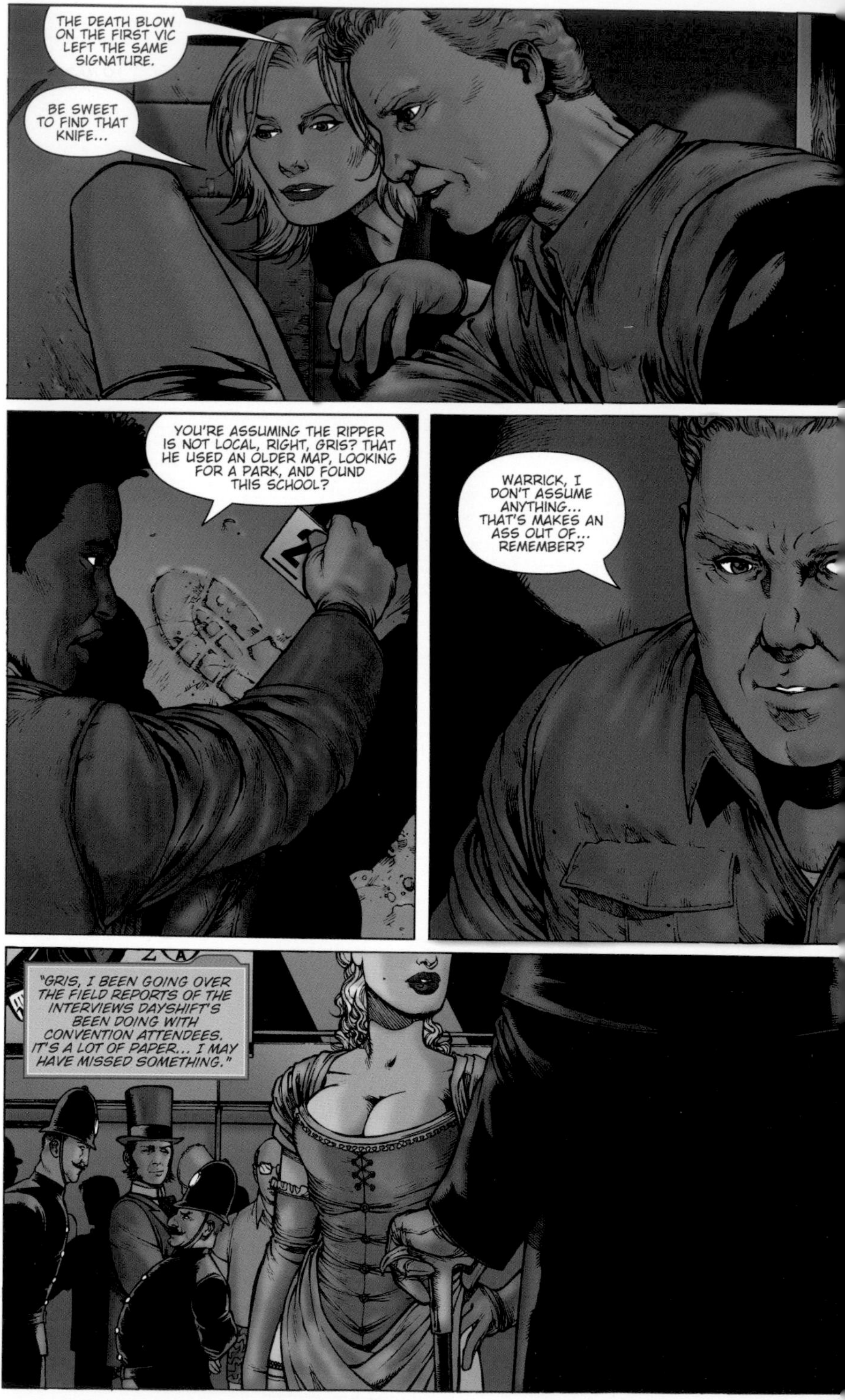
THE DEATH BLOW ON THE FIRST VIC LEFT THE SAME SIGNATURE.
BE SWEET TO FIND THAT KNIFE...
YOU'RE ASSUMING THE RIPPER IS NOT LOCAL, RIGHT, GRIS? THAT HE USED AN OLDER MAP, LOOKING FOR A PARK, AND FOUND THIS SCHOOL?
WARRICK, I DON'T ASSUME ANYTHING... THAT'S MAKES AN ASS OUT OF... REMEMBER?
"GRIS, I BEEN GOING OVER THE FIELD REPORTS OF THE INTERVIEWS DAYSHIFT'S BEEN DOING WITH CONVENTION ATTENDEES. IT'S A LOT OF PAPER... I MAY HAVE MISSED SOMETHING."

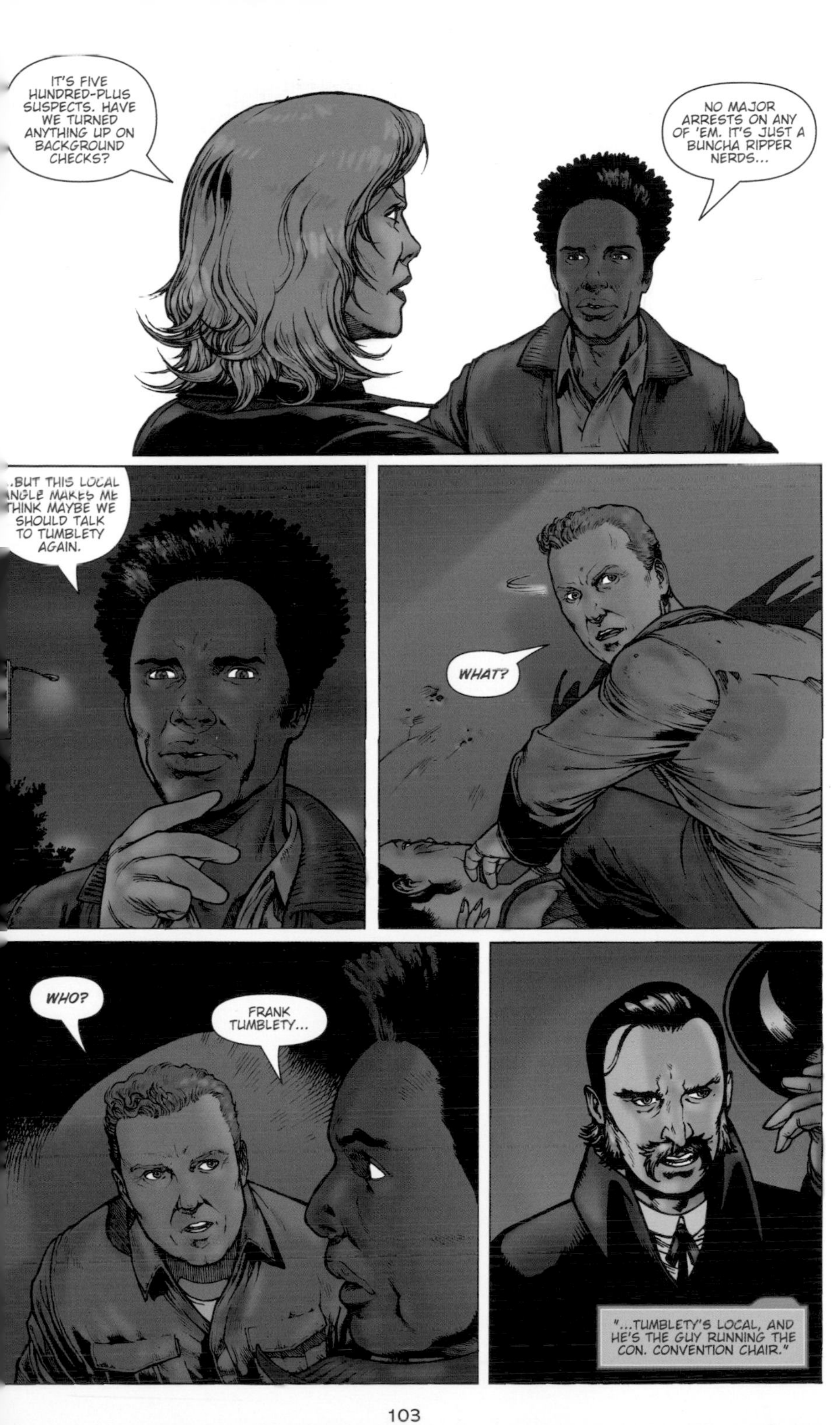
IT'S FIVE HUNDRED-PLUS SUSPECTS. HAVE WE TURNED ANYTHING UP ON BACKGROUND CHECKS?
NO MAJOR ARRESTS ON ANY OF 'EM. IT'S JUST A BUNCHA RIPPER NERDS...
..BUT THIS LOCAL ANGLE MAKES ME THINK MAYBE WE SHOULD TALK TO TUMBLETY AGAIN.
WHAT?
WHO?
FRANK TUMBLETY...
"...TUMBLETY'S LOCAL, AND HE'S THE GUY RUNNING THE CON. CONVENTION CHAIR."

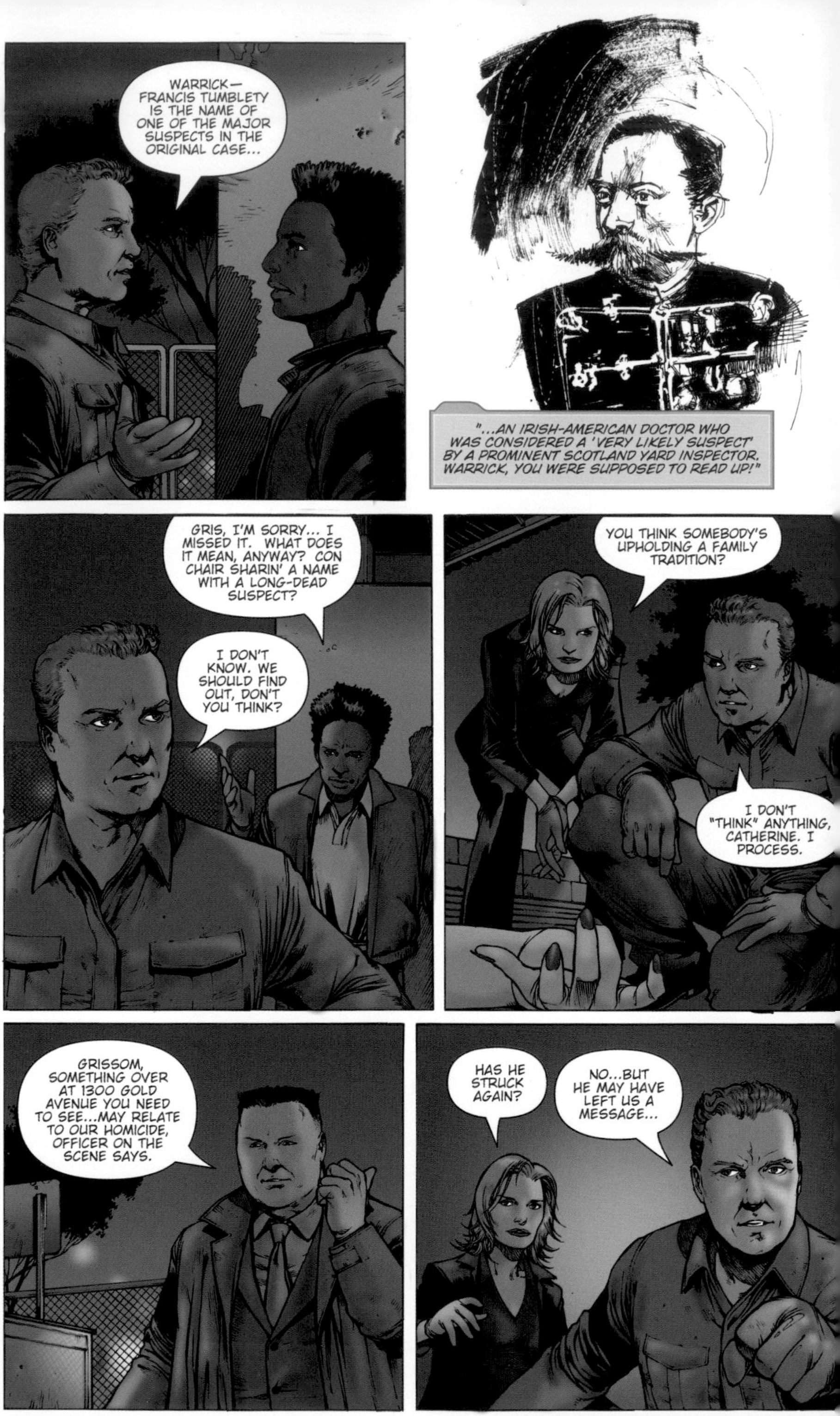
WARRICK— FRANCIS TUMBLETY IS THE NAME OF ONE OF THE MAJOR SUSPECTS IN THE ORIGINAL CASE...
"...AN IRISH-AMERICAN DOCTOR WHO WAS CONSIDERED A 'VERY LIKELY SUSPECT' BY A PROMINENT SCOTLAND YARD INSPECTOR. WARRICK, YOU WERE SUPPOSED TO READ UP!"
GRIS, I'M SORRY... I MISSED IT. WHAT DOES IT MEAN, ANYWAY? CON CHAIR SHARIN' A NAME WITH A LONG-DEAD SUSPECT?
I DON'T KNOW. WE SHOULD FIND OUT, DON'T YOU THINK?
YOU THINK SOMEBODY'S UPHOLDING A FAMILY TRADITION?
I DON'T "THINK" ANYTHING, CATHERINE. I PROCESS.
GRISSOM, SOMETHING OVER AT 1300 GOLD AVENUE YOU NEED TO SEE...MAY RELATE TO OUR HOMICIDE, OFFICER ON THE SCENE SAYS.
HAS HE STRUCK AGAIN?
NO...BUT HE MAY HAVE LEFT US A MESSAGE...

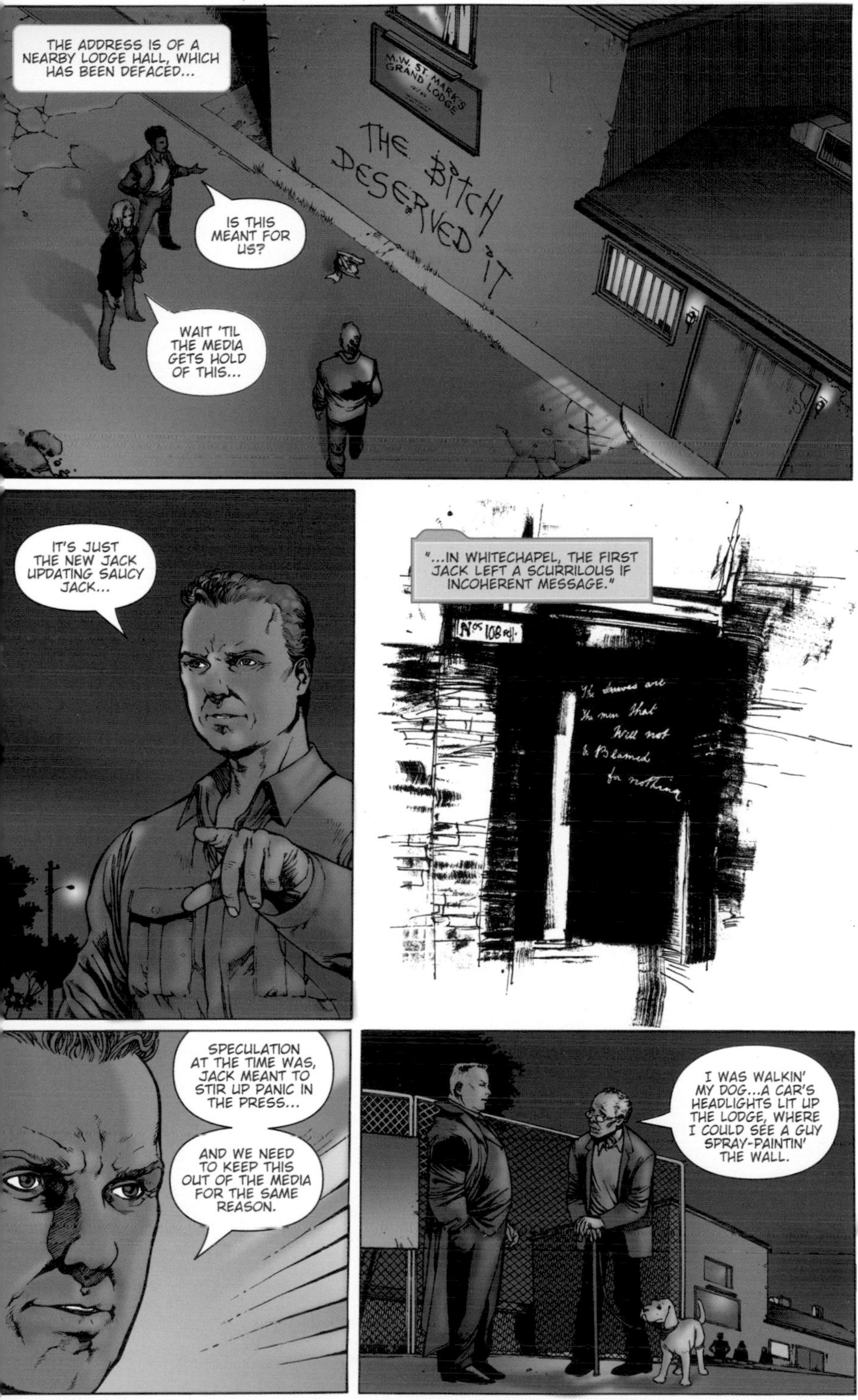
THE ADDRESS IS OF A NEARBY LODGE HALL, WHICH HAS BEEN DEFACED...
M.W. ST. MARK'S GRAND LODGE
THE BITCH DESERVED IT
IS THIS MEANT FOR US?
WAIT 'TIL THE MEDIA GETS HOLD OF THIS...
IT'S JUST THE NEW JACK UPDATING SAUCY JACK...
"...IN WHITECHAPEL, THE FIRST JACK LEFT A SCURRILOUS IF INCOHERENT MESSAGE."
The Juwes are
The men that
Will not
be Blamed
for nothing
SPECULATION AT THE TIME WAS, JACK MEANT TO STIR UP PANIC IN THE PRESS...
AND WE NEED TO KEEP THIS OUT OF THE MEDIA FOR THE SAME REASON.
I WAS WALKIN' MY DOG...A CAR'S HEADLIGHTS LIT UP THE LODGE, WHERE I COULD SEE A GUY SPRAY-PAINTIN' THE WALL.

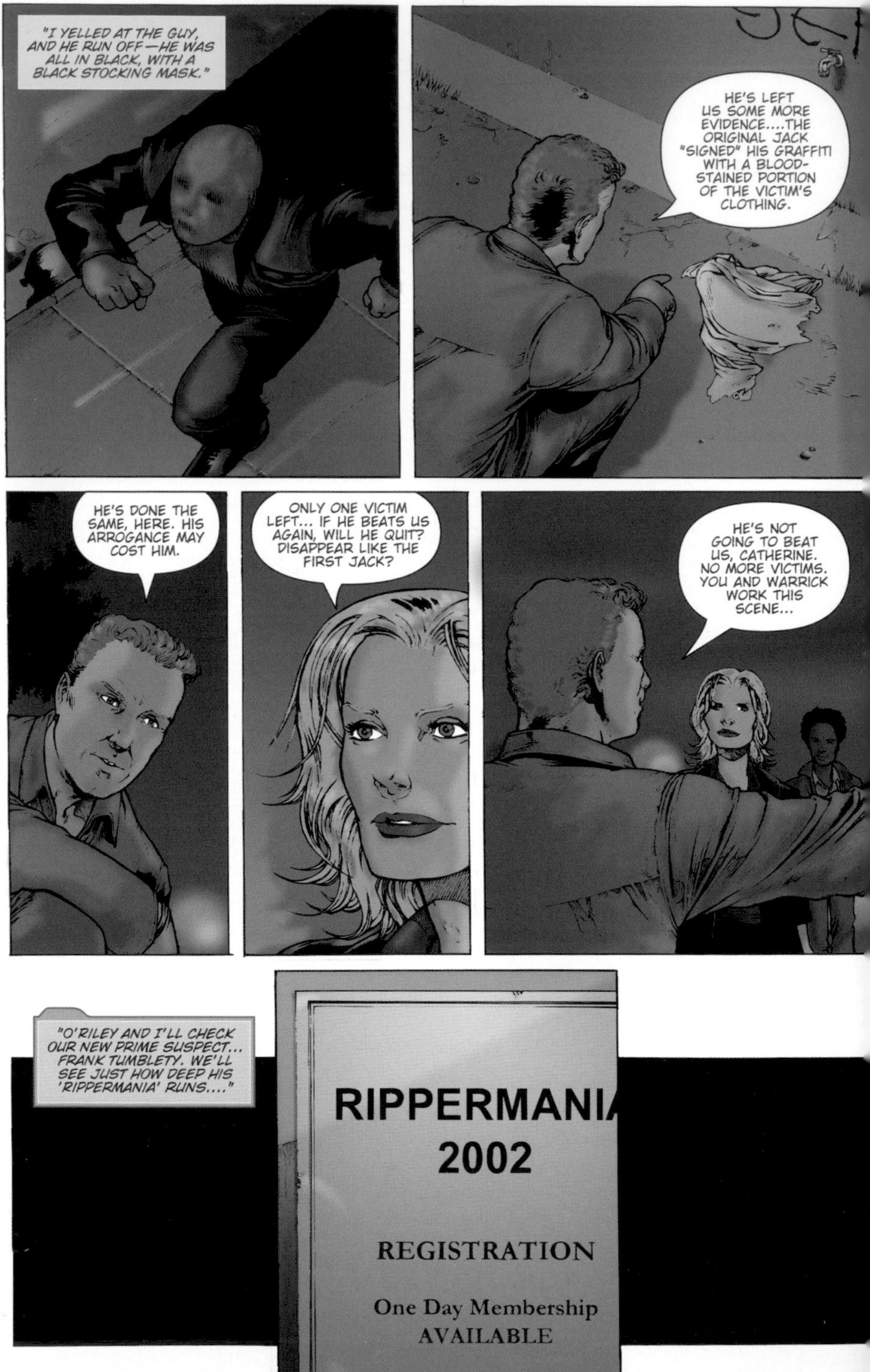
"I YELLED AT THE GUY, AND HE RUN OFF—HE WAS ALL IN BLACK, WITH A BLACK STOCKING MASK."
HE'S LEFT US SOME MORE EVIDENCE....THE ORIGINAL JACK "SIGNED" HIS GRAFFITI WITH A BLOOD-STAINED PORTION OF THE VICTIM'S CLOTHING.
HE'S DONE THE SAME, HERE. HIS ARROGANCE MAY COST HIM.
ONLY ONE VICTIM LEFT... IF HE BEATS US AGAIN, WILL HE QUIT? DISAPPEAR LIKE THE FIRST JACK?
HE'S NOT GOING TO BEAT US, CATHERINE. NO MORE VICTIMS. YOU AND WARRICK WORK THIS SCENE...
"O'RILEY AND I'LL CHECK OUR NEW PRIME SUSPECT... FRANK TUMBLETY. WE'LL SEE JUST HOW DEEP HIS 'RIPPERMANIA' RUNS...."
RIPPERMANIA
2002
REGISTRATION
One Day Membership
AVAILABLE

chapter five

Jack Be Nimble

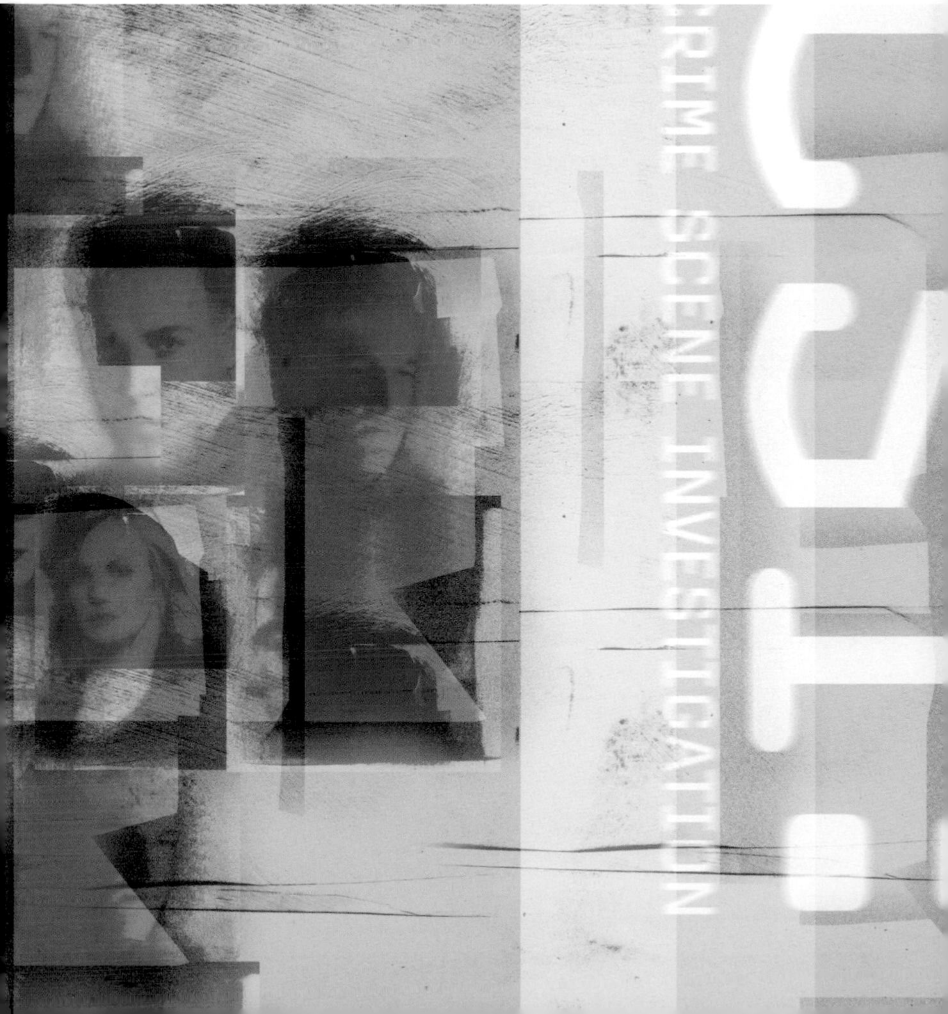
CRIME SCENE INVESTIGATION

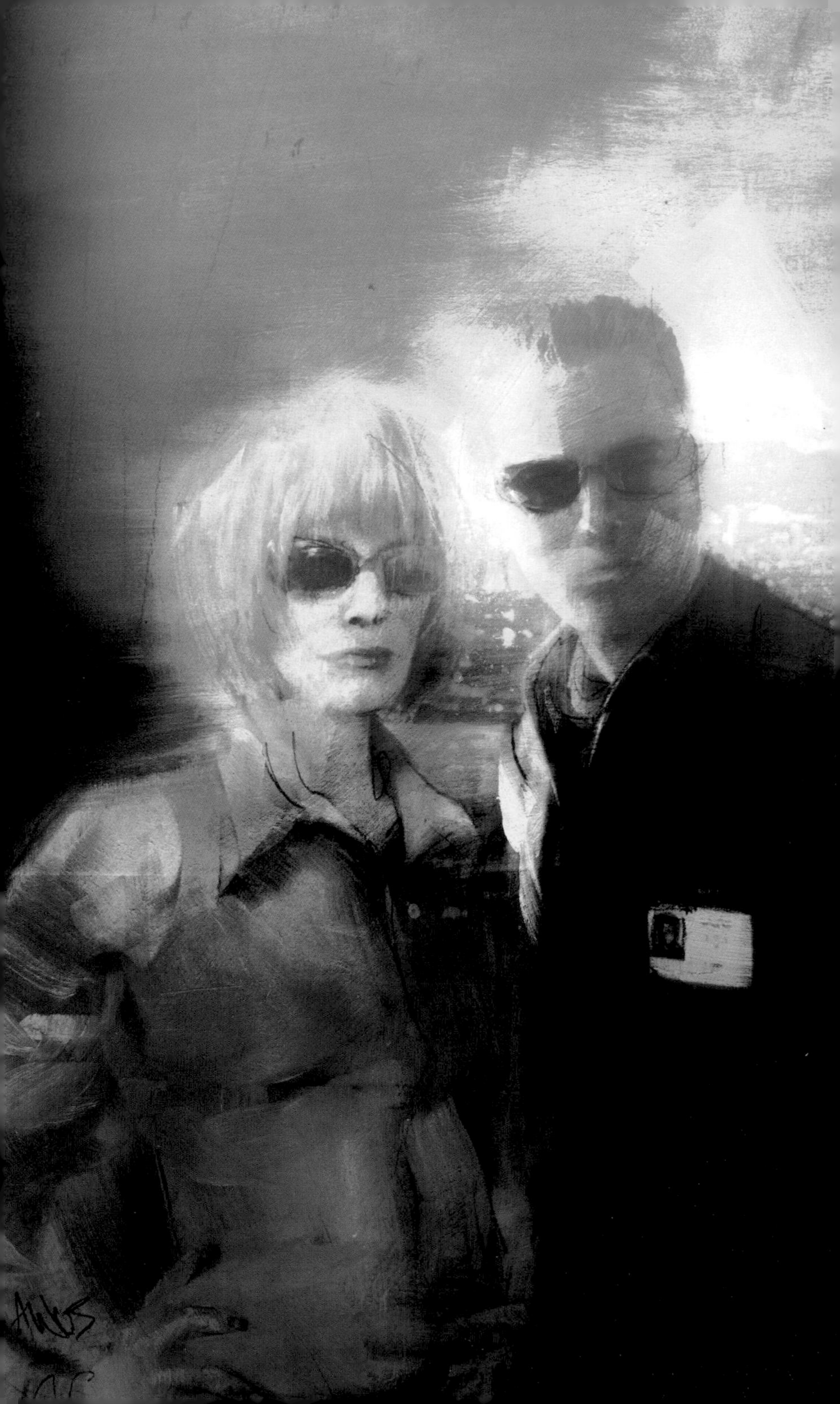

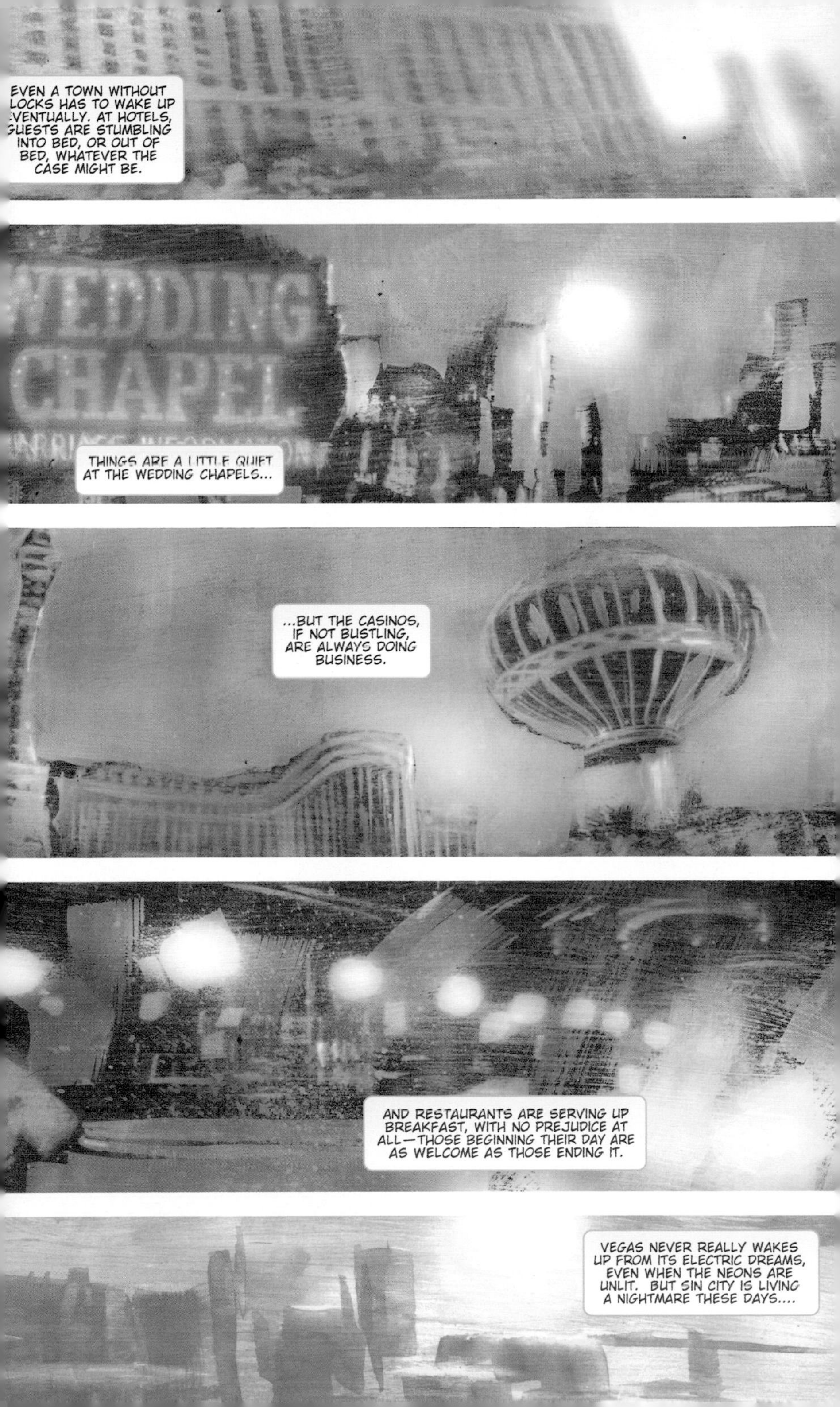
EVEN A TOWN WITHOUT LOCKS HAS TO WAKE UP EVENTUALLY. AT HOTELS, GUESTS ARE STUMBLING INTO BED, OR OUT OF BED, WHATEVER THE CASE MIGHT BE.
WEDDING CHAPEL
THINGS ARE A LITTLE QUIET AT THE WEDDING CHAPELS...
...BUT THE CASINOS, IF NOT BUSTLING, ARE ALWAYS DOING BUSINESS.
AND RESTAURANTS ARE SERVING UP BREAKFAST, WITH NO PREJUDICE AT ALL—THOSE BEGINNING THEIR DAY ARE AS WELCOME AS THOSE ENDING IT.
VEGAS NEVER REALLY WAKES UP FROM ITS ELECTRIC DREAMS, EVEN WHEN THE NEONS ARE UNLIT. BUT SIN CITY IS LIVING A NIGHTMARE THESE DAYS....

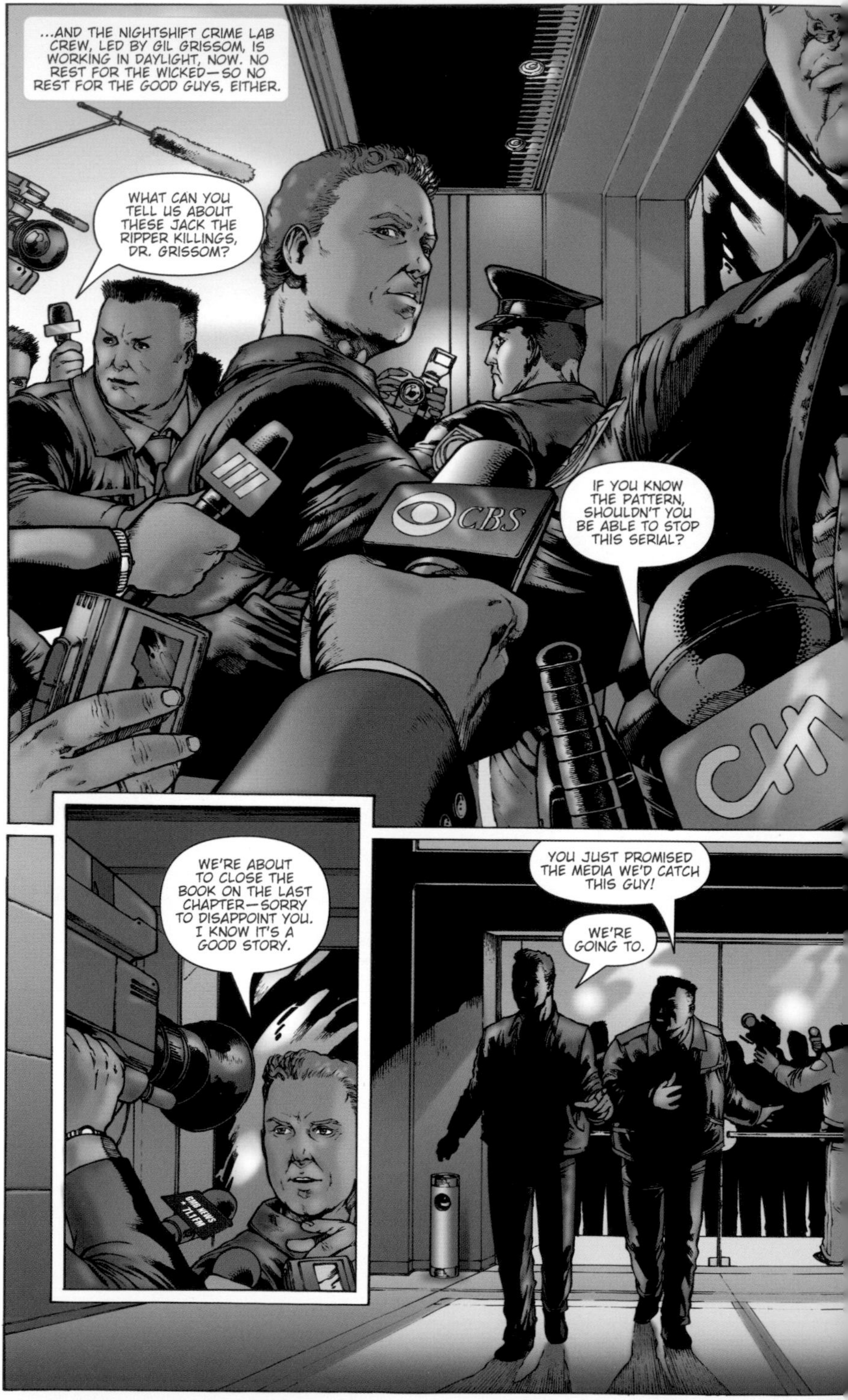
...AND THE NIGHTSHIFT CRIME LAB CREW, LED BY GIL GRISSOM, IS WORKING IN DAYLIGHT, NOW. NO REST FOR THE WICKED—SO NO REST FOR THE GOOD GUYS, EITHER.
WHAT CAN YOU TELL US ABOUT THESE JACK THE RIPPER KILLINGS, DR. GRISSOM?
CBS
IF YOU KNOW THE PATTERN, SHOULDN'T YOU BE ABLE TO STOP THIS SERIAL?
WE'RE ABOUT TO CLOSE THE BOOK ON THE LAST CHAPTER—SORRY TO DISAPPOINT YOU. I KNOW IT'S A GOOD STORY.
YOU JUST PROMISED THE MEDIA WE'D CATCH THIS GUY!
WE'RE GOING TO.

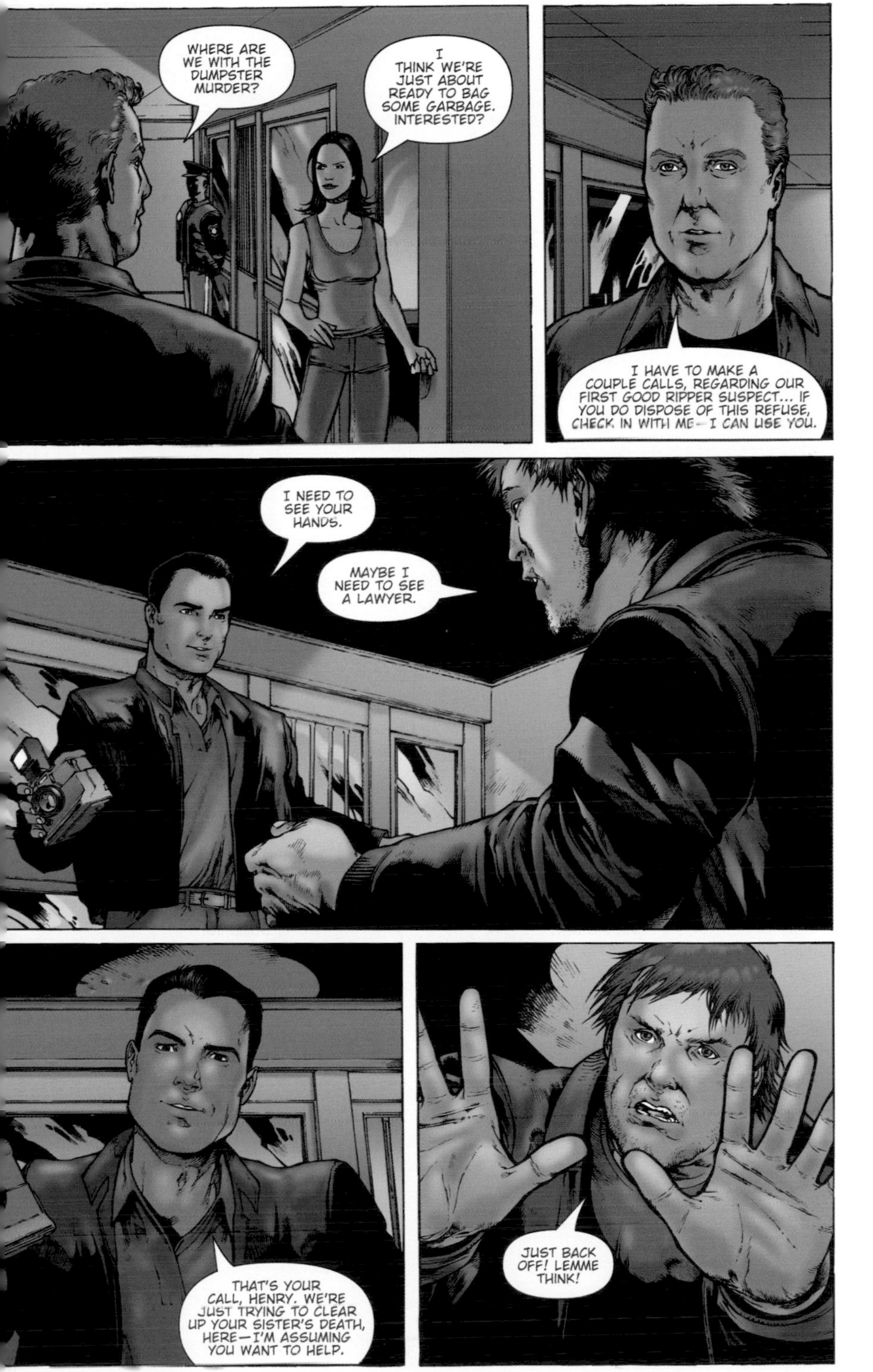
WHERE ARE WE WITH THE DUMPSTER MURDER?
I THINK WE'RE JUST ABOUT READY TO BAG SOME GARBAGE. INTERESTED?
I HAVE TO MAKE A COUPLE CALLS, REGARDING OUR FIRST GOOD RIPPER SUSPECT... IF YOU DO DISPOSE OF THIS REFUSE, CHECK IN WITH ME— I CAN USE YOU.
I NEED TO SEE YOUR HANDS.
MAYBE I NEED TO SEE A LAWYER.
THAT'S YOUR CALL, HENRY. WE'RE JUST TRYING TO CLEAR UP YOUR SISTER'S DEATH, HERE— I'M ASSUMING YOU WANT TO HELP.
JUST BACK OFF! LEMME THINK!

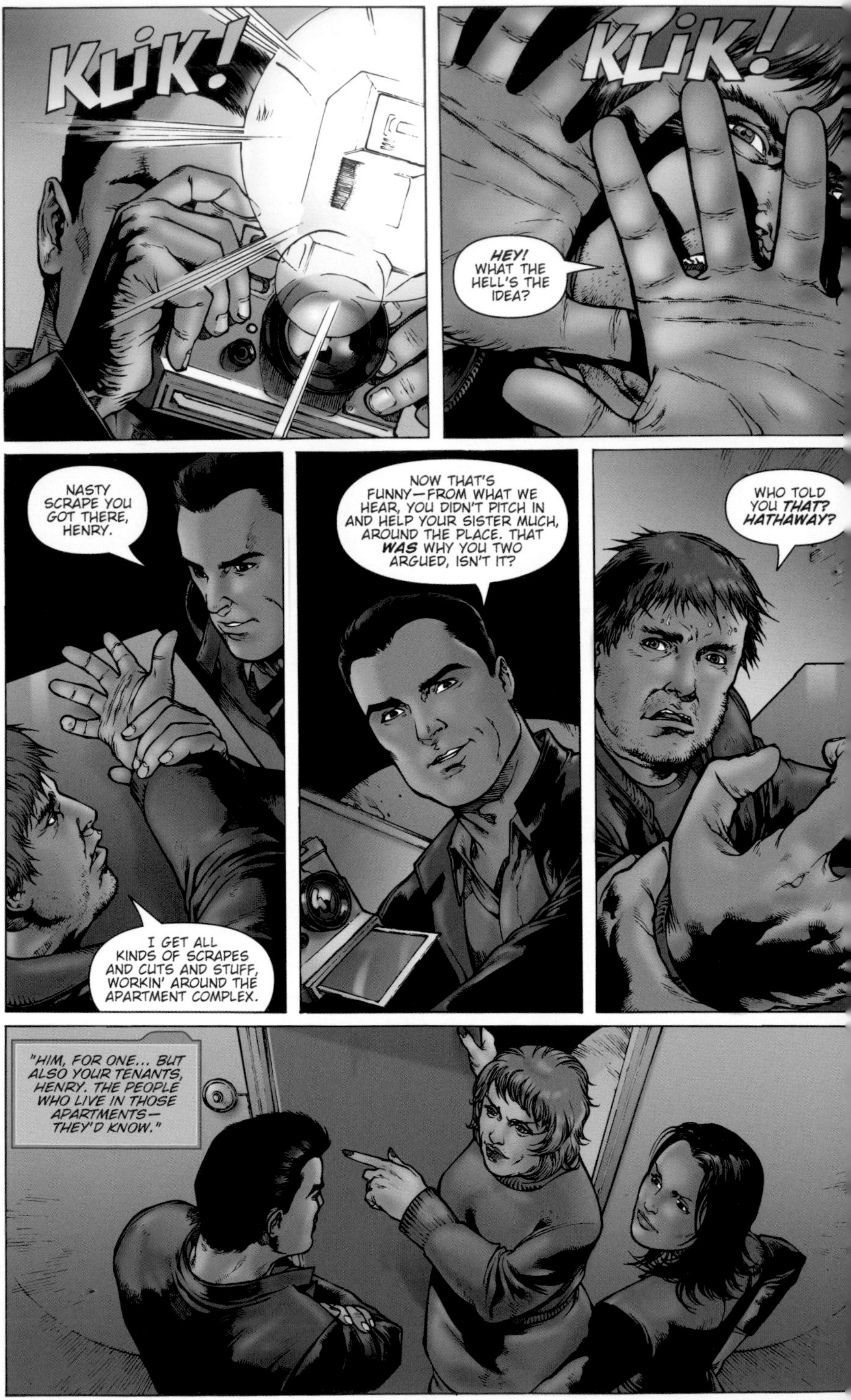
KLIK!
KLIK!
HEY! WHAT THE HELL'S THE IDEA?
NASTY SCRAPE YOU GOT THERE, HENRY.
I GET ALL KINDS OF SCRAPES AND CUTS AND STUFF, WORKIN' AROUND THE APARTMENT COMPLEX.
NOW THAT'S FUNNY—FROM WHAT WE HEAR, YOU DIDN'T PITCH IN AND HELP YOUR SISTER MUCH, AROUND THE PLACE. THAT WAS WHY YOU TWO ARGUED, ISN'T IT?
WHO TOLD YOU THAT? HATHAWAY?
"HIM, FOR ONE... BUT ALSO YOUR TENANTS, HENRY. THE PEOPLE WHO LIVE IN THOSE APARTMENTS—THEY'D KNOW."

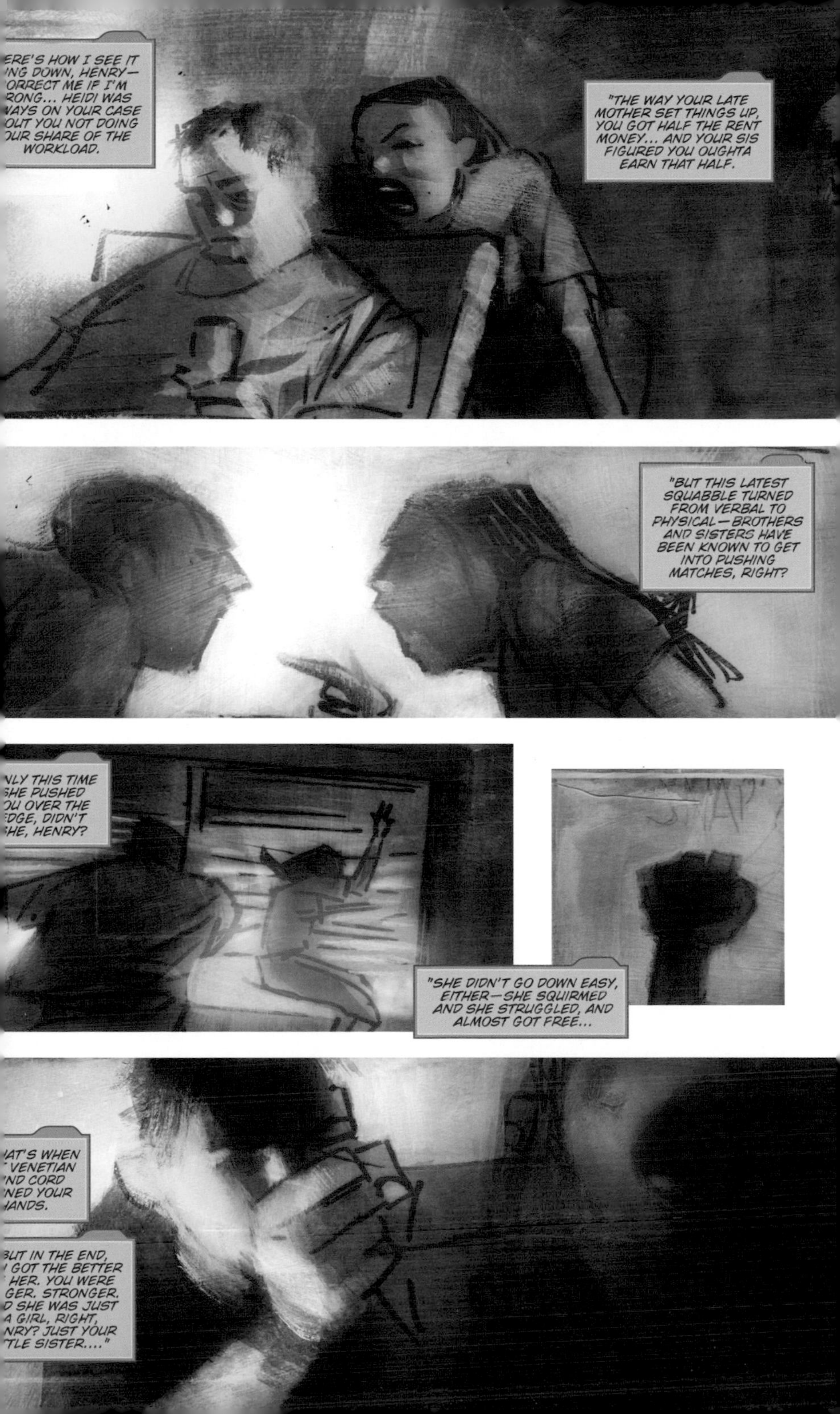
ERE'S HOW I SEE IT
NG DOWN, HENRY—
ORRECT ME IF I'M
RONG... HEIDI WAS
WAYS ON YOUR CASE
OUT YOU NOT DOING
OUR SHARE OF THE
WORKLOAD.
"THE WAY YOUR LATE MOTHER SET THINGS UP, YOU GOT HALF THE RENT MONEY... AND YOUR SIS FIGURED YOU OUGHTA EARN THAT HALF.
"BUT THIS LATEST SQUABBLE TURNED FROM VERBAL TO PHYSICAL—BROTHERS AND SISTERS HAVE BEEN KNOWN TO GET INTO PUSHING MATCHES, RIGHT?
NLY THIS TIME
SHE PUSHED
OU OVER THE
EDGE, DIDN'T
SHE, HENRY?
"SHE DIDN'T GO DOWN EASY, EITHER—SHE SQUIRMED AND SHE STRUGGLED, AND ALMOST GOT FREE...
AT'S WHEN
VENETIAN
ND CORD
NED YOUR
HANDS.
BUT IN THE END,
GOT THE BETTER
HER. YOU WERE
GER. STRONGER.
D SHE WAS JUST
A GIRL, RIGHT,
NRY? JUST YOUR
TLE SISTER...."

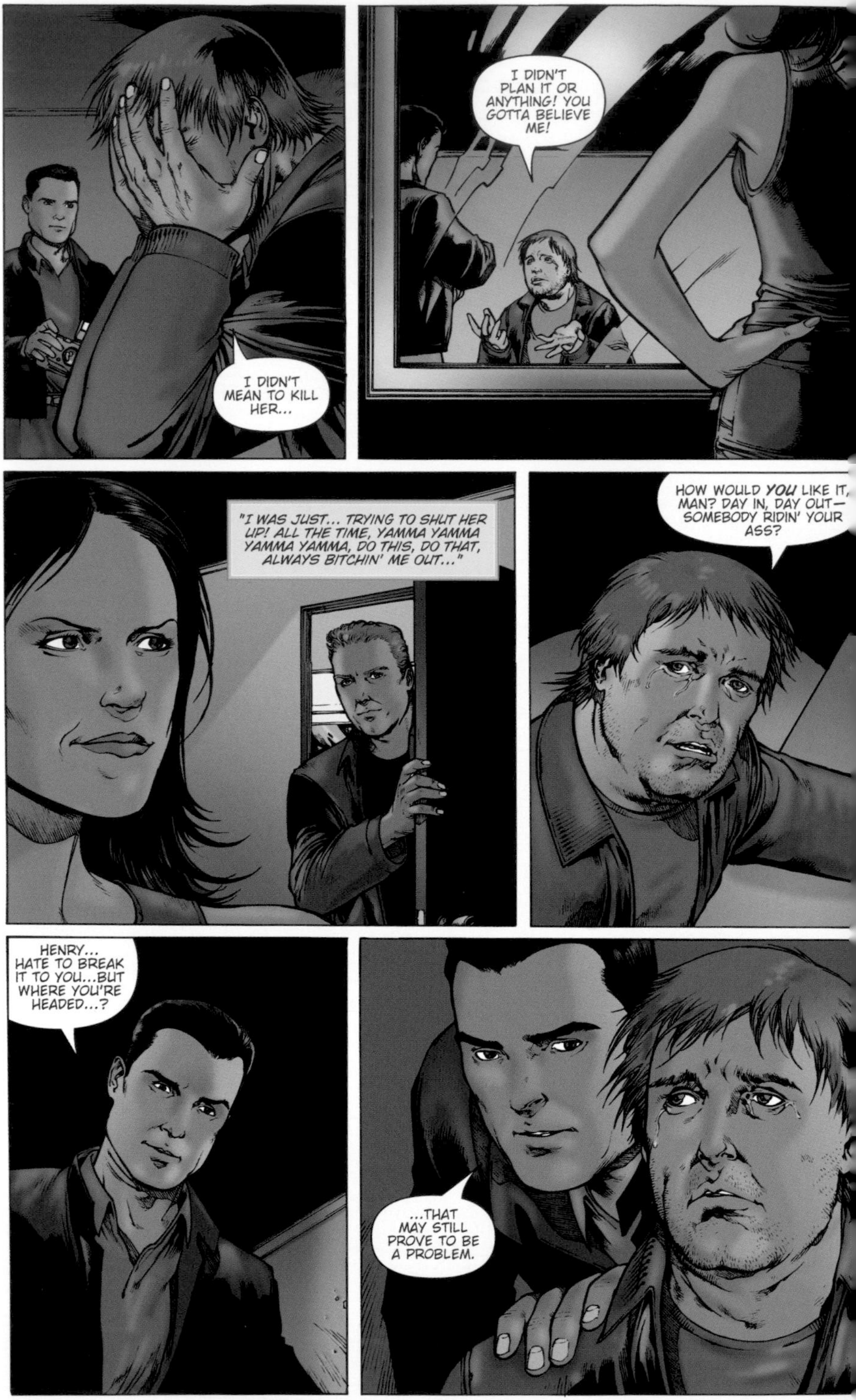
I DIDN'T MEAN TO KILL HER...
I DIDN'T PLAN IT OR ANYTHING! YOU GOTTA BELIEVE ME!
"I WAS JUST... TRYING TO SHUT HER UP! ALL THE TIME, YAMMA YAMMA YAMMA YAMMA, DO THIS, DO THAT, ALWAYS BITCHIN' ME OUT..."
HOW WOULD *YOU* LIKE IT, MAN? DAY IN, DAY OUT— SOMEBODY RIDIN' YOUR ASS?
HENRY... HATE TO BREAK IT TO YOU...BUT WHERE YOU'RE HEADED...?
...THAT MAY STILL PROVE TO BE A PROBLEM.

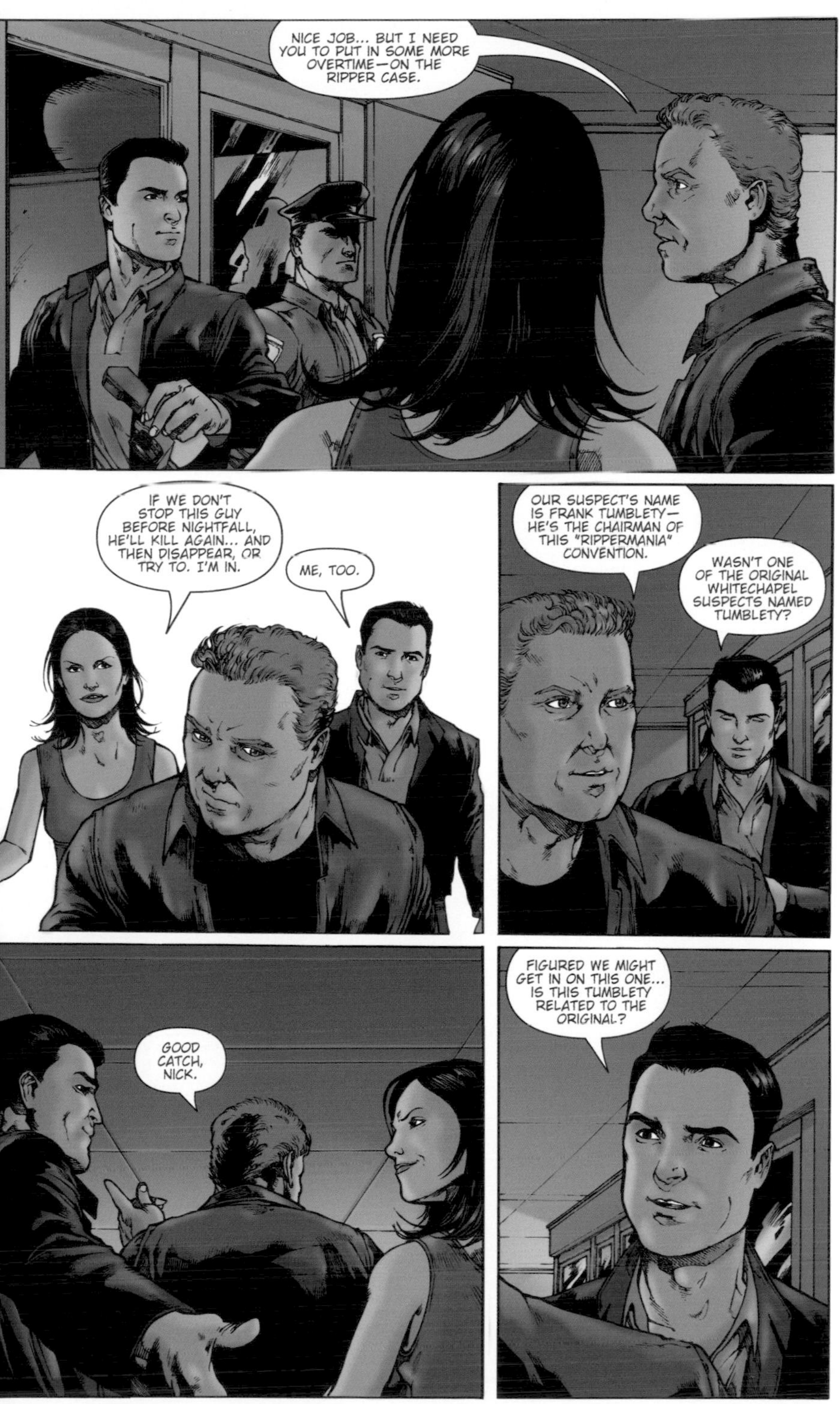
NICE JOB... BUT I NEED YOU TO PUT IN SOME MORE OVERTIME—ON THE RIPPER CASE.
IF WE DON'T STOP THIS GUY BEFORE NIGHTFALL, HE'LL KILL AGAIN... AND THEN DISAPPEAR, OR TRY TO. I'M IN.
ME, TOO.
OUR SUSPECT'S NAME IS FRANK TUMBLETY—HE'S THE CHAIRMAN OF THIS "RIPPERMANIA" CONVENTION.
WASN'T ONE OF THE ORIGINAL WHITECHAPEL SUSPECTS NAMED TUMBLETY?
GOOD CATCH, NICK.
FIGURED WE MIGHT GET IN ON THIS ONE... IS THIS TUMBLETY RELATED TO THE ORIGINAL?

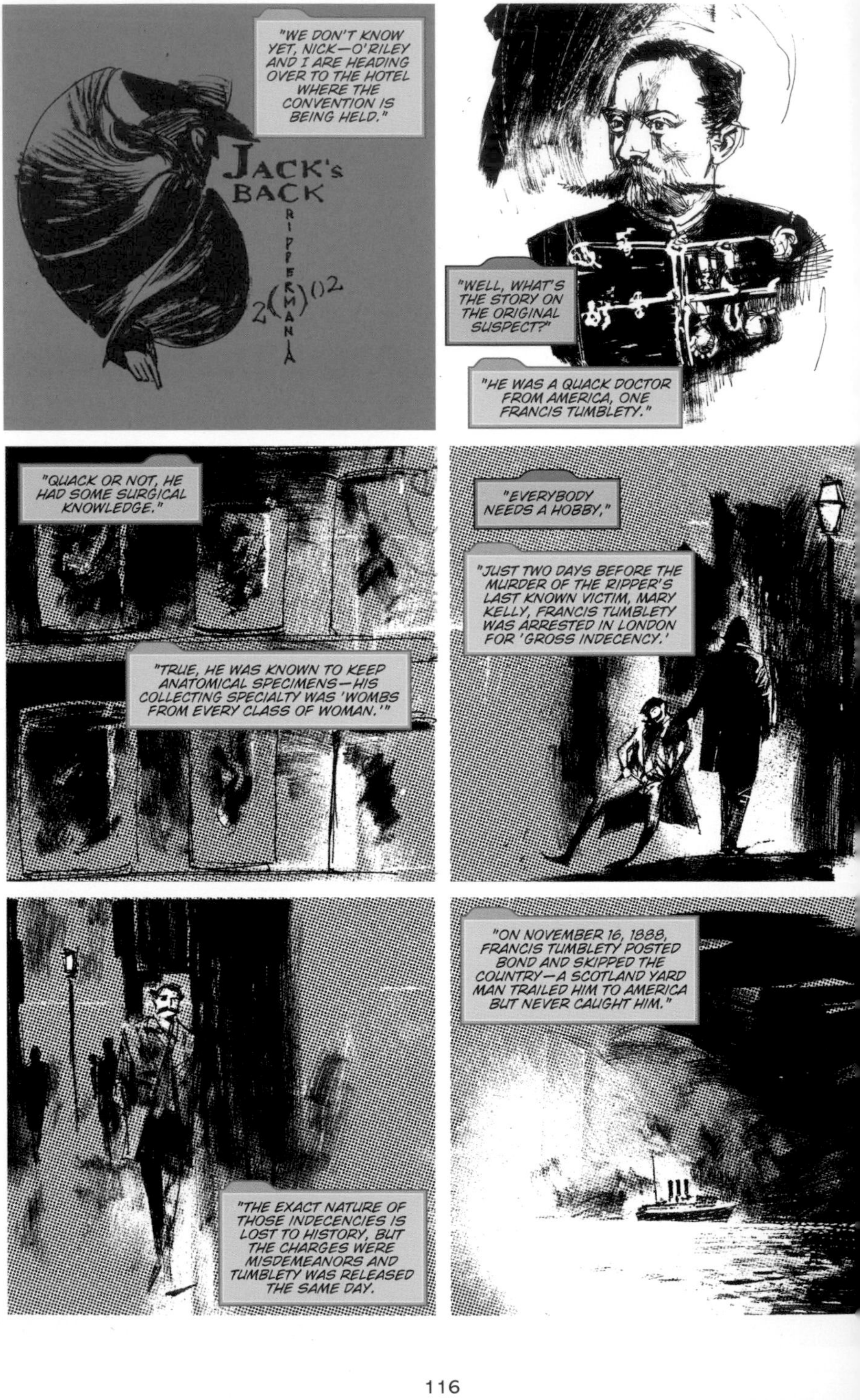
"WE DON'T KNOW YET, NICK—O'RILEY AND I ARE HEADING OVER TO THE HOTEL WHERE THE CONVENTION IS BEING HELD."
JACK's BACK
RIPPERMANIA
"WELL, WHAT'S THE STORY ON THE ORIGINAL SUSPECT?"
"HE WAS A QUACK DOCTOR FROM AMERICA, ONE FRANCIS TUMBLETY."
"QUACK OR NOT, HE HAD SOME SURGICAL KNOWLEDGE."
"TRUE, HE WAS KNOWN TO KEEP ANATOMICAL SPECIMENS—HIS COLLECTING SPECIALTY WAS 'WOMBS FROM EVERY CLASS OF WOMAN.'"
"EVERYBODY NEEDS A HOBBY."
"JUST TWO DAYS BEFORE THE MURDER OF THE RIPPER'S LAST KNOWN VICTIM, MARY KELLY, FRANCIS TUMBLETY WAS ARRESTED IN LONDON FOR 'GROSS INDECENCY.'
"THE EXACT NATURE OF THOSE INDECENCIES IS LOST TO HISTORY, BUT THE CHARGES WERE MISDEMEANORS AND TUMBLETY WAS RELEASED THE SAME DAY.
"ON NOVEMBER 16, 1888, FRANCIS TUMBLETY POSTED BOND AND SKIPPED THE COUNTRY—A SCOTLAND YARD MAN TRAILED HIM TO AMERICA BUT NEVER CAUGHT HIM."

AND ONCE TUMBLETY LEFT ENGLAND, THE RIPPER MURDERS CEASED.

AND THE THINKING IS, OUR TUMBLETY IS PICKING UP WHERE HIS ANCESTOR LEFT OFF?

WHY DON'T WE FIND T? HERE'S TUMBLETY'S DRESS—WAIT THERE FOR LOCKWOOD. HE'LL BE ALONG SOON WITH A WARRANT.

WILL TUMBLETY BE HOME, YOU THINK?

WHAT'S WRONG, NICK? SHY ABOUT POPPING IN ON JACK THE RIPPER?

HE'S BEEN STAYING AT THE HOTEL THROUGHOUT THE CONVENTION. AS THE CHAIRMAN, HE APPARENTLY WANTED TO BE AVAILABLE 24/7, FOR WHATEVER MIGHT COME UP.

AND LESS THAN AN HOUR LATER...

JACK BACK RIPPERMANIA 2002

SO WITH ALL DUE RESPECT TO MY FELLOW RIPPER ENTHUSIASTS...

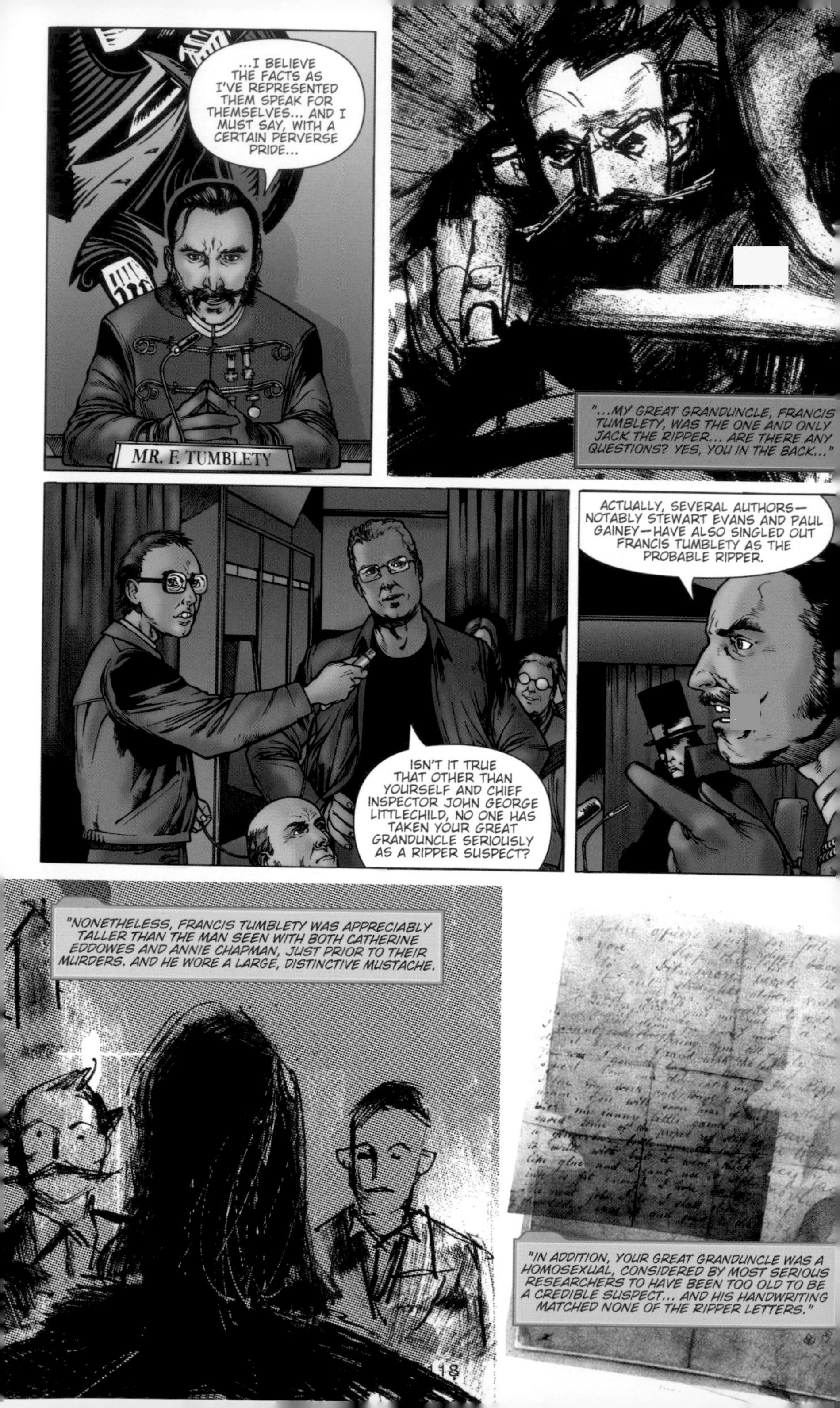

...I BELIEVE THE FACTS AS I'VE REPRESENTED THEM SPEAK FOR THEMSELVES... AND I MUST SAY, WITH A CERTAIN PERVERSE PRIDE...
MR. F. TUMBLETY
"...MY GREAT GRANDUNCLE, FRANCIS TUMBLETY, WAS THE ONE AND ONLY JACK THE RIPPER... ARE THERE ANY QUESTIONS? YES, YOU IN THE BACK..."
ISN'T IT TRUE THAT OTHER THAN YOURSELF AND CHIEF INSPECTOR JOHN GEORGE LITTLECHILD, NO ONE HAS TAKEN YOUR GREAT GRANDUNCLE SERIOUSLY AS A RIPPER SUSPECT?
ACTUALLY, SEVERAL AUTHORS—NOTABLY STEWART EVANS AND PAUL GAINEY—HAVE ALSO SINGLED OUT FRANCIS TUMBLETY AS THE PROBABLE RIPPER.
"NONETHELESS, FRANCIS TUMBLETY WAS APPRECIABLY TALLER THAN THE MAN SEEN WITH BOTH CATHERINE EDDOWES AND ANNIE CHAPMAN, JUST PRIOR TO THEIR MURDERS. AND HE WORE A LARGE, DISTINCTIVE MUSTACHE.
"IN ADDITION, YOUR GREAT GRANDUNCLE WAS A HOMOSEXUAL, CONSIDERED BY MOST SERIOUS RESEARCHERS TO HAVE BEEN TOO OLD TO BE A CREDIBLE SUSPECT... AND HIS HANDWRITING MATCHED NONE OF THE RIPPER LETTERS."

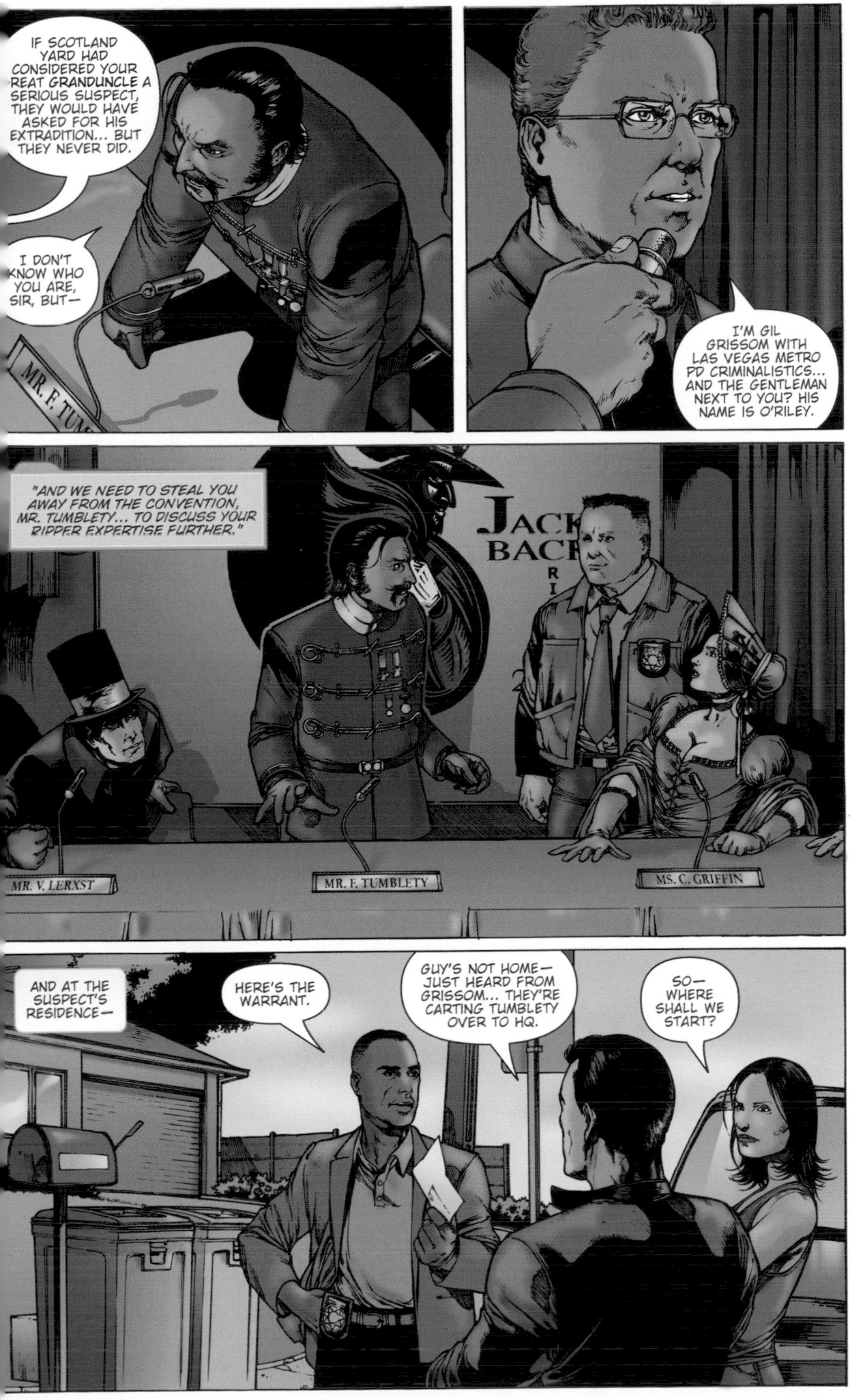

IF SCOTLAND YARD HAD CONSIDERED YOUR GREAT GRANDUNCLE A SERIOUS SUSPECT, THEY WOULD HAVE ASKED FOR HIS EXTRADITION... BUT THEY NEVER DID.
I DON'T KNOW WHO YOU ARE, SIR, BUT—
MR. F. TUM
I'M GIL GRISSOM WITH LAS VEGAS METRO PD CRIMINALISTICS... AND THE GENTLEMAN NEXT TO YOU? HIS NAME IS O'RILEY.
"AND WE NEED TO STEAL YOU AWAY FROM THE CONVENTION, MR. TUMBLETY... TO DISCUSS YOUR RIPPER EXPERTISE FURTHER."
JACK
BACK
MR. V. LERXST
MR. F. TUMBLETY
MS. C. GRIFFIN
AND AT THE SUSPECT'S RESIDENCE—
HERE'S THE WARRANT.
GUY'S NOT HOME— JUST HEARD FROM GRISSOM... THEY'RE CARTING TUMBLETY OVER TO HQ.
SO— WHERE SHALL WE START?

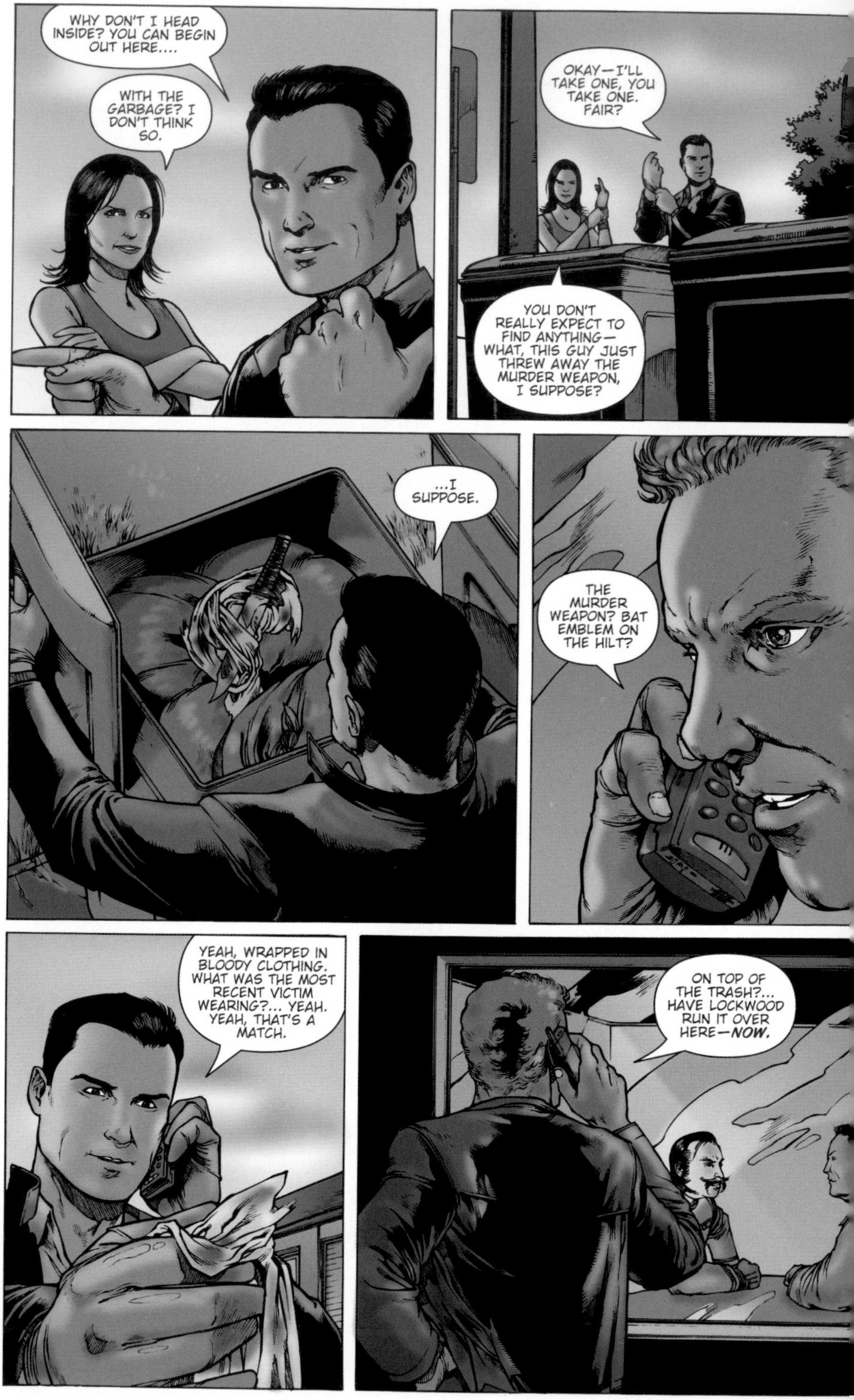
WHY DON'T I HEAD INSIDE? YOU CAN BEGIN OUT HERE....
WITH THE GARBAGE? I DON'T THINK SO.
OKAY—I'LL TAKE ONE, YOU TAKE ONE. FAIR?
YOU DON'T REALLY EXPECT TO FIND ANYTHING—WHAT, THIS GUY JUST THREW AWAY THE MURDER WEAPON, I SUPPOSE?
...I SUPPOSE.
THE MURDER WEAPON? BAT EMBLEM ON THE HILT?
YEAH, WRAPPED IN BLOODY CLOTHING. WHAT WAS THE MOST RECENT VICTIM WEARING?... YEAH. YEAH, THAT'S A MATCH.
ON TOP OF THE TRASH?... HAVE LOCKWOOD RUN IT OVER HERE—*NOW.*

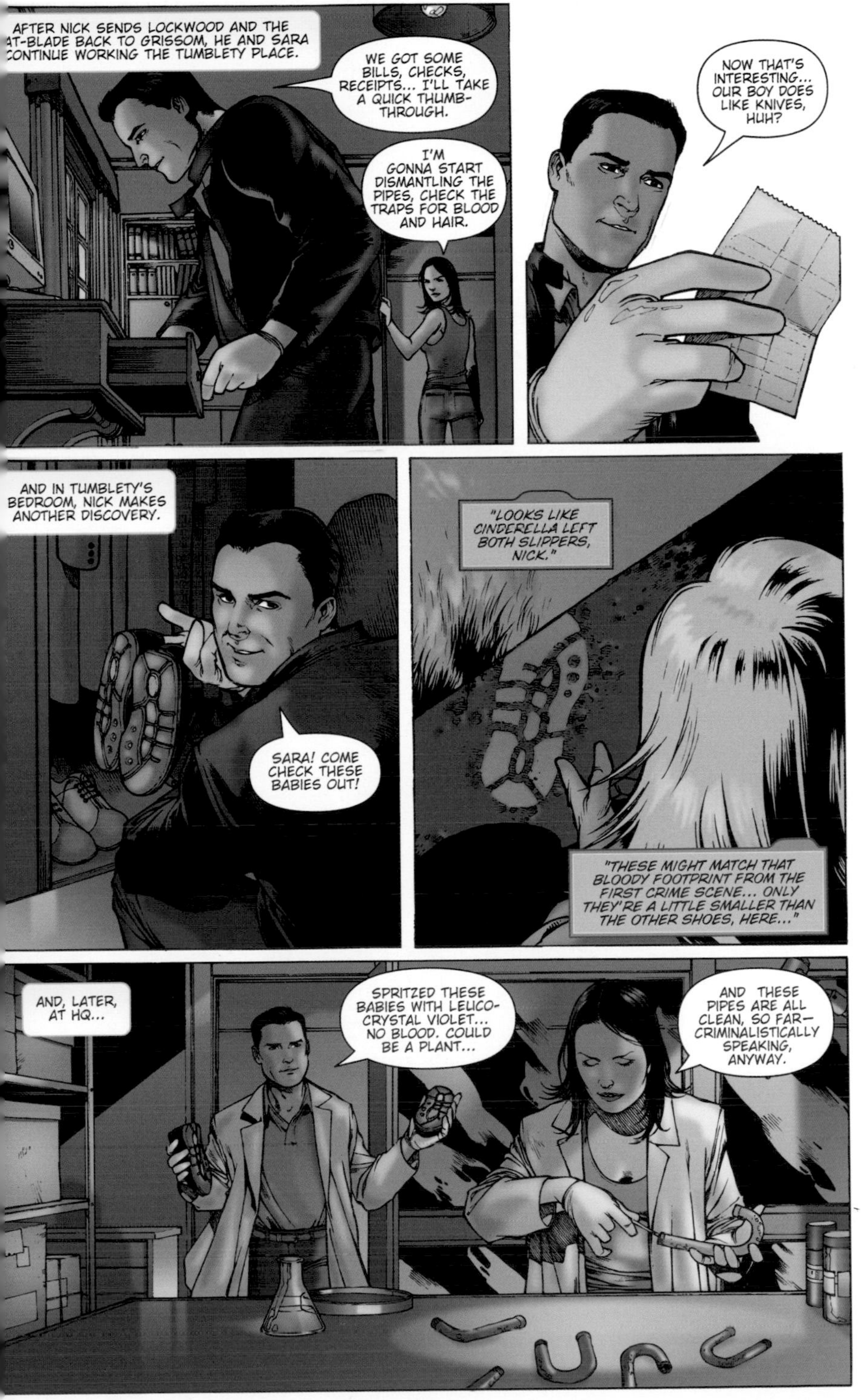

AFTER NICK SENDS LOCKWOOD AND THE AT-BLADE BACK TO GRISSOM, HE AND SARA CONTINUE WORKING THE TUMBLETY PLACE.
WE GOT SOME BILLS, CHECKS, RECEIPTS... I'LL TAKE A QUICK THUMB-THROUGH.
I'M GONNA START DISMANTLING THE PIPES, CHECK THE TRAPS FOR BLOOD AND HAIR.
NOW THAT'S INTERESTING... OUR BOY DOES LIKE KNIVES, HUH?
AND IN TUMBLETY'S BEDROOM, NICK MAKES ANOTHER DISCOVERY.
SARA! COME CHECK THESE BABIES OUT!
"LOOKS LIKE CINDERELLA LEFT BOTH SLIPPERS, NICK."
"THESE MIGHT MATCH THAT BLOODY FOOTPRINT FROM THE FIRST CRIME SCENE... ONLY THEY'RE A LITTLE SMALLER THAN THE OTHER SHOES, HERE..."
AND, LATER, AT HQ...
SPRITZED THESE BABIES WITH LEUCO-CRYSTAL VIOLET... NO BLOOD. COULD BE A PLANT...
AND THESE PIPES ARE ALL CLEAN, SO FAR—CRIMINALISTICALLY SPEAKING, ANYWAY.

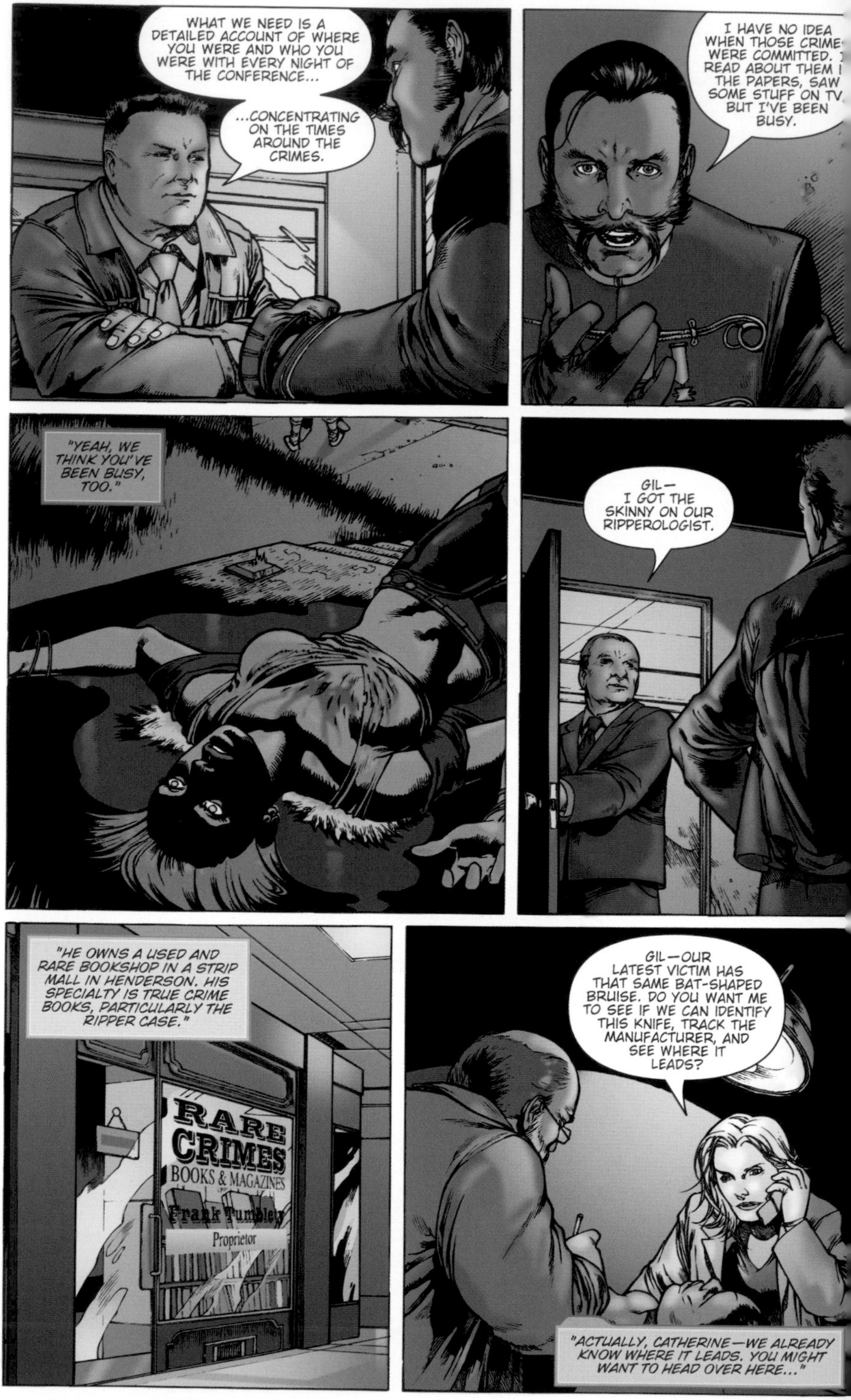
WHAT WE NEED IS A DETAILED ACCOUNT OF WHERE YOU WERE AND WHO YOU WERE WITH EVERY NIGHT OF THE CONFERENCE...
...CONCENTRATING ON THE TIMES AROUND THE CRIMES.
I HAVE NO IDEA WHEN THOSE CRIMES WERE COMMITTED. I READ ABOUT THEM IN THE PAPERS, SAW SOME STUFF ON TV, BUT I'VE BEEN BUSY.
"YEAH, WE THINK YOU'VE BEEN BUSY, TOO."
GIL— I GOT THE SKINNY ON OUR RIPPEROLOGIST.
"HE OWNS A USED AND RARE BOOKSHOP IN A STRIP MALL IN HENDERSON. HIS SPECIALTY IS TRUE CRIME BOOKS, PARTICULARLY THE RIPPER CASE."
RARE CRIMES
BOOKS & MAGAZINES
Frank Tumbley
Proprietor
GIL—OUR LATEST VICTIM HAS THAT SAME BAT-SHAPED BRUISE. DO YOU WANT ME TO SEE IF WE CAN IDENTIFY THIS KNIFE, TRACK THE MANUFACTURER, AND SEE WHERE IT LEADS?
"ACTUALLY, CATHERINE—WE ALREADY KNOW WHERE IT LEADS. YOU MIGHT WANT TO HEAD OVER HERE..."

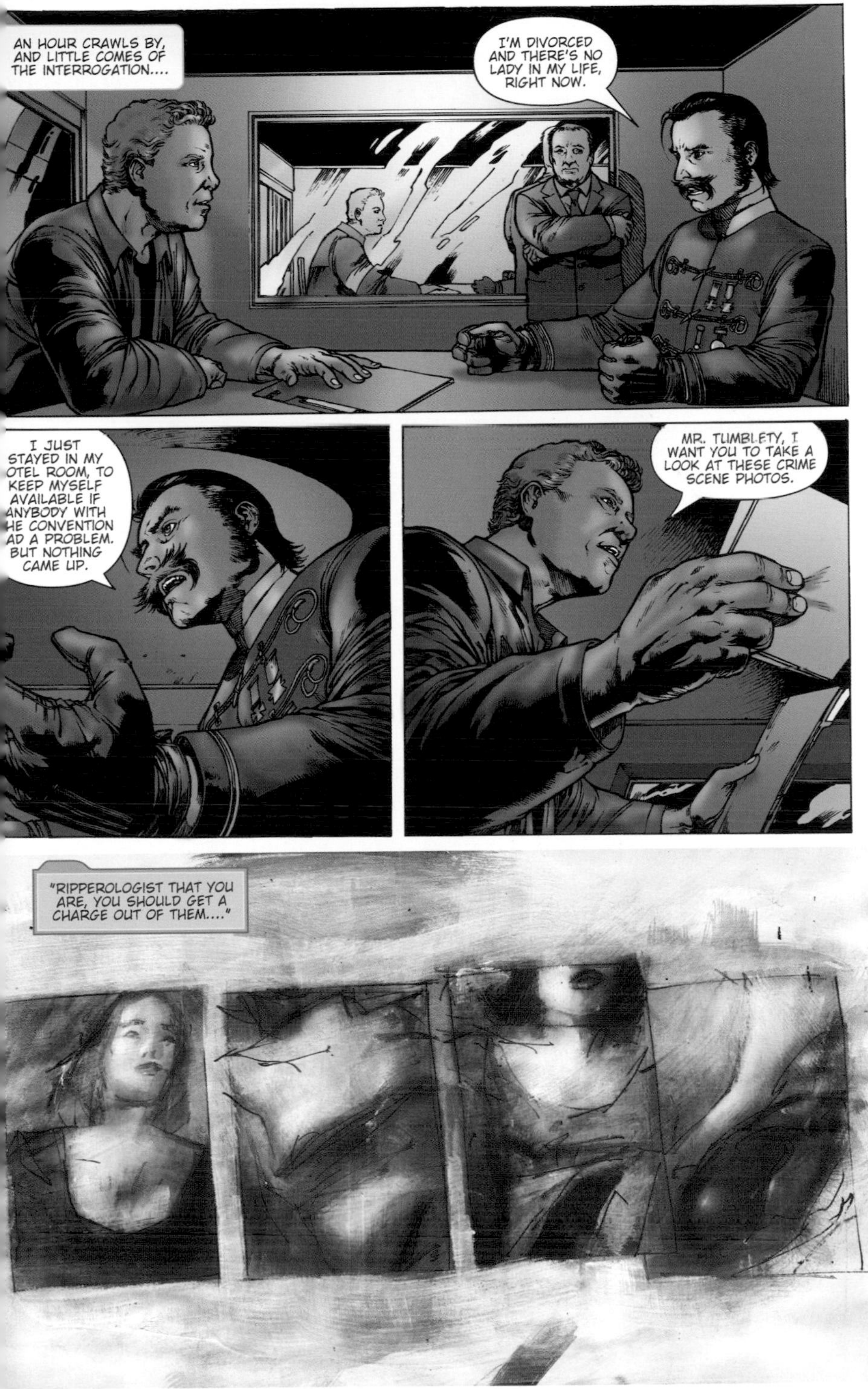
AN HOUR CRAWLS BY, AND LITTLE COMES OF THE INTERROGATION....
I'M DIVORCED AND THERE'S NO LADY IN MY LIFE, RIGHT NOW.
I JUST STAYED IN MY OTEL ROOM, TO KEEP MYSELF AVAILABLE IF ANYBODY WITH HE CONVENTION AD A PROBLEM. BUT NOTHING CAME UP.
MR. TUMBLETY, I WANT YOU TO TAKE A LOOK AT THESE CRIME SCENE PHOTOS.
"RIPPEROLOGIST THAT YOU ARE, YOU SHOULD GET A CHARGE OUT OF THEM...."

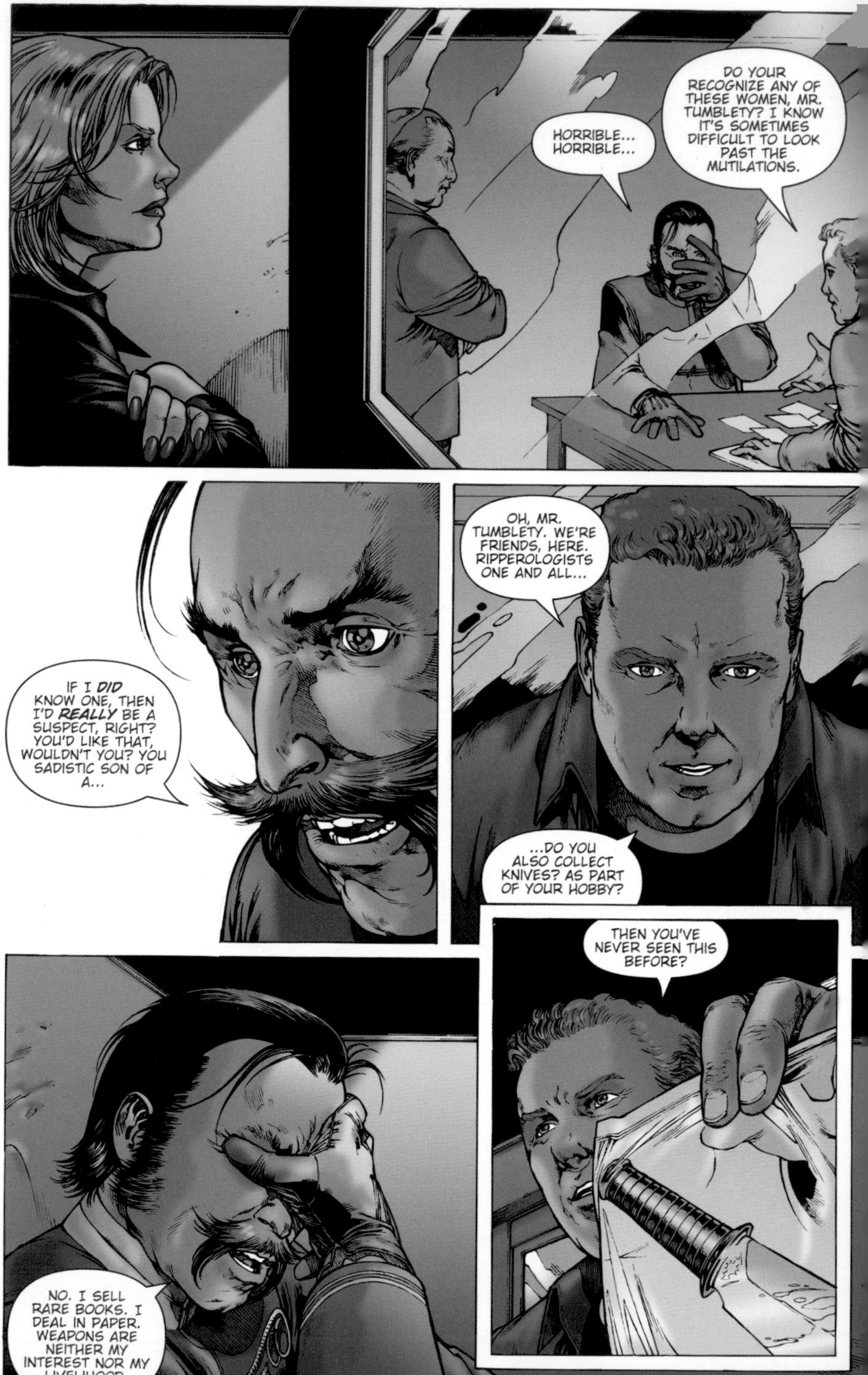
HORRIBLE... HORRIBLE...
DO YOUR RECOGNIZE ANY OF THESE WOMEN, MR. TUMBLETY? I KNOW IT'S SOMETIMES DIFFICULT TO LOOK PAST THE MUTILATIONS.
IF I *DID* KNOW ONE, THEN I'D ***REALLY*** BE A SUSPECT, RIGHT? YOU'D LIKE THAT, WOULDN'T YOU? YOU SADISTIC SON OF A...
OH, MR. TUMBLETY. WE'RE FRIENDS, HERE. RIPPEROLOGISTS ONE AND ALL...
...DO YOU ALSO COLLECT KNIVES? AS PART OF YOUR HOBBY?
NO. I SELL RARE BOOKS. I DEAL IN PAPER. WEAPONS ARE NEITHER MY INTEREST NOR MY LIVELIHOOD.
THEN YOU'VE NEVER SEEN THIS BEFORE?

I... I HAVE SEEN THAT KNIFE BEFORE.

BUT IT'S NOT MINE... I *DID* BUY IT, THOUGH.

I KNOW. ONE OF OUR CSIs FOUND THE RECEIPT IN A DESK IN YOUR HOUSE... WE HAD A WARRANT.

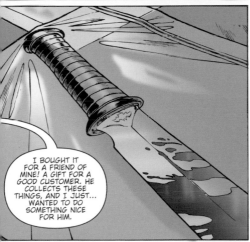

I BOUGHT IT FOR A FRIEND OF MINE! A GIFT FOR A GOOD CUSTOMER. HE COLLECTS THESE THINGS, AND I JUST... WANTED TO DO SOMETHING NICE FOR HIM.

WHO IS THIS GOOD CUSTOMER?

WELL, HE'S NOT YOUR JACK THE RIPPER, I CAN TELL YOU THAT. HE'S A RESPECTED CITIZEN... A GOOD GUY, A FINE MAN, AND A PERSONAL FRIEND. I'M NOT GOING TO GET HIM IN TROUBLE.

WOULD YOUR GOOD FRIEND HAPPEN TO BE A DOCTOR?

WHY... YES.

DR. GERALD MAYFIELD?

THIS KNIFE YOU GAVE YOUR FRIEND, BY THE WAY—TURNED UP ON TOP OF YOUR TRASH, WRAPPED IN BLOODY APPAREL FROM LAST NIGHT'S VICTIM.

LET ME SEE THOSE PHOTOS AGAIN... JUST THE ONE AT THE PARKING GARAGE....

AND MOMENTS LATER...

I DO KNOW THIS WOMAN. KNEW HER... GAIL KELLY. SHE USED TO HELP DR. MAYFIELD'S WIFE WITH HER DOGS. THEY'RE SHOW DOGS.

WAS THAT *ALL* GAIL KELLY WAS TO DR. MAYFIELD?

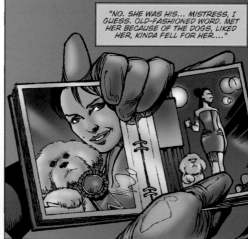

"NO. SHE WAS HIS... MISTRESS, I GUESS. OLD-FASHIONED WORD. MET HER BECAUSE OF THE DOGS, LIKED HER, KINDA FELL FOR HER...."

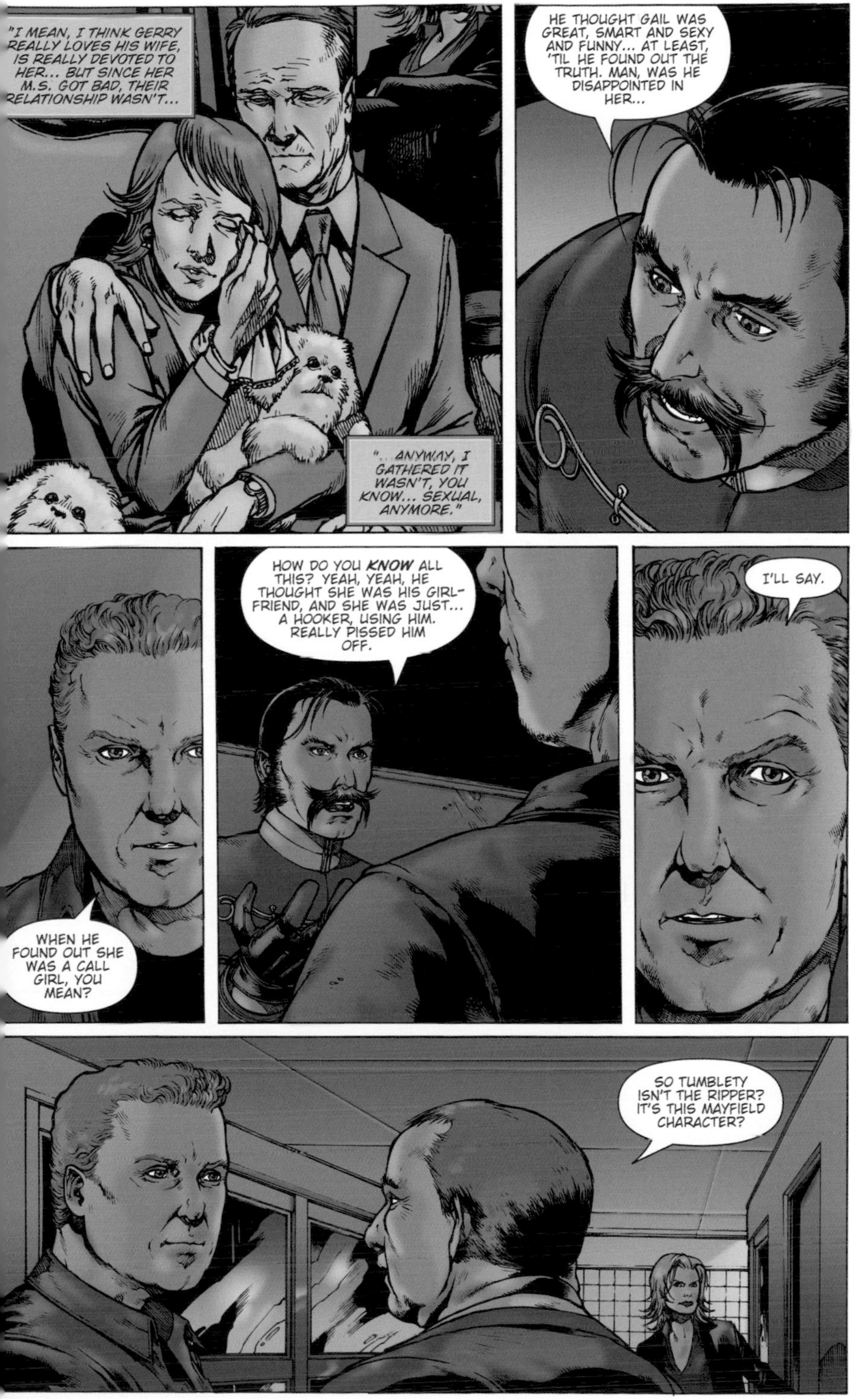
"I MEAN, I THINK GERRY REALLY LOVES HIS WIFE, IS REALLY DEVOTED TO HER... BUT SINCE HER M.S. GOT BAD, THEIR RELATIONSHIP WASN'T...
"... ANYWAY, I GATHERED IT WASN'T, YOU KNOW... SEXUAL, ANYMORE."
HE THOUGHT GAIL WAS GREAT, SMART AND SEXY AND FUNNY... AT LEAST, 'TIL HE FOUND OUT THE TRUTH. MAN, WAS HE DISAPPOINTED IN HER...
WHEN HE FOUND OUT SHE WAS A CALL GIRL, YOU MEAN?
HOW DO YOU KNOW ALL THIS? YEAH, YEAH, HE THOUGHT SHE WAS HIS GIRL-FRIEND, AND SHE WAS JUST... A HOOKER, USING HIM. REALLY PISSED HIM OFF.
I'LL SAY.
SO TUMBLETY ISN'T THE RIPPER? IT'S THIS MAYFIELD CHARACTER?

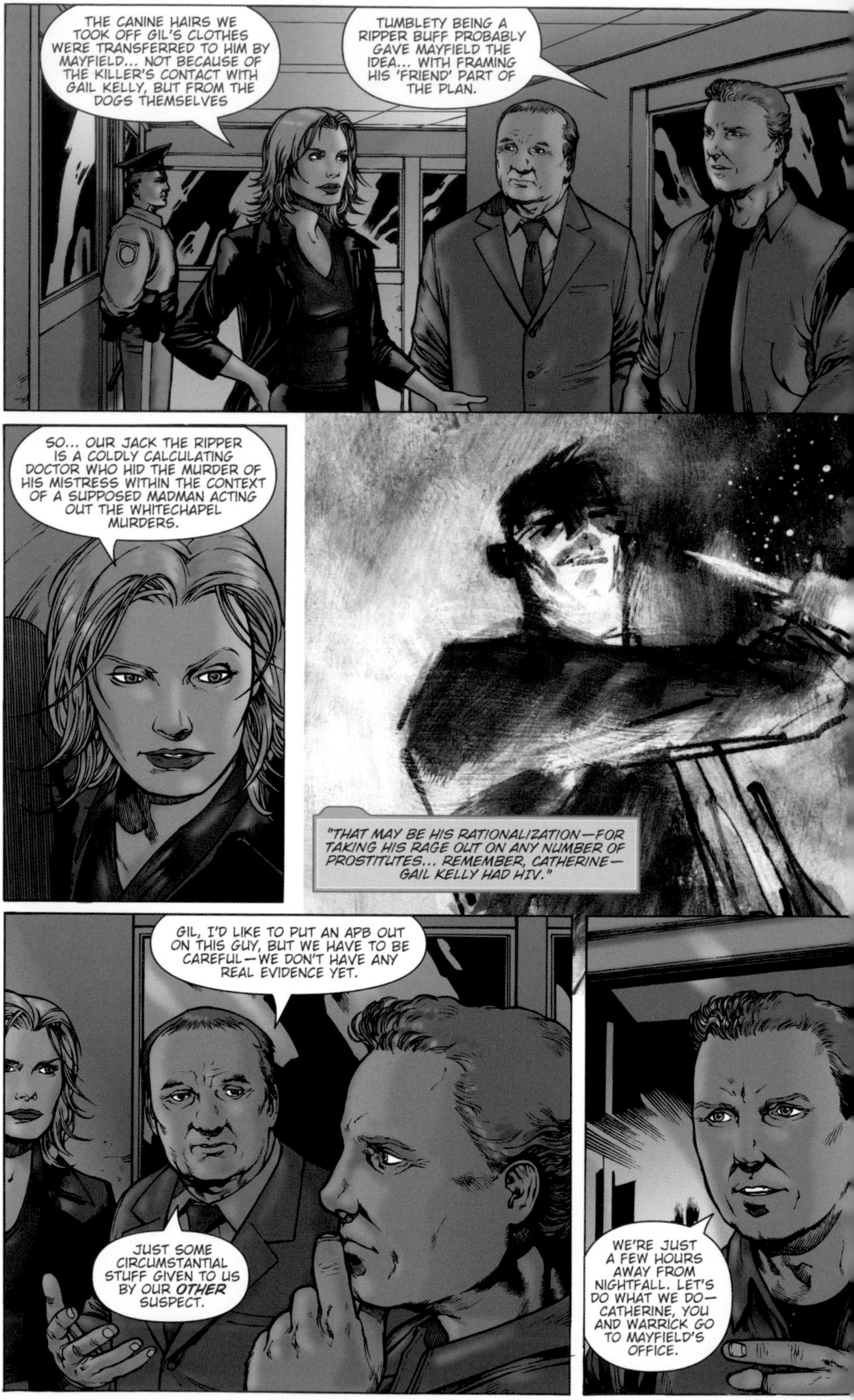

THE CANINE HAIRS WE TOOK OFF GIL'S CLOTHES WERE TRANSFERRED TO HIM BY MAYFIELD... NOT BECAUSE OF THE KILLER'S CONTACT WITH GAIL KELLY, BUT FROM THE DOGS THEMSELVES
TUMBLETY BEING A RIPPER BUFF PROBABLY GAVE MAYFIELD THE IDEA... WITH FRAMING HIS 'FRIEND' PART OF THE PLAN.
SO... OUR JACK THE RIPPER IS A COLDLY CALCULATING DOCTOR WHO HID THE MURDER OF HIS MISTRESS WITHIN THE CONTEXT OF A SUPPOSED MADMAN ACTING OUT THE WHITECHAPEL MURDERS.
"THAT MAY BE HIS RATIONALIZATION—FOR TAKING HIS RAGE OUT ON ANY NUMBER OF PROSTITUTES... REMEMBER, CATHERINE—GAIL KELLY HAD HIV."
GIL, I'D LIKE TO PUT AN APB OUT ON THIS GUY, BUT WE HAVE TO BE CAREFUL—WE DON'T HAVE ANY REAL EVIDENCE YET.
JUST SOME CIRCUMSTANTIAL STUFF GIVEN TO US BY OUR *OTHER* SUSPECT.
WE'RE JUST A FEW HOURS AWAY FROM NIGHTFALL. LET'S DO WHAT WE DO—CATHERINE, YOU AND WARRICK GO TO MAYFIELD'S OFFICE.

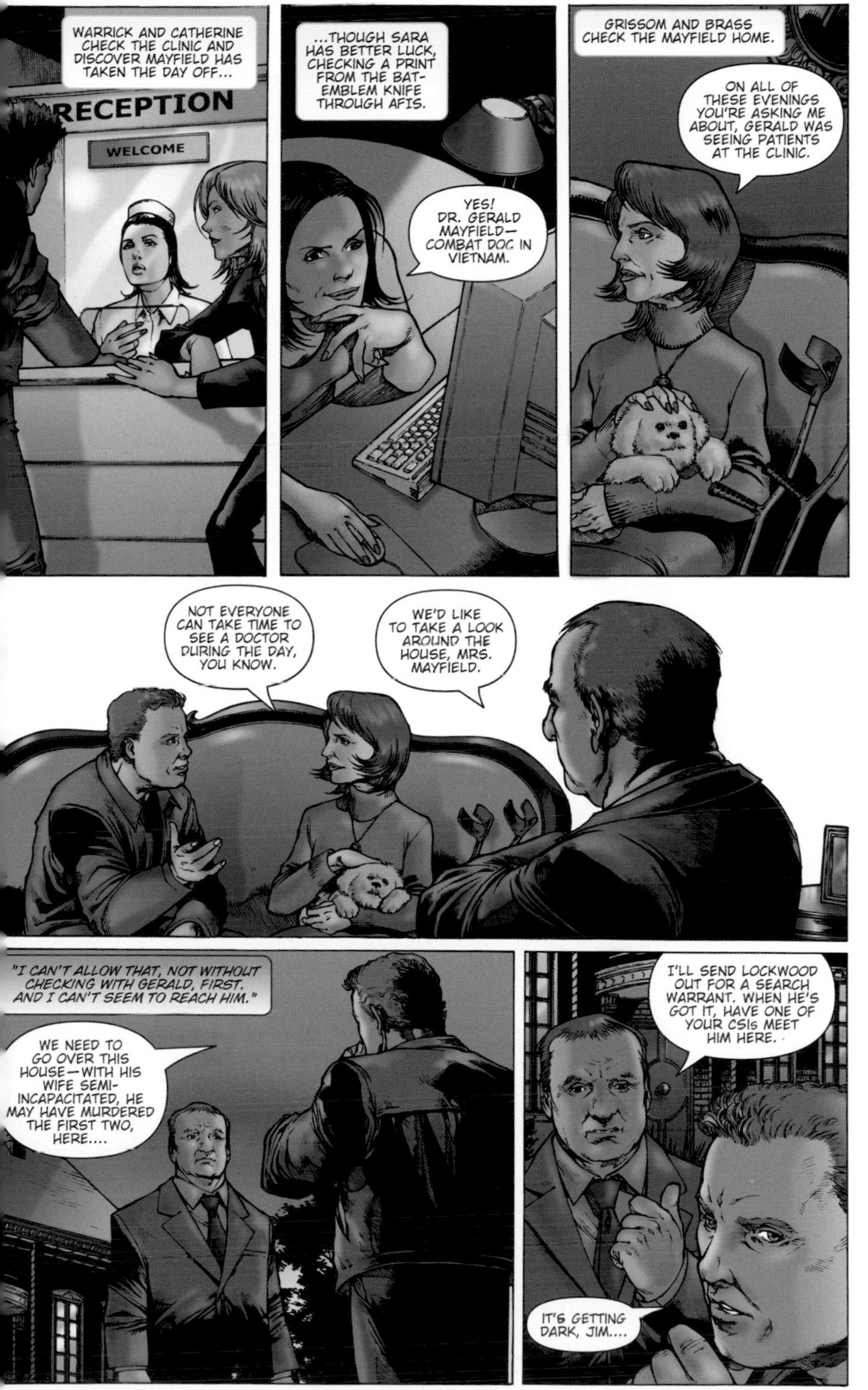

WARRICK AND CATHERINE CHECK THE CLINIC AND DISCOVER MAYFIELD HAS TAKEN THE DAY OFF...
RECEPTION
WELCOME
...THOUGH SARA HAS BETTER LUCK, CHECKING A PRINT FROM THE BAT-EMBLEM KNIFE THROUGH AFIS.
YES! DR. GERALD MAYFIELD—COMBAT DOC IN VIETNAM.
GRISSOM AND BRASS CHECK THE MAYFIELD HOME.
ON ALL OF THESE EVENINGS YOU'RE ASKING ME ABOUT, GERALD WAS SEEING PATIENTS AT THE CLINIC.
NOT EVERYONE CAN TAKE TIME TO SEE A DOCTOR DURING THE DAY, YOU KNOW.
WE'D LIKE TO TAKE A LOOK AROUND THE HOUSE, MRS. MAYFIELD.
"I CAN'T ALLOW THAT, NOT WITHOUT CHECKING WITH GERALD, FIRST. AND I CAN'T SEEM TO REACH HIM."
WE NEED TO GO OVER THIS HOUSE—WITH HIS WIFE SEMI-INCAPACITATED, HE MAY HAVE MURDERED THE FIRST TWO, HERE....
I'LL SEND LOCKWOOD OUT FOR A SEARCH WARRANT. WHEN HE'S GOT IT, HAVE ONE OF YOUR CSIs MEET HIM HERE.
IT'S GETTING DARK, JIM....

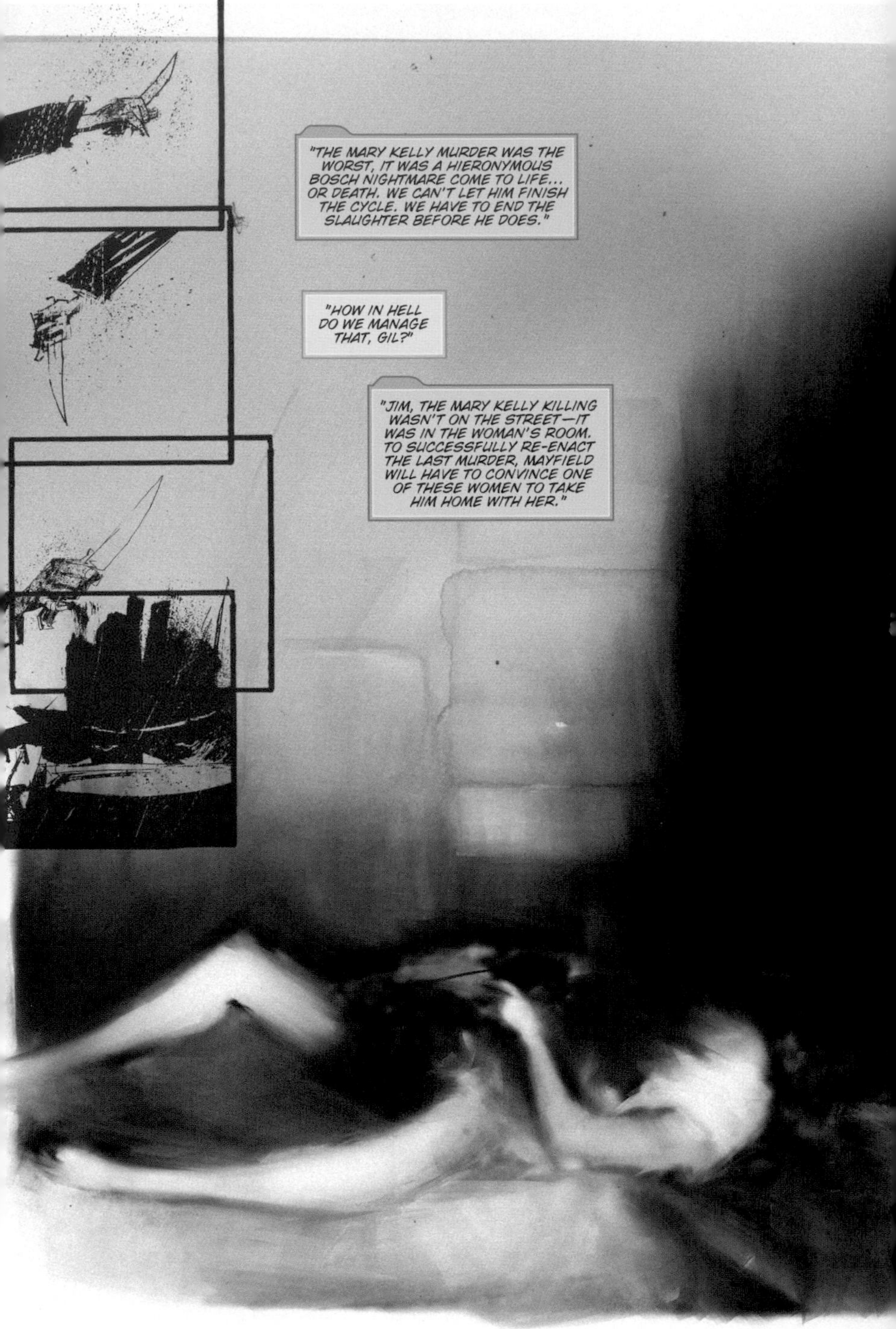
"THE MARY KELLY MURDER WAS THE WORST, IT WAS A HIERONYMOUS BOSCH NIGHTMARE COME TO LIFE... OR DEATH. WE CAN'T LET HIM FINISH THE CYCLE. WE HAVE TO END THE SLAUGHTER BEFORE HE DOES."
"HOW IN HELL DO WE MANAGE THAT, GIL?"
"JIM, THE MARY KELLY KILLING WASN'T ON THE STREET—IT WAS IN THE WOMAN'S ROOM. TO SUCCESSFULLY RE-ENACT THE LAST MURDER, MAYFIELD WILL HAVE TO CONVINCE ONE OF THESE WOMEN TO TAKE HIM HOME WITH HER."

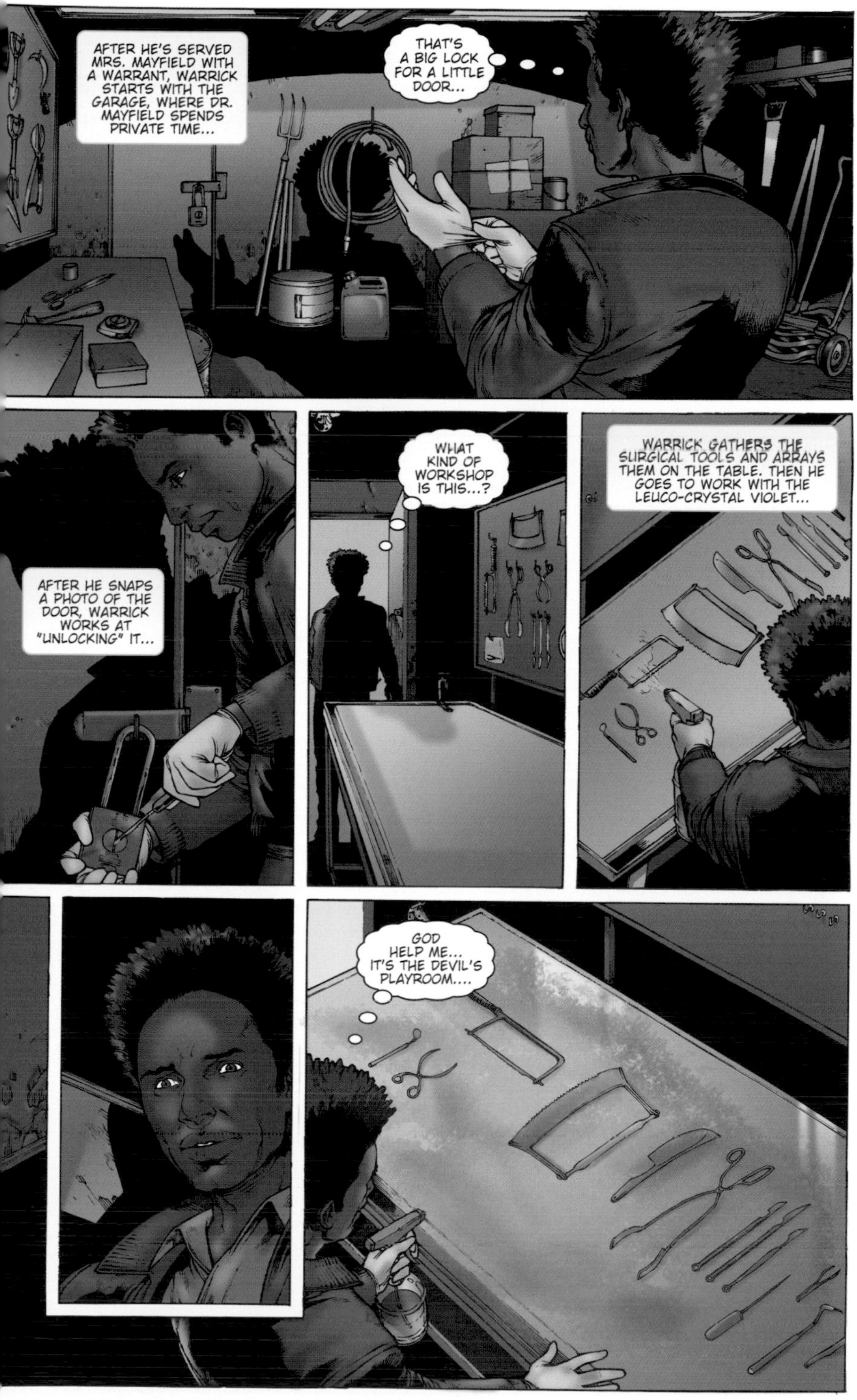
AFTER HE'S SERVED MRS. MAYFIELD WITH A WARRANT, WARRICK STARTS WITH THE GARAGE, WHERE DR. MAYFIELD SPENDS PRIVATE TIME...
THAT'S A BIG LOCK FOR A LITTLE DOOR...
AFTER HE SNAPS A PHOTO OF THE DOOR, WARRICK WORKS AT "UNLOCKING" IT...
WHAT KIND OF WORKSHOP IS THIS...?
WARRICK GATHERS THE SURGICAL TOOLS AND ARRAYS THEM ON THE TABLE. THEN HE GOES TO WORK WITH THE LEUCO-CRYSTAL VIOLET...
GOD HELP ME... IT'S THE DEVIL'S PLAYROOM....

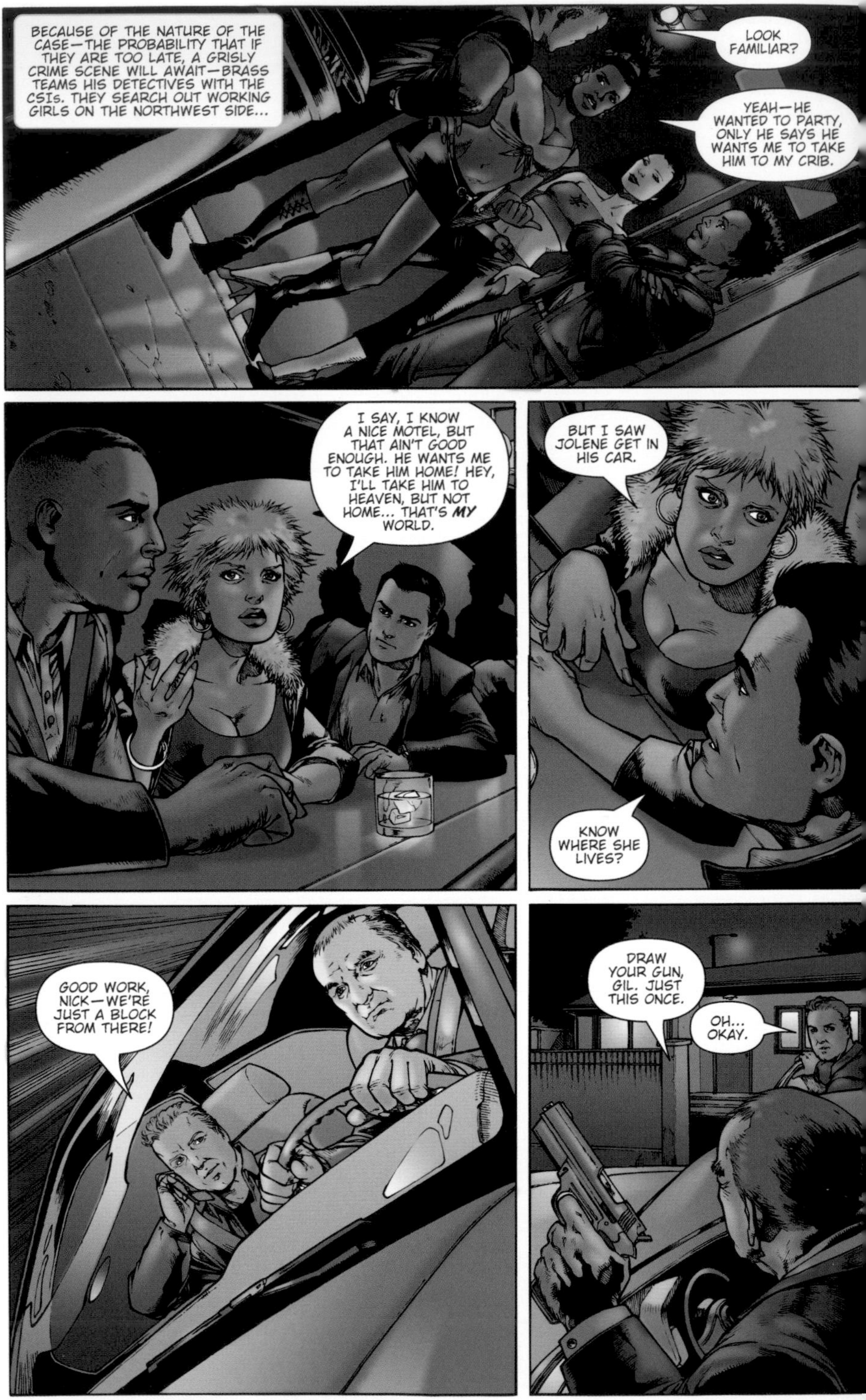
BECAUSE OF THE NATURE OF THE CASE—THE PROBABILITY THAT IF THEY ARE TOO LATE, A GRISLY CRIME SCENE WILL AWAIT—BRASS TEAMS HIS DETECTIVES WITH THE CSIs. THEY SEARCH OUT WORKING GIRLS ON THE NORTHWEST SIDE...
LOOK FAMILIAR?
YEAH—HE WANTED TO PARTY, ONLY HE SAYS HE WANTS ME TO TAKE HIM TO MY CRIB.
I SAY, I KNOW A NICE MOTEL, BUT THAT AIN'T GOOD ENOUGH. HE WANTS ME TO TAKE HIM HOME! HEY, I'LL TAKE HIM TO HEAVEN, BUT NOT HOME... THAT'S MY WORLD.
BUT I SAW JOLENE GET IN HIS CAR.
KNOW WHERE SHE LIVES?
GOOD WORK, NICK—WE'RE JUST A BLOCK FROM THERE!
DRAW YOUR GUN, GIL. JUST THIS ONCE.
OH... OKAY.

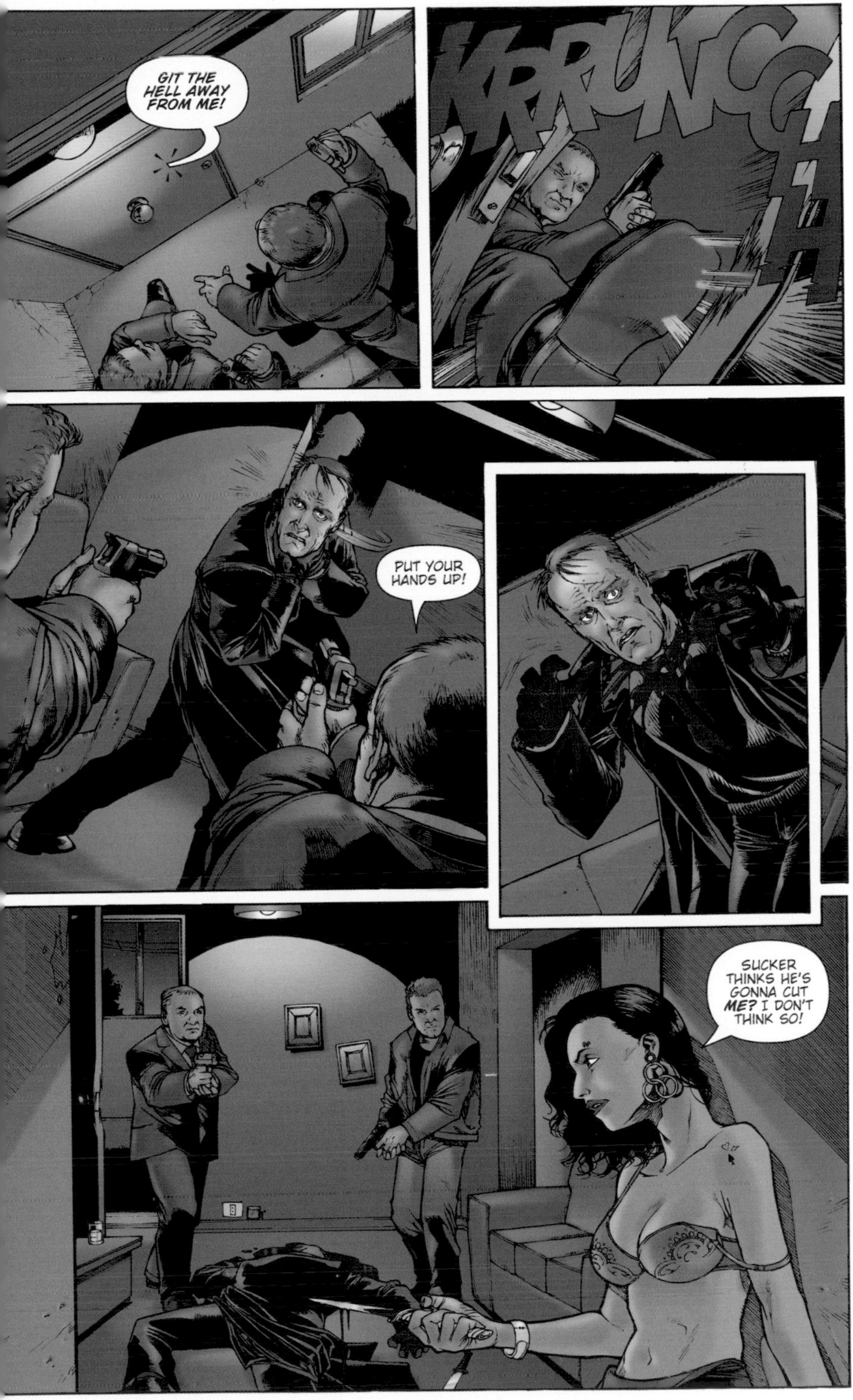
GIT THE HELL AWAY FROM ME!
KRRUNGGH
PUT YOUR HANDS UP!
SUCKER THINKS HE'S GONNA CUT **ME?** I DON'T THINK SO!

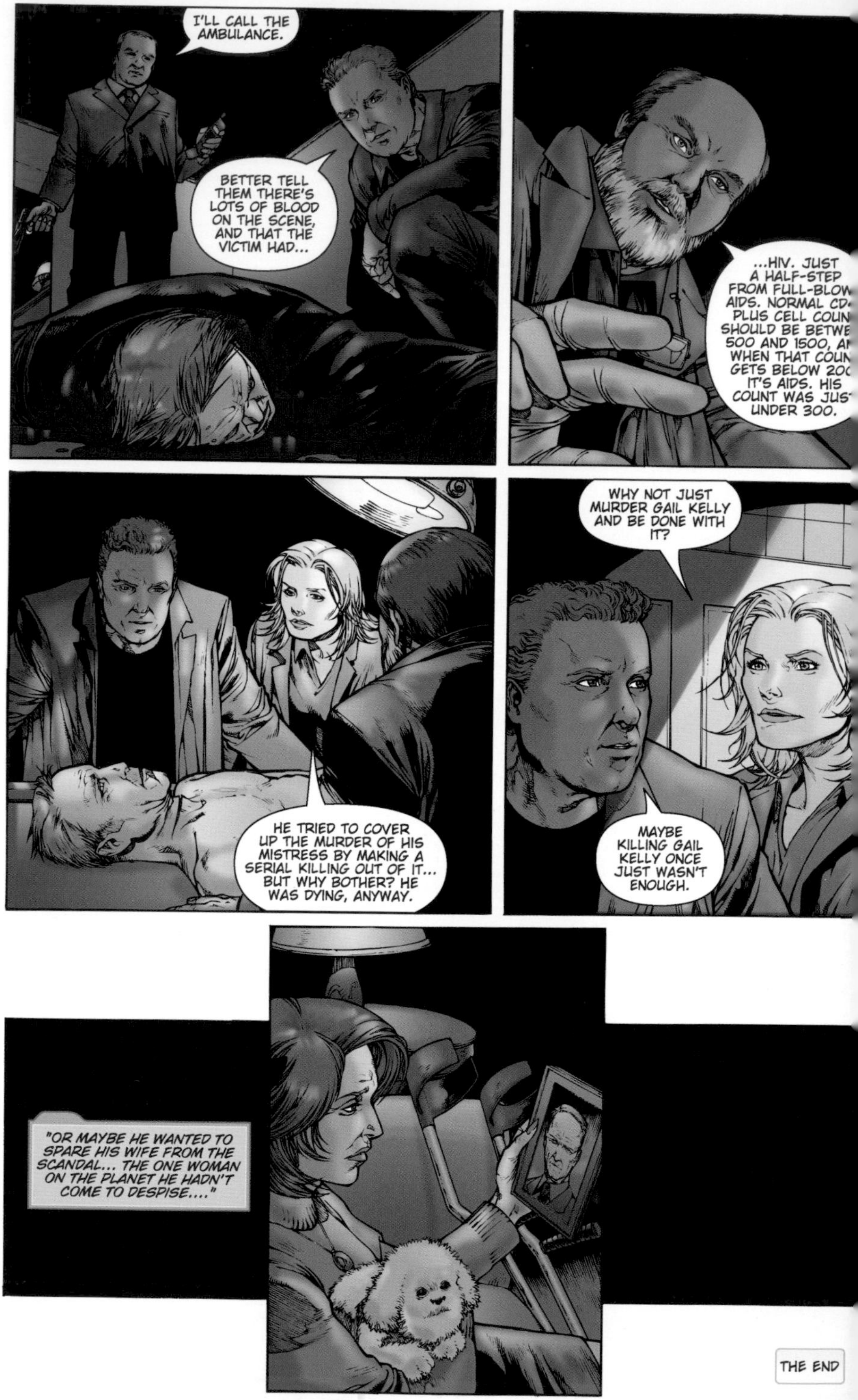

I'LL CALL THE AMBULANCE.
BETTER TELL THEM THERE'S LOTS OF BLOOD ON THE SCENE, AND THAT THE VICTIM HAD...
...HIV. JUST A HALF-STEP FROM FULL-BLOW AIDS. NORMAL CD PLUS CELL COUN SHOULD BE BETWE 500 AND 1500, A WHEN THAT COUN GETS BELOW 20 IT'S AIDS. HIS COUNT WAS JUS UNDER 300.
HE TRIED TO COVER UP THE MURDER OF HIS MISTRESS BY MAKING A SERIAL KILLING OUT OF IT... BUT WHY BOTHER? HE WAS DYING, ANYWAY.
WHY NOT JUST MURDER GAIL KELLY AND BE DONE WITH IT?
MAYBE KILLING GAIL KELLY ONCE JUST WASN'T ENOUGH.
"OR MAYBE HE WANTED TO SPARE HIS WIFE FROM THE SCANDAL... THE ONE WOMAN ON THE PLANET HE HADN'T COME TO DESPISE...."
THE END

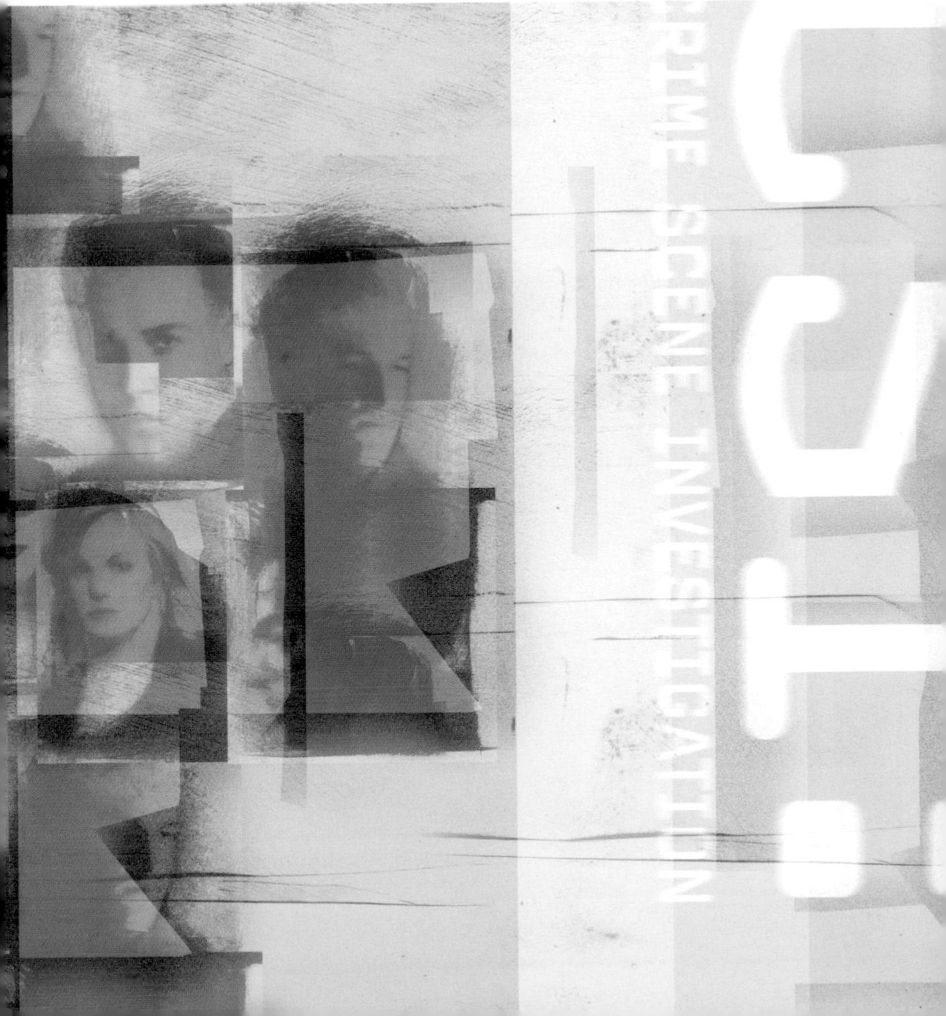

CSI:
CRIME SCENE INVESTIGATION™

Presented here for the fir
time anywhere is a brief CS
Crime Scene Investigation bon
story, by Max Allan Colli
and Ashley Wood!

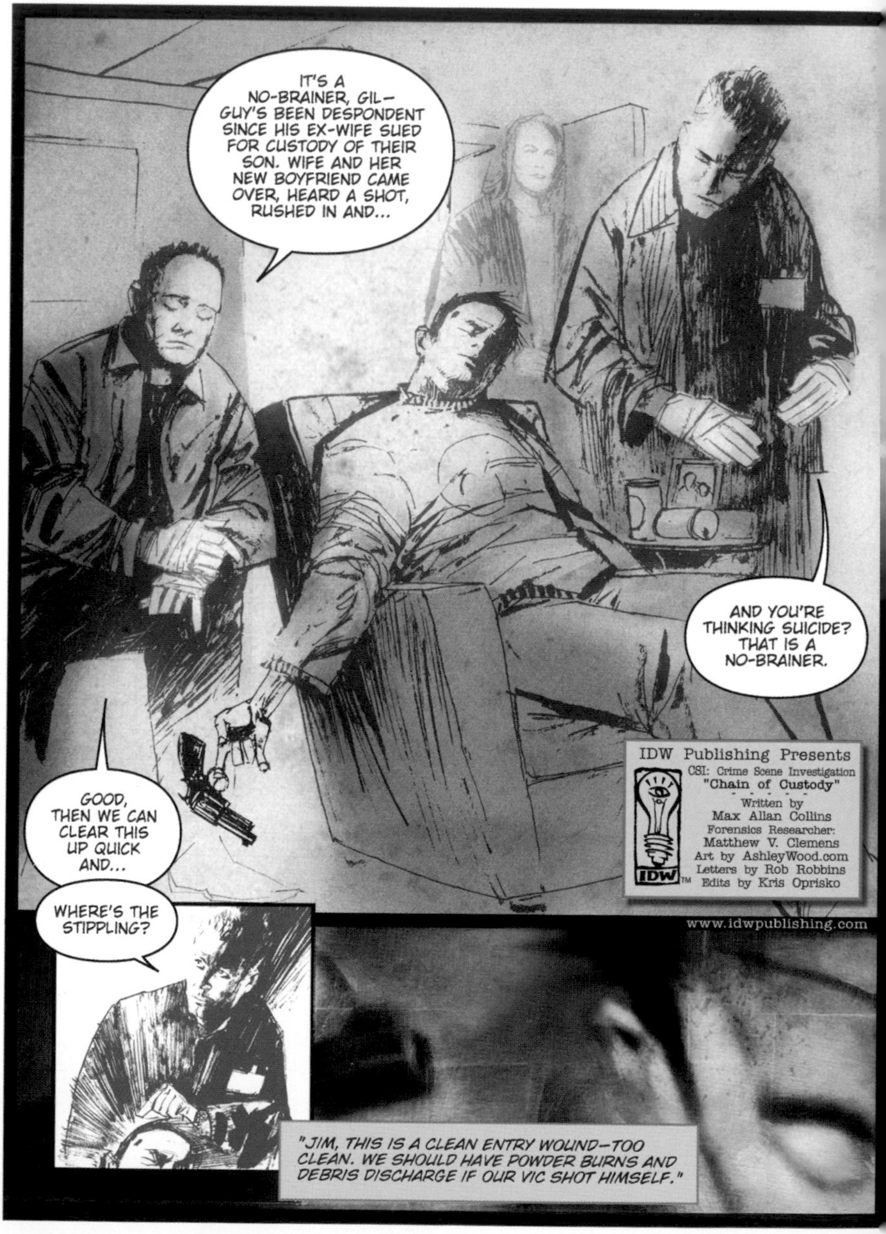
IT'S A NO-BRAINER, GIL-- GUY'S BEEN DESPONDENT SINCE HIS EX-WIFE SUED FOR CUSTODY OF THEIR SON. WIFE AND HER NEW BOYFRIEND CAME OVER, HEARD A SHOT, RUSHED IN AND...
AND YOU'RE THINKING SUICIDE? THAT IS A NO-BRAINER.
GOOD, THEN WE CAN CLEAR THIS UP QUICK AND...
IDW Publishing Presents
CSI: Crime Scene Investigation
"Chain of Custody"
Written by
Max Allan Collins
Forensics Researcher:
Matthew V. Clemens
Art by AshleyWood.com
Letters by Rob Robbins
Edits by Kris Oprisko
IDW™
www.idwpublishing.com
WHERE'S THE STIPPLING?
"JIM, THIS IS A CLEAN ENTRY WOUND--TOO CLEAN. WE SHOULD HAVE POWDER BURNS AND DEBRIS DISCHARGE IF OUR VIC SHOT HIMSELF."

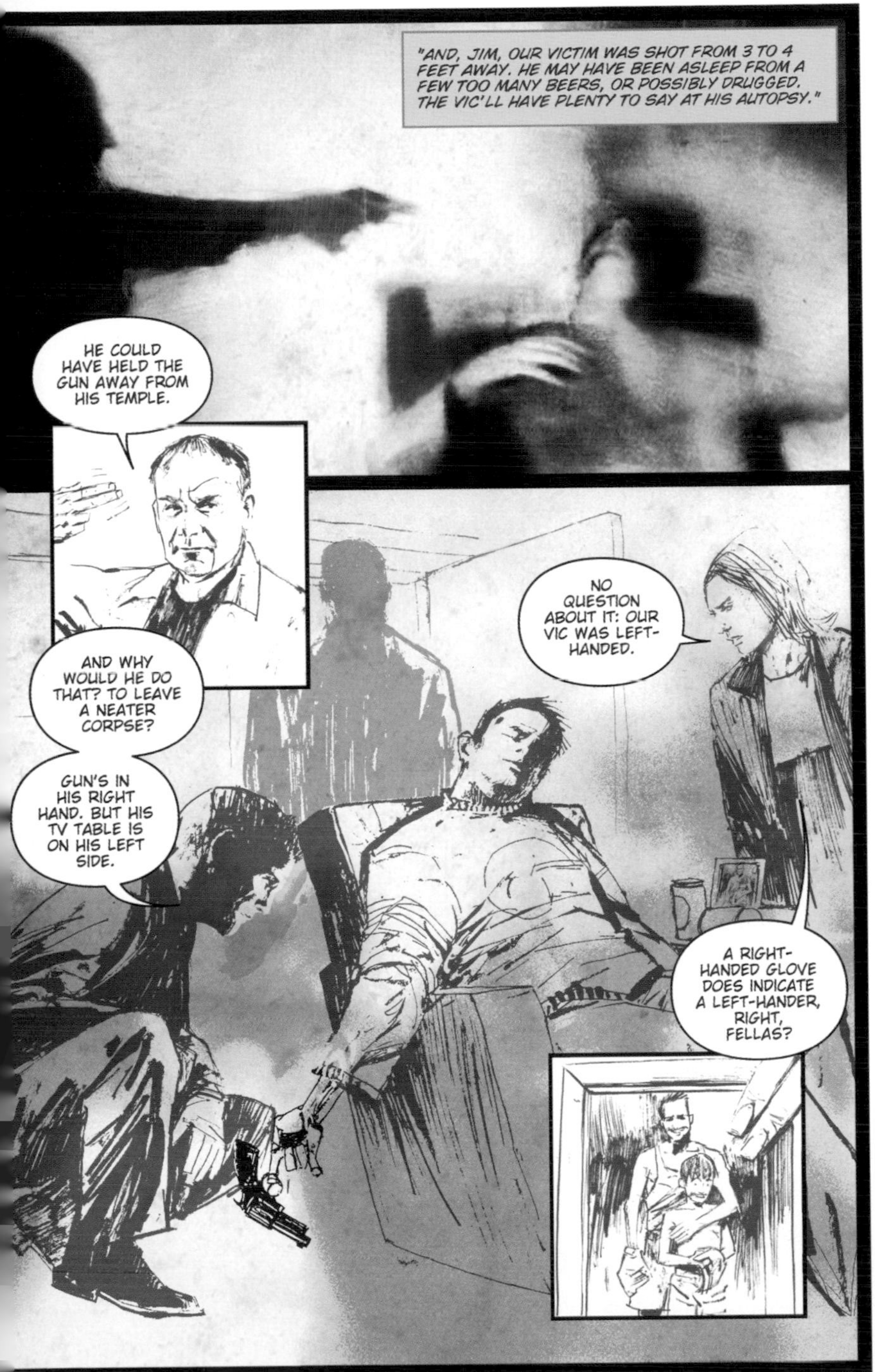
"AND, JIM, OUR VICTIM WAS SHOT FROM 3 TO 4 FEET AWAY. HE MAY HAVE BEEN ASLEEP FROM A FEW TOO MANY BEERS, OR POSSIBLY DRUGGED. THE VIC'LL HAVE PLENTY TO SAY AT HIS AUTOPSY."
HE COULD HAVE HELD THE GUN AWAY FROM HIS TEMPLE.
AND WHY WOULD HE DO THAT? TO LEAVE A NEATER CORPSE?
GUN'S IN HIS RIGHT HAND. BUT HIS TV TABLE IS ON HIS LEFT SIDE.
NO QUESTION ABOUT IT: OUR VIC WAS LEFT-HANDED.
A RIGHT-HANDED GLOVE DOES INDICATE A LEFT-HANDER, RIGHT, FELLAS?

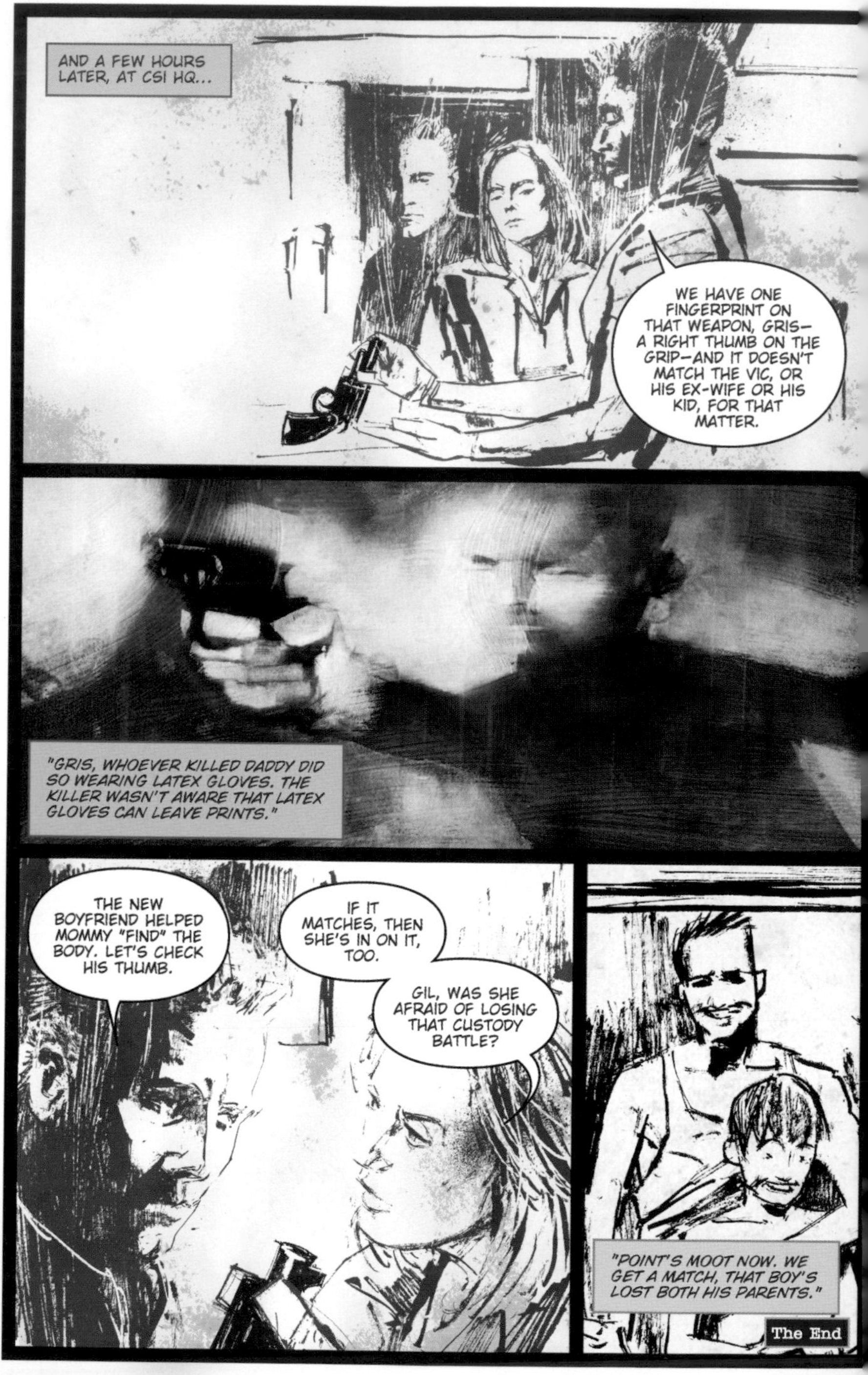
AND A FEW HOURS LATER, AT CSI HQ...
WE HAVE ONE FINGERPRINT ON THAT WEAPON, GRIS—A RIGHT THUMB ON THE GRIP—AND IT DOESN'T MATCH THE VIC, OR HIS EX-WIFE OR HIS KID, FOR THAT MATTER.
"GRIS, WHOEVER KILLED DADDY DID SO WEARING LATEX GLOVES. THE KILLER WASN'T AWARE THAT LATEX GLOVES CAN LEAVE PRINTS."
THE NEW BOYFRIEND HELPED MOMMY "FIND" THE BODY. LET'S CHECK HIS THUMB.
IF IT MATCHES, THEN SHE'S IN ON IT, TOO.
GIL, WAS SHE AFRAID OF LOSING THAT CUSTODY BATTLE?
"POINT'S MOOT NOW. WE GET A MATCH, THAT BOY'S LOST BOTH HIS PARENTS."
The End

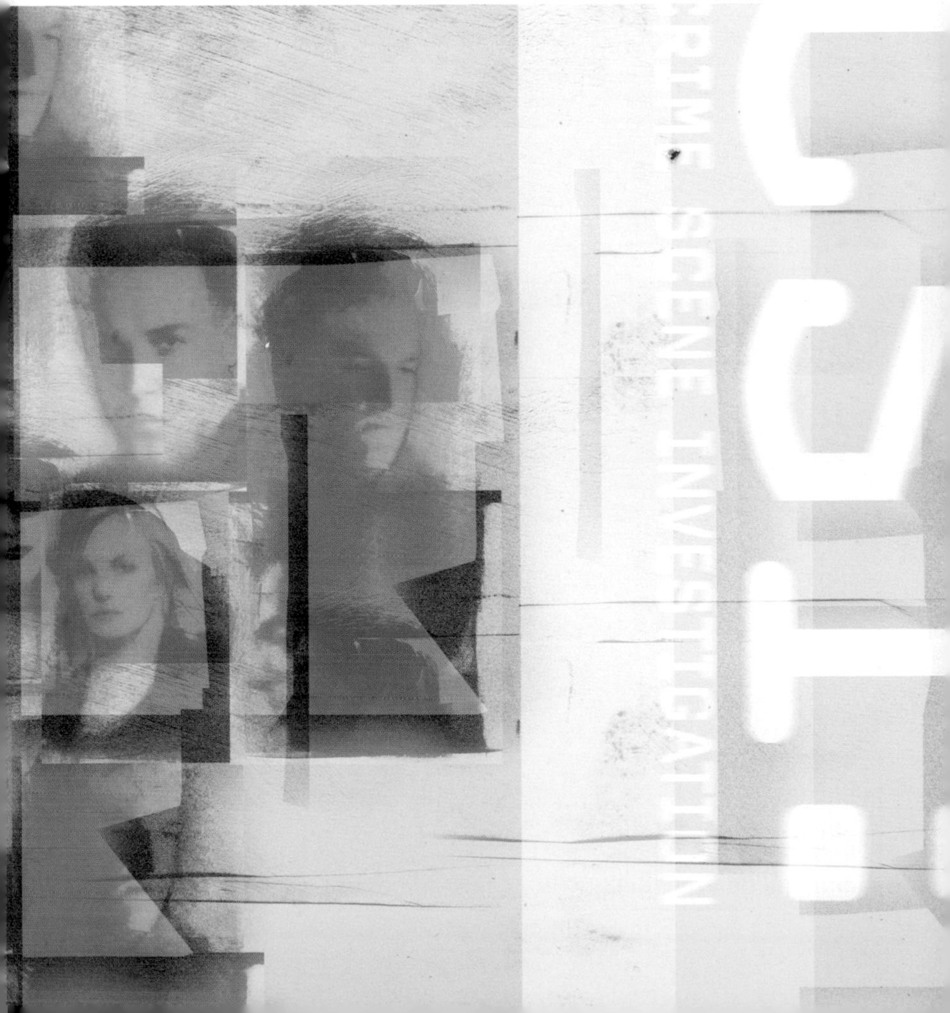
SCENE

www.**idw**publishing.com